IRELAND
UNHINGED

OTHER BOOKS BY DAVID MONAGAN:

Jaywalking with the Irish

Journey into the Heart

IRELAND UNHINGED

Encounters with a Wildly Changing Country

DAVID MONAGAN

A KANBAR & CONRAD BOOK

COUNCIL
OAK
BOOKS

SAN FRANCISCO & TULSA

www.counciloakbooks.com

First edition, first printing 2011

Type and cover design by Tom Morgan

Printed in Canada

The author gratefully acknowledges permission granted him to reprint from others' work the material named here:

 P. VII. "The Dawn Chorus" poem by Derek Mahon, used with the kind permission of Derek Mahon.

 P. 11. Lyrics of the song "Happy Talk" by Richard Rodgers and Oscar Hammerstein II, used by permission.

 PP. 100-11. JP Donleavy has kindly given permission for use of his work.

 P. 197. Paul Muldoon has kindly given permission for use of his poem "The Old Country."

 P. 271. Lines from Patrick Kavanagh's "On Raglan Road" used by permission of the Trustees of the Estate of the late Katherine B. Kavanagh, through the Jonathan Williams Literary Agency.

 P. 274. The Phil Colclough song "The Call and The Answer" quoted by permisson.

LIBRARY OF CONGRESS CATALOGING-IN-PUBLICATION DATA

Monagan, David.

Ireland unhinged : encounters with a wildly changing country / David Monagan. — 1st ed.

 p. cm.

"A Kanbar & Conrad Book."

ISBN 978-1-57178-252-6 (hardcover : alk. paper)

1. Monagan, David--Homes and haunts. 2. Ireland–Economic conditions–21st century. 3. Ireland–Social life and customs–21st century. 4. Cork (Ireland–Social life and customs–21st century. I. Title.

DA966.M66 2011

941.70824--dc22

         2010047429

FOR BARNABY CONRAD III,
MY EDITOR AND FRIEND OF MANY YEARS.

It is not sleep but dreams we miss,
Say the psychologists and the poets too.
We yearn for that reality in this.

If we could only achieve a synthesis
Of the archaic and the entirely new . . .

From *The Dawn Chorus*, by Derek Mahon

Where will be the best place to live in 2005? The World in 2005 turned to the Economist Intelligence Unit, which has devised a 2005 "quality of life" index for 111 countries. Result: Ireland comfortably tops the league.

The Economist, November 17, 2004

The Irish are now the most pessimistic people in Europe, thanks to the economic gloom. After years of poll-topping optimism, the feel-good factor has gone into reverse . . .

Irish Evening Herald, December 20, 2008

Having now fully absorbed the shock of the crash, we have the opportunity to ask the question that was not asked in the dizzy days of apparently endless growth: who and what are we as a people?

The Irish Times, Janaury 1, 2011

Chapter I

S pring was dawning. Wife was away. Whorls of light were doo-
dling through evening clouds. Birds were trilling, maybe even
fouling our laundry on the back garden line.

And here I was looking out over the conundrum called Cork City,
trying once again to make sense of life. Other people came to Ireland
for a week or two, unlimbered their bank cards, got drunk in a castle,
bashed golf balls through the rain, then followed their post cards home
to reality: the office, the landscaping business, the spreadsheets, and
lawsuits in L.A. or London.

Oh no, not me. I had to seek the whole *Tír na nÓg*. That's the isle
of the happy, the land of eternal youth, the mystical reality that fabled
Irish dreamers from St. Brendan onwards quested for in order to stop
time. Until the year 2000, I had been running my herd in exemplary
order: three kids with perfect American teeth, big Connecticut house
with heated swimming pool, mortgage paid like clockwork. But I
was stuck with a sense of the repetition of mid-life and wanted an
adventure. My very Irish-American wife felt the same, and so, one day
we up and moved our children to the land of our forebears. There I
learned that *Tír na nÓg* could appear without warning.

The phone rang, then stopped. I was musing by my bay window
when it rang again.

"You're coming to the cathedral tonight, right?" This was not a vicar or a priest calling, but a former oil rigger who graduated to selling oil fields, and then chucked that career to become an oil painter, a calling he pursued with his fingers, rather than a brush. It had come to pass that Bill Griffin was holding an exhibition of his artwork in the most hallowed church in Cork City, the sombre French-Gothic styled fantasia of St. Finbarr's.

"Of course, Bill. I'm looking at it this moment," I said, which was true. My house high on a hill offered a panoramic view of the entire city, from its inner warrens wrapped by twin branches of the River Lee to the spires of St. Finbarr's soaring like exclamation points.

"Good, because I'm stuck. I need a bartender."

"You *what?*"

Here he roared with his trademark mead-hall laughter.

"At St. Finbarr's. We're serving wine and it's going to be packed. Can you come early?"

"Well I guess so," I agreed. My teenaged daughter and son were ensconced in their Irish boarding schools, while our youngest at twelve, Owen, was at his rowing club and had a lift home arranged. My wife Jamie was attending a theater opening in Dublin.

"Give me a few minutes," I said and hurried toward the door. By now, I had enjoyed many adventures in my adopted land, but this one took the biscuit—*serving as the first bartender in a cathedral in the history of Ireland!* The thought nonetheless gave me pause. St. Finbarr's was an iconic place. It stood on ground first sanctified by a seventh-century mystic who had spent years praying by the mountain source of the River Lee, where he lived on an islet in a lake that came to be called Gougane Barra ("the rocky cave of Fionbharr"). A worker of miracles, the saint eventually travelled downriver to build a monastery whence to spread the word of God to his fellow Celts. That priory is considered the birthplace of Cork City, and the cathedral was built on its ruins.

And I was supposed to serve as its bartender?

To get to St. Finbarr's, I first had to traverse our neighborhood. This was a curious world in itself, a red brick terrace that was watchful as a moving curtain, and a far cry from the forest solitude my children had enjoyed in their previous lives back in Connecticut.

It was a challenge to exit my cul de sac without being detained. Ahead, a bearded poet prepared for his evening run, and beside him a gentle old man sat murmuring to himself in the spring sun. Little boys kicked a soccer ball between the parked cars. Beyond them all, a white-haired grandmother was sweeping her stoop so I knew it was between 6:00 and 6:10 p.m., the precise time she did this every evening. Her job was to brush aside chaos, which blows around Ireland like a supernatural force.

At the next corner I came to an escarpment with a prodigious, if more cockeyed view. Below sat the island of downtown Cork with its eighteen bridges. From its enormous outer harbor a procession of trawlers and container ships pushed up the estuary toward the docklands where the River Lee splits into its twin branches that encase the town. Over the rooflines below, all I could see was a progression of the boats' smokestacks sliding forward as if my adopted city were being invaded by top hats.

Step by step, I proceeded down the escarpment and, for no apparent reason, began thinking of an art video I had just seen of a man who starts walking across town and finds that he is beginning to defy gravity. He is so very light that he maneuvers sideways and begins planting his feet up a tree. At its pinnacle he realises the most beautiful thing of all—*he is free.*

That is what one gets from moving abroad—a strange and fresh new perspective, I thought, as I headed down to Cork's main drag, Patrick Street.

"How are ye, boy?" several citizens greeted me in the native style. Everybody in boisterous Cork, including broken-down octogenarians, can and will be hailed with that aural slap on the back. We had found no such exuberance in chilly Connecticut, and Jamie and I prayed that the madcap spontaneity of Ireland would enrich our children, too.

As always, Patrick Street was abuzz: a frazzle-haired Russian electric guitarist blasted Jimi Hendrix agonistas while Jamaican acrobats tossed each other around like mutual irritants; a few yards beyond, the local Peruvian bunch worked their Pipes of Pan act into Andean dimensions of monotony even Prozac could not channel. Fore and aft of these buskers, Romanian gypsy women sat on their squares of cardboard, whimpering, "Help me please, Mister!"

Such was the new life I had found.

BILL GRIFFIN WAS STANDING IN FRONT OF THE CATHEDRAL, his vast greying beard cascading over a brown sports jacket that he had jobbed onto his formidable frame. He chatted with two friends, laughing uproariously in his distinctive manner that often ends with a wistful, faraway yearning in his eyes. So goes Ireland, I thought the first time I met him—euphoria and sadness walking arm and arm.

Bill thinks big. So when he decided to have a gala exhibition of his paintings, he ignored Gallery This and Gallery That and walked about, scanning the horizon. With under a quarter of a million people, Cork is a small canvas whose focal points are vivid. Its most magnificent are the towering 240-foot spires of St. Finbarr's, which first started climbing into the sky in 1865.

"That might do," Bill thought, brushing aside the fact that the cathedral was a high seat of the Church of Ireland, which means Protestant, and that tribe in this country tends to venerate both order and tradition. In short, St. Finbarr's was the last place anyone would expect to host a raucous event such as Bill had in mind.

But Bill loved this Gothic shrine, from its gargoyles leering beneath soaring spires, to its vaulted entrances wreathed by haunting bas relief figures from the Last Judgement. Carved by nineteenth-century master masons, those tableaux cast uncompromising eyes upon every human who prepares to venture past to seek God. The cathedral's seventh-century patron saint was said to be so holy that he was called into heaven to be consecrated while still alive. To this day, pilgrims visit Finbarr's island hermitage in West Cork to parade around his holy well, always in the direction of the sun, and leave strips of cloth—called "clooties"—as tokens of devotion. A few miles away rests another holy well—one of three thousand in Ireland—where Finbarr's confessor Olan prayed away as well. Beside this arises a rune-inscribed standing stone capped in quartz. Suppliants used to make their so-called "pattern" circles there with that heavy quartz stone on their heads, seeking healing and fertility from pagan and Christian spirits according to their whims.

Bill was pursuing spirits himself, occasionally letting his paintings be guided by visions that come to him after ingesting psychotropic mushrooms. These mycological agents have flourished in Ireland since the ages of the Druids and may explain more ancient religious ecstasy than the modern world can comprehend. Bill works with his fingers for fear that a brush slows inspiration and often composes in darkness as if to make room for a higher light. He thus had no trouble approaching the Protestant bishop of Cork and pronouncing that he, too, was drawn to the sacred. "This cathedral's beauty is stunning," said Bill. "But I believe thousands of people in Cork have never even been inside it. Maybe a showing of modern art will draw a lot in."

The Right Reverend scrutinized the odd suppliant and responded, "This isn't a circus we're running here."

Bill played a clever card. "Aren't cathedrals also shrines to human art? Hasn't that always been their role—to display our highest strivings? Why must they only host art that is old?"

The Bishop was stuck with a predicament: Two thirds of the urban Irish had stopped going to church, and the crisis of observance had become especially acute for Protestants, since that dwindling breed comprises just over two percent of the Republic of Ireland's population. It is hard to inspire crescendos of worshipping plainsong when the pews are nearly vacant.

So it was that a lordly vicar and profane oil rigger broke bread. Bill closed the deal and his inner wheels began to spin. Soon, he convinced a certain liquor distributor to provide free cases of wine and persuaded half the mad, party-loving town—the Irish equivalent to New Orleans—to think that his was to be a premier cultural event.

"How could I not love Cork?" I thought as I shook Bill's hand and eased into the cathedral. My work table at the front of the church was draped in linen, just like the one on the altar three hundred feet away. But I guessed only one bottle of sacramental wine was kept on hand back there. Under mine, there appeared to be dozens. After uncorking a few, I ventured down the side aisle, where Bill's paintings hung under subdued lighting, and I filed past dozens more stationed at the transept with its magnificent organ. Many of Bill's works looked magical to me—there were pictures of confused dunces, dazed mariners, Hindu holy men, all finger-daubed as if from visions and yearnings of unfettered immediacy.

Suddenly, the vaulted doors started groaning open and banging shut. Here in short order appeared the curiosity shop of Cork life: the Lord Mayor with her necklace of heavy gold chain; charming ladies with their suited barristers; newly wealthy entrepreneurs with trousers flecked with plaster drippings from their latest building sites; and motley denizens of Bill's favorite pubs, many of whom had never paused over a painting before in their lives. Soon I discovered that the one thing they had in common was thirst.

I poured a polite glass of wine for an attractive woman of my acquaintance and proffered it with a smile. This was met with disdain.

"You're in Ireland for God's sakes," said Aoife. "We don't serve half glasses here, certainly not when they're free."

A man called "The Bird" asked for two.

"Why do you want two, Bird?" I asked.

"Because I have two hands," he said.

"The IRA shot a man on the street outside this door, just for being a Protestant," someone with similarly urgent fingers said. It was a fellow called "World War," who knew too much about every battle in history.

"Oh, my God," I thought, shovelling him a helping of red without making eye contact.

Things got worse.

I stopped filling glasses and switched to merely uncorking the bottles, at a rate of perhaps two a minute. Still, I could not keep up. Two hundred tippling Catholics had invaded this sanctuary of the formerly ruling Anglo-Irish gentry, and a sizeable minority were having their rollicking revenge. Word spread to the homeless shelter and that adventurous bunch came to my linen-draped table with hands outstretched. One fellow lay down for a snooze in a crypt outdoors. Finally, two women set to fighting before the altar, and the distraught bishop appeared in a flurry of green and white robes.

"This is very bad form! I'm afraid you must all leave now!" he said and threw open the exit doors. Bang went the lever on the latest Irish attempt at a grace note.

On the way home, I climbed past a handsome brick-faced Victorian-era hotel that was once known as "The Hospital for the Incurables." Now it had a wide screen TV in its comfy bar and a health club, as countless ones had sprouted across the country.

Below loomed the current hospice, within whose lawns there often shuffled the apparent last nuns in Ireland, tiny, age-bent creatures like the remnants of a lost tribe.

Outside, a cluster of young Polish construction workers clambered past uttering their "Zs" and "Cs", four of the four hundred thousand Eastern Europeans who had poured into Ireland, a country of just four million, after their homelands gained accession to the EU in

2004. Twelve hundred years of Viking, Norman, and English invasions brought fewer immigrants to this island. But the country mostly just shrugged and hired the flood of Poles, Lithuanians, and Latvians en masse to tend to its pubs, scrub its floors, and feed a construction boom that would eventually become a fiendish Pandora's box.

I MET BILL GRIFFIN OVER PINTS A FEW WEEKS LATER, and we laughed at the irreverence of his event, which talk around town had transmuted into that separate reality known as an Irish Story.

Finally, I told the truth. "There was too much jackass behavior that night in the cathedral, and I'm getting tired of all that. It's like everybody's play acting to try to be more Irish or something than the next, and maybe I am doing the same thing myself."

Bill squinted my way. His fingers tonight were blue. "It's the feckin' drink that infests the whole culture. It turns us all into fools, and I was embarrassed by some of what went on as well."

I suddenly blurted out my concerns. "Sometimes I worry about the direction this country is going in and even whether it's the right place for my family. I have this fantasy about finding some bolt-hole in the country to share with Jamie and the kids. I've been looking around West Cork a lot but the prices there have gone through the roof."

Cork City had become our only home, but lately the place was beginning to worry me, as was the country itself. From the amphi-theatre of surrounding hills to the bustle of the city center, nearly every quadrant of my vision was peppered by a frenzy of cranes swinging wrecking balls. The gold rush economy of modern Ireland had reached a ravenous peak. Never in my life had I seen a culture change so rapidly, and I feared that much of its soul was being lost.

Bill quaffed his Beamish, a locally brewed stout. "I hear you," he said, "and I am consulting my crystal ball."

When you stir reflections in an Irish dreamer, you are stirring clouds, water and sun. When you petition guidance from Bill Griffin, you prepare to receive parables. So he said: "I will tell you of one place I have always loved, it's called the Blackwater. Half the history of Ireland played out there. It is so close to Cork, and yet it is worlds away. The beauty of that valley stuns me. And property there is not quite so dear either."

"Hmmh," I said, confessing that I barely knew it.

"The lower part in Waterford is like a secret valley," added Bill.

The topics switched on into the night, for Bill Griffin is a man who spins tales. He said he had a potential commission to do a portrait of Fidel Castro, and seeing as all three of us had beards, would I like to come? Yes, I said, and the fantasy was vividly explored.

Finally, what I saw in his eyes, framed by many crows' feet, was both wizened and sadly touching. That he supposedly helped sort out a few oil fields for the Libyan dictator, Moammar Gaddafi, didn't overly bother me. That he claimed to have laid flat-out drunk on a Shell Oil executive's desk in Amsterdam when negotiating drilling rights in Siberia made me laugh. His spirit was large.

Bill ultimately leaned close and said, "You know, I love you."

I gasped, sensing trouble. The words made me tremulous and not from untoward connotations—for Bill was a ladies' man—but because every time anyone in Ireland said them to me, they soon fell down. And there was no matador posture I found that could stop it—down stairs, over stools, and across banquettes, three or four friends had fallen just lately. Madcap and tragic, the Irish extend their arms to sudden visions and then their balance goes.

Bill tottered, but he did not fall. Like so many others, he would dust himself off in the morning and search again for the divine or the sublime, some transport at any cost. For now, we said goodnight.

Chapter 2

The next morning Jamie was rummaging about in the kitchen, preparing for work at the Cork Opera House, where she had landed her personal dream job in Ireland—introducing school groups to the magic of live theatre and musical performances. My commute involved shuffling down the stairs.

"I'm itchy and thinking of heading into the country," I said.

"Just like that, free as a bird? Well, you wouldn't have a better day for it, so go on," she said, pouring a cup of coffee.

Out the back window, I glanced at the massive trampoline we had bought for the boys—and our daughter Laura when she felt like it—a couple of years before. The idea was to offer some zest for the outdoors in their transplanted and now urban lives. Though dominating our meagre slice of lawn, the trampoline looked like a launching pad for happiness when they first began to bounce upon it, often surrounded by packs of gleeful friends.

The summer of 2000 was when we first landed at our never-before-seen rental house on this hill. The question "Why?" still lurked. After all, my impoverished progenitors had headed across the ocean to New England in the 1840s without much hope of returning to their native land. Like three million others, my wife's ancestors later did the same, destination New Jersey. Now here we were in reverse mode. Perhaps, I sometimes teased Jamie, it all had to do with her zany renditions of that Rodgers and Hammerstein song from "South Pacific": *Happy talk, keep talkin' happy talk, talk about things you'd like to do. You gotta have a dream, if you don't have a dream, how you gonna have a dream come true?*

Ireland was no Bali Hai, but we had reasons to select it for our adventure. One was that I myself had grown enamored of the place upon enrolling for a year at Trinity College, Dublin, as a student in 1973.

My first stop then was a bed and breakfast ridden with a crucifix, pope portraits, and photos of JFK. There I shivered in an igloo-like cabaña off the kitchen. In the middle of the night the man and woman of the house got up or rather down to do something on the dining room table ten feet away. This involved much grunting and moaning with pots and pans being kicked every which way. Cries of "Harder, HARDER!" arose between the smashing glassware, and likely the demise of an odd papal portrait or two. My ancestral race had to reproduce itself somehow, I figured.

On a ten-miles-distant headland called Howth, I found a rustic gate lodge beside a winding drive the next day. Below this lay the "big house" with formal gardens and a balustraded terrace offering sweeping views across Dublin's brooding bay. Purplish mountains elbowed up from the south.

If you don't have a dream, how you gonna have a dream come true?

A rangy figure named Bun Wilkinson led me about. A former farmer turned stone carver and recently widowed, he was managing the otherwise uninhabited place for now. What Bun did best was tell stories, and I laughed so readily at them he quickly handed over the keys and soon adopted me like a second son.

His real one, Paddy, was renovating a pub in a village called Terryglass by the shores of Tipperary's Loch Derg, and as our friendship grew, Bun and I often went there to help. On Sunday evenings a crowd of farmers would tumble in from Galway to drink and sing.

One said, "You know, I am not much for formal religion but I am a religious man. I am after the farming every day, and you would think what I see would be the same, but it is not. I see things growing every hour that I didn't see before. I look in a hedgerow and there I see God. I see him in the white thorn, in the spring lambs, in my crops."

Bun brought me everywhere, to the mountains and midlands and to an island off Connemara called Inishbofin, to ancient stone towers and colorful Dublin pubs. Then I hitchhiked from remote Donegal to Cork City where crones in black shawls sold cabbage and carrots from makeshift stalls. Life was so much poorer—with a third of the population scraping to get by—but also so much more vivid than anything I had known. Of course, they were also brutal times, with sectarian bombs riddling Belfast, London, and one May Day killing and wounding scores of innocents on the streets of Dublin.

Jamie and I honeymooned in Ireland a decade later, and she became smitten with the country, too. A Donnelly with a grandfather born in Roscommon, this land was in her genes. Onward flew time and our family grew. Finally, our vision of an extended Irish safari stirred.

To be sure, we had a good life in Cornwall, Connecticut. Our house there was surrounded by five-hundred acres of forest full of deer, coyote, bobcat, wild turkey, and even the odd bear—along with Harris's treasured snakes, frogs, and magical red newts. Below this lay a pristine lake where the children could swim by summer and skate by winter without hearing a single car. Five minutes off lay a small, family-run ski area, which local kids used for free.

But something vital was missing. Neighbors had little reason to greet each other as they drove off to jobs in faraway cities, and the eternity of New England winter added to a pervasive sense of chill. The local café was owned by a woman who hated men. The convenience store was run by a man who sneered at all comers. The dump could be a challenge when its attendant swore at people for parking at the wrong angle.

In time, Cornwall, Connecticut, began to feel like a cold comfort farm, splintered into rival subgroups, with a heavy influx of snooty New York weekenders spearheading much of the divisiveness. Worse, multiple couples we knew began divorcing, their unions shattering like hurled crockery. As our children got bigger our little town seemed to grow ever smaller, and crankier. So what then was the solution?

Talk about things you'd like to do. Have a dream.

Going to Ireland for a year or two became ours.

AT FIRST, WE SAVOURED THE POSTCARD SIDE OF THINGS and took the kids everywhere—to offshore islands, hidden waterfalls, and ancient forts, hurling matches and horse races on silver strands. And because our spirits were open, we quickly made a remarkable number of new friends.

Of course, the country's baffling aspects became apparent, too. Some were showcased in a bar which manifested all the weird eccentricity for which Cork is famous—the Hi-B. At the crest of a dingy stairwell, it sports a windowless black door such as might lead to a morgue. On my first visit, the wispy-haired owner was blasting a Mahler recording and waving an imaginary conductor's baton, while scowling my way.

"You are a fairly tall fellow," said Brian O'Donnell, the publican.

I shrugged.

"You are within an inch of the limit," he observed.

"I beg your pardon?"

"My ceiling is not so high, and your head is close to it and therefore obstructing my light," he said.

A half-dozen souls along the small crescent bar sniggered into their pints.

The owner helped himself to a large brandy, and his prosecutorial eyes again set to twisting my way. His cadence was peptic. "I was just saying now, there was a man in here recently who was six-foot-three. He blocked my light and had to leave."

"Permanently!" blurted a customer into his drink to a roar of laughter from his mates. "You barred him for life!"

"I shortened his wick anyway," quoth Brian.

"Er, ah, I presume you are in search of fluids?"

"Yes, a Murphy's please," I said.

Time passed as Brian poured. Two minutes became ten. The way he fussed with the creamy head of my pint with a plastic spatula resembled some primary-school science experiment.

At last, I had my drink and settled in for a chat. Brian's bar proved to be a mother lode of inanity. One day he introduced me to a ginger-headed midget called Small Denis, a leprechaun if ever there was one. Not proud of being small, Denis had recently visited one of the "adult shops" that were suddenly arising in every Irish town. There, Small Denis discovered a new world of gadgetry, including suction devices that supposedly extend the length of the male anatomy.

Denis is not what would be called a high wage earner. So he came up with an alternative which involved a kind of economy-class docking-in-space act with his home vacuum cleaner. Alas, he possessed one very powerful Hoover and this nearly sucked all of him in with such a vehemence that he fell onto the floor. Flailing about there, he finally succeeded in ripping the electric cord out of its socket and began the tortuous process of self-extrication.

As a result, Small Denis was limping when we met. But how he laughed as he told his story and that laughter spread. Ireland was my tonic in those days—improvisational, wickedly fresh, and so very human—just what the doctor ordered after the New England chill.

To be sure, there were hard times, too—the trials by fire that come with moving abroad. The worst were inflicted by a throng of thirteen-year-olds who harassed our household with xenophobic vindictiveness. God save you when the wrath of "knackers" falls upon your door, hurling apples and rocks and even pissing upon it—all because you weren't born in the neighborhood. They had a field day after 9/11, screaming, "Ye had it coming to you, Yanks!" at our windows in reaction to the horrors of the Twin Towers—this in a country which generations of families like mine considered their spiritual homeland. Our neighbors' guidance was as old as Irish stoicism—ignore them, and this too will pass. In time, they proved right; the bullies set off for fresh targets, then grew up.

Also problematic was the clannish coolness to outsiders that a good few Corkonians still brandish like a grump's shillelagh. The latter begins with a comatose-looking stare and an ear cocked to discern every word you are exchanging with some one else twenty feet down the bar.

Finally, your man walks by, his eyes darkening with the centripetal pull of his own eternal mental stew. This type is known as The Messer. His primary job is to spot The Stranger.

"You're not from here are you?"

"No, but I live here now."

"Oh, do you, now? What do you think of this place?"

"It's mad, but it's fun. I love it."

The Messer's next task is to rampage through the fragile china of your mind. "What right do you have to an opinion about our country?"

"But you asked."

In fact, any answer is wrong, since The Messer is born with a special gift: He knows everything.

"Your country is nothing." His sullen lips purse; he is tasting eight centuries of bitterness against assorted invaders and a great-great uncle who didn't send sufficient currency back from his digging on the Erie Canal. "You're nothing but imperialists."

It goes on from there. Pascal had it right: "All of man's troubles come from not staying in his own room."

IN TRUTH, SUCH PROVOCATIONS SOON DIED OUT. By any balance sheet, the entire family was recharged. Owen, a boisterous seven-year-old then, was a hit in his new primary school, and when asked to do any little thing took to mouthing in the quintessential Cork sing-song, "I will, yeah," which means "I won't." Harris, filling out at ten, dove into the sport of rugby at the same close-by Christian Brothers College and thrilled to at last have friends at his doorstep. Red-haired Laura, twelve, responded to the challenge of dawn bus commuting to a distant secondary school with aplomb. I myself kept busy writing, increasingly about the heady surprises of our new Irish life.

A year turned into two and our lease came up. Jamie and I were unsure what to do next. So many good souls had opened their hearts to us and now a chorus of them insisted, "You must stay!"

Finally, a neighbor named Shaun sauntered over with an Answer Man click to his heels—we should buy a property across the street! And never mind the toilet in the kitchen or that it had no heat, nonsensical wiring, no paint, and a lawn that looked like Berlin after the Allied bombers and Russians were done. It did have two-foot thick walls and very high ceilings, some boasting plasterwork from the 1880s, and splendid views.

The dwelling nested in the middle of a long terrace built for British army officers like the young Montgomery of later WWII fame and that legendary loser of Singapore, Arthur Percival. Jamie thought it had "good bones."

"So does a mausoleum," I responded at the first inspection.

The owner had been single-handedly renovating the place for

fifteen years, in the manner of the Looney Tunes character, Wile E. Coyote, churning ever deeper into the dirt without getting ten feet from the starting block. Much of his time was spent collecting dubious treasures, such as old cinderblocks, rotting boards, broken slates, mismatched sections of fence, cylinders of truck and tractor motor oil, and dozens upon inexplicable dozens of fertilizer sacks. All these he deposited in heaps out back. Inside, he crammed the place with more keepsakes—salvaged doors stacked among sheets of plywood, wallboard, and Styrofoam insulation by the score; boxes of plumbing bits, forty-year-old fuses, broken telephones, chipped doorknobs, and the circuitry for what appeared to be a ham radio. It was a Tinker's paradise packed with radiators in four reclamation-sale sizes, old glass by the hundred pane, and enough piping to cross Arabia.

Here, I supposed, still lay the old famine-haunted Ireland, ever patiently and stoically saving against future want.

Another neighbor strolled over to inspect this eccentric at work. "What are you doing there today, Tim?" asked the bemused Pat O'Leary. He found the renovator digging a three-foot trench between various heaps in the back garden.

"I was thinking of starting an extension?" said Tim.

"An extension to what?"

"To the kitchen."

"But sure you have no kitchen, Tim. There are things growing in there."

Pat went back to his garage and made ready for his next project. After a while he emerged and looked up to see a figure toiling on the steeply pitched roof across the way.

"How's it going there, boy?" hailed Pat.

"Tipping away," hollered Tim. "Now that it's dry, I am thinking I will re-slate the roof. Yerrah, I can nearly see to Cobh." He was referring to the port town ten miles distant, which fronts on Cork's magnificent harbor. Three million Irish departed there never to return, at first on typhoid-ridden so-called Coffin Ships to North America and later to Australia.

Everyone in our cul de sac worried that Tim was attempting the impossible in single-handedly renovating an exhausted house with three floors and a back annex, and with an utter inability to complete one job before moving onto the next.

That was when our friend Shaun stepped forward.

A boxer when young, and then a professional ballet dancer who performed on Broadway, Shaun was a raconteur of the Irish Order Most High, with an operatic singing voice. "It's time to make a deal," commanded Shaun the Beguiler.

Tim smiled the wary Irish smile of a man certain he is about to be blindsided by a truckload of charm.

Then Shaun had at him with the knowing glances and the rest.

"I don't know," waffled Tim, his resistance puddling at his feet.

His subject finally obliged. Shaun stroked a pen across his blank sheet to suggest a selling price. A little trading of notes, and there it was. Both parties produced the exact same figure, and we were informed that our future had been decided.

"Properties in this terrace come available only rarely, and this would be the deal of your life. Nobody ever loses on Irish property," Shaun proclaimed.

He was reciting Ireland's intoxicated mantra just a few years ago. The country's house prices had been doubling, tripling, and in some cases quadrupling in the last decade. Everybody wanted in, and in short, we jumped too. In six bank account-draining months, our house was restored. Our builder Liam Hurley brought in his supporting cast: wiry, tireless labourers with thick country accents; feckless carpenters whom he fired one-by-one until none was left. Then there was a gold chain-wearing plumber with six apprentices, a holiday home in the Canary Islands, and a massive SUV. He managed to install toilets that didn't flush, radiators and kitchen fixtures that leaked, a tub suspended in gravity-defiance an inch above the floor, and hot water taps marked cold.

If you want to understand a country, renovate a house in it. One late autumn afternoon, I was feeling the usual mix of delirium and exhaustion and stopped by the Hi-B.

Esther, the bartender there, could be counted on to unleash jolliness in spigot-force. She introduced me to a late-fiftyish woman on a neighboring stool and explained what I was up to.

"Oh, *mein Gott*," the gal said with a distinct German accent. "Ve did this also."

"Really?" I smiled the smile of a fellow traveller.

"Yes, ve first came to Ireland twenty years ago and thought it was the most beautiful country on earth, with the most beautiful people and spirit."

"And?"

"Und then ve started renovating an old house, a lovely old house."

"How did it go?"

"My husband had three heart attacks," she began sniffling, then sobbed. "Und now he is *dead*. Ze house *killed* him."

The nearby citizenry gasped. Then Esther whispered, "Don't mind her. She cries a lot. That's why she's called 'Waterfall.'"

I understood Waterfall's point of view. Our builder, like many during the boom, took frequent leaves. So I attempted to take control. The phrase drips with irony.

One day, I was standing by an open fire in the back garden, burning rotten boards. Now Paddy, a prodigious labourer, wove back to me and said there was a fresh carpenter at the door.

"Bring him on," I said.

The apprentice plumbers had gone a bit quiet, and I guessed they were pausing for a banana break. One of the quirks of Irish building sites is that they feature an enormous amount of banana eating. This likely has to do with the attraction of leaving the peels on the floor, and a 5 p.m. trail of spent banana peels is a Cork specialty. They usually led to the nearest pub.

In any case, the fresh carpenter sashayed forward and said he was named Pat. Of course he was. I had twelve people working in the house now and seven of them were either named Pat, Paddy, Pádraig, or Pad. The new Pat had a whiskered face and blinkered eyes. I wanted to talk to him about built-in book shelves.

Pat swayed forward, reeking of alcohol. "Do you want sixteen-inch separations, or eighteen or twenty-four, I need to know what you want? And where will the wall be?"

"I was just thinking about getting a preliminary sketch."

"*A what?*"

Pat was tacking southwest now, circling more or less straight toward a pile of sawdust and banana peels I had just swept together. In its midst he planted a foot and registered his passionate objection to the insanity of my foreign brain.

"I am not sure that you know what you are after," Pat declaimed.

Well, some of our workmen were excellent, and neighbors pitched in to finish off many projects for which they would take no pay. Then others gave us furniture, carpets, and curtains, since nobody tops the generosity of the good Irish neighbor. So in the end, our house was renovated beyond Tim's dreams, and there my family began to extend its roots.

Chapter 3

Watching Owen bouncing on our trampoline one afternoon with his friends, I suddenly realized that they were metaphors. The Irish economy in the early 2000s was defying gravity with an annual growth rate that was roughly two times higher than that of the U.S. and three times that of France or the U.K. Newspapers claimed the country now had more millionaires per capita than about anywhere in the world. People were splurging on ever larger houses and ever flashier cars. Four-wheel-drive SUVs became *de rigueur* in a country that has almost no snow, while Ireland enjoyed the highest per-capita acquisition rate of Mercedes Benzes in all of Europe. So the nagging question was: what do you get the kids?

Contraptions that defy gravity were the answer. From Dublin to Donegal, inflatable jump-stations, called Bouncy Castles, cropped up beside thousands of homes. The things came with pumped-up walls on three sides and an inflatable turreted roof on top. When deflated, they could be rolled up into half-nothing and easily transported, creating an opportunity for small-time entrepreneurs with a van to rent them out. The secret to their success turned out to be the Catholic sacraments.

In Ireland, these used to be observed before the altar, the youthful rites of passage followed by a sign of the cross flittered over the chest and a modest family gathering at home. But with the spreading of Celtic Tiger riches, the hallowed rituals turned into something else. Anyone with a gift for marketing could see the new commercial potential in sacraments. Cake bakers, champagne sellers, and dress makers stepped forward to help, but the Bouncy Castle reigned supreme—the signature statement of the pumped-up boom.

As the Bouncy Castle Era flourished, the traders in the inflatable arts set to hard-selling. They quickly understood that the three big sacraments—Baptism, First Holy Communion, and Confirmation— are each packed with separate bouncing potential.

As Owen's First Communion neared, we asked him what he wanted for the party afterwards. The answer was no surprise.

"A Bouncy Castle!"

The man with the white van arrived with his giant air-compression pump, and soon two dozen kids yanked off their shoes, preparing to get high.

"Are you having a good time?" I asked when our First Communicant was three feet above the curvature of the earth as it presented itself on our lawn.

"Yeah, yeah, yeah," Owen said from mid-air, his lips grimacing like an astronaut's on the way up and up and out of this world. Beneath him lay a fall-out of candy wrappers and loose change, which was to be expected seeing as friends and neighbors at the height of the boom were stuffing money into kids' pockets at every important religious ritual. Many had little choice, since the darlings in white dresses and dark suits often knocked door-to-door with their hands out.

Back in the kitchen, I was uncorking a bottle of champagne when a neighbor sidled forward.

"How much did he get?" Ger asked.

"Maybe four hundred," I confided sheepishly.

"That's nothing," Ger smirked. "My nephew got eleven hundred last week."

"Well at my First Communion, I got rosary beads and a pink cardigan sweater, and I treasured them," said Jamie.

What happened next was inevitable. As a more emphatic expression of *upward mobility*, permanent backyard trampolines soon sprouted on tens of thousands of lawns. Our kids demanded theirs—and got one.

Things kept tripping along. Laura had become a boarder in her secondary school in the West Cork town of Bandon, built by the Duke of Devonshire in 1651 for that region's "planted" British stock. Nowadays, Bandon Grammar School serves as a magnet for remnants of the Anglo-Irish gentry and many foreigners. More numerous still are ordinary but free-thinking modern Irish looking for a small, coeducational school (still rare in Ireland) that fosters an easy civility. Laura loved the place.

Harder challenges hit Harris as he finished his nurturing little Catholic primary school. Alas, the transition to secondary school occurs in Ireland at the vulnerable age of twelve. His destination now was but a hundred feet up the hill—the massive Christian Brothers fortress of stern study.

The first morning that Jamie and I delivered Harris into that hallowed Cork institution of 925 boys and zero girls, we saw panic in his eyes. Christian Brothers College, a.k.a. CBC, was a rigorous institution that was supposed to offer a ticket to the top Irish universities. But our son began hyperventilating, and for good reason. First of all, he didn't smoke. The road outside the school was ringed by circles of Irish lads in blue blazers and white shirts and striped ties, sucking cigarettes in manly style. Between puffs, they scowled in contempt at the new arrivals.

Harris had another problem. This had to do with the fact that the car he was incarcerated in was my ten-year-old heap of an Opel. Worse, our white family station wagon, which for some reason is called an "estate," had grown a film of relentlessly spreading moss. The interior still reeked of gasoline from the night that young thugs had broken into our original rental house while we slept upstairs, stole the keys from the kitchen table, and free-wheeled the banger homeward. There, the police interrupted the hooligans as they doused the car with petrol for the torching.

A painting of an all-caring Jesus greeted Harris at CBC's door, but our son drew no solace from it. Since not a single Christian Brother had been ordained in Ireland in the last five years, owing to a succession of sordid scandals about the order's former penchant for pedophilia, there were no men of the cloth left to teach the Good Book in that school. Nor was the situation about to change—the following year would see thirteen new Catholic priests ordained in all of Ireland, an astonishing ninety-seven percent decline from 1965.

So what awaited my son was a thoroughly secular torment in the form of twelve different subjects rendered by twelve different teachers, a couple as severe as their priestly predecessors. He responded by alternately playing the clown or withdrawing into a shell and sank to the bottom of his class.

We tried various motivational techniques, including buying him snakes—those symbols of evil St. Patrick once banished—which the pet stores were now importing to the wonderment of local lads. They would gather around their cages, saying "Ah, he's a massive slimy ting, dat one." To oohs and ahs, Harris would reach in and cradle some writhing foot-long creature between his fingers as if it were a kitten. So, for fifty quid, we bought him a corn snake, the same pink and white species he used to pluck out of the American woods for free. Within a week, it disappeared. And there was no progress on the studying, either.

Desperate for inspiration, we brought the kids to view the remains of an ancient monastery in a seaside village called Ardmore. It had an enormous round tower within which the monks could draw up the ladder when weathering Viking raids. Owen, now ten, looked it over and said, "Do you see how every layer of stone leans a bit back from the one before? That's how they made these towers go up and up without falling down."

"I never thought about that."

He held Jamie's hand as we walked through the village, commenting on the structural hallmarks of every building of interest. "You know I want to be an architectologist," he offered. His brother and sister howled at the boy's latest malapropism, but my wife and I felt proud. Already, it was clear that he was meant to solve puzzles, a nice talent considering what we had done to his life.

I ARRANGED SOME SPECIAL OUTINGS just for Harris and me. One involved checking out an absurdly ritualized form of Thai kick boxing, called *Muay Thai*, which had become a small rage in Ireland. Off we went to a hotel ballroom at the edge of town, which sported the usual roped gladiatorial platform. Approaching it was a wiry tough with his skin drenched in oil and with mean little eyes. But this particular pugilist wore a garland of red flowers around his head and sported a necklace of still gaudier blossoms and beads. He leapt over the ropes and landed in the ring with a prodigious bound. The crowd roared.

Next, the flowered fighter proceeded to lie flat on the floor with his arms outstretched. Then he got up on one knee, stretched out the other leg, and raised his gloved hands to either side of his chin.

"What's he doing?" asked Harris.

"Beats me," I responded, as the fellow in the red shorts finally stood and began ceremoniously bowing to each corner of the ring, which of course was square.

Another barefoot youth in a white robe and blue trunks leapt over the ropes to muted cheers—muted because he was from Belgium, a place that doesn't overly excite the Irish or anyone else.

Boy Blue started his personal bowing and prayer thing and the crowd was not impressed. "Yur man's fierce tall," said a blonde gal in a black bustier beside me.

"He's a stiff looking ting," said a dolly bird to my left.

On the platform, the pre-fight posturing grew weirder. The native son moved along the ropes with a little brush whisking away invisible objects on the floor. His oiled body gleamed as he rhythmically shuffled and strutted like some Hare Krishna lost in trance and kicked away some more atoms with his bare feet.

"What's he doing now, Dad?" asked a bewildered Harris.

I scanned the program. "They call this *Wai Kru*, or invoking spirits. I think he's trying to banish bad karma or something away from the fight."

Now two men began parading around with an enormous red banner that said "Bridgestone Tyres." Meanwhile the loudspeakers blasted "In-A-Gadda-Da-Vida," the 1968 Iron Butterfly heavy metal anthem that is arguably the worst song ever written.

I read out loud. "Muay Thai is called 'The art of the eight limbs' because you can use both hands, shins, elbows, and knees. But there's no biting, no eye gouging, no spitting or head butting, no swearing or kicks to the groin allowed."

"That's not how they fight on Cork's streets, Dad," said Harris, and he was right. The level of personal assaults in Ireland had risen by 350 percent in the last ten years, the ugliness of the hooliganism growing worse. Biting earlobes off was a fashionable new technique, kicking in the head and groin when a victim was already prone a commonplace finishing-off procedure. That predilection had just left two hapless college students in Cork in permanent comas.

"Maybe things are changing," I said.

Bam! The Cork lad delivered a stunning kick to the side of Blue Boy's face.

Wham! He spun all the way around and dropped a backwards kick from out of nowhere into the foreigner's chest.

"Ye Belgian waffle, ye!" bellowed the girl in fishnet stockings, as if a blow had been struck for Ireland against a thousand years of invaders from points far.

But Boy Blue had a trick up his knee which he promptly thudded into the dead center of the Native Son's stomach.

Backing off, the Cork conquistador bowed in appreciation. Then he shot his opponent a right upside the chin.

Eventually, the Belgian was indeed waffled, and I began wondering about the meaning of the night's madness with its cocked-up religious trappings. Was Ireland losing its bearings altogether? Not long ago, a priest would have found his way to any convocation of youths, and pugilists would be making the sign of the cross before touching gloves—but that was unthinkable now.

We came to a traffic light, and I asked Harris, "What did you make of that stuff tonight?"

"It was pretty strange," came his small voice.

"You're darn right," I began, before fumbling for some moral lesson. "But the Cork guy's whole thing was about confidence, and that's something to think about. Maybe you should act just like him at CBC, just believe in yourself more, and things will get better."

"But I'm doing fine, Dad," Harris said. Of course, it wasn't true.

Another semester passed and finally we were called in to meet the principal. "Perhaps Harris would fare better in a different school?" offered the not very kindly chap.

As it happened, our Irish saga nearly ended that summer. When my mother became gravely ill, we returned to our Connecticut house near her, which we had been renting out for the last three years. That July and August we visited her often and spent other weekends with Jamie's mother in New Jersey as well. It was a time of reconnecting.

Laura initially padded around our spacious Connecticut home as if she were reclaiming her birthright. "I love this house. This is who I am. What made you ever think of leaving all this for Ireland?" she pronounced with a directness not easily answered.

Meanwhile, she and the boys savoured sunny days at the local lake, where they initially regarded the blazing heat of American summer with a kind of wonder. Jamie and I, however, rediscovered our weariness of the pretentious New York weekenders who infested the beach.

As summer advanced, even our children could not be dragged to the lake on weekends either. They too sensed something more shadowy than they had ever encountered in gregarious Ireland. Laura, with adolescent moods swinging, abruptly snarled one morning, "I hate it there. It is like totally status. Why did we ever leave Ireland?"

Such is parenthood. And such had our family become—caught between two worlds.

As parents, we debated endlessly about what to do next. We had each lost our fathers within the last few years, both of whom deeply identified with their Irish ancestry. All we had left was mothers—mothers who, though hurt by our absence, cared enough that they would support us in whatever we felt we must do. But adding to our confusion was the fact Jamie's sister had suffered a paralyzing car accident when young and was confined to a wheelchair. Yet her mother and brother and his wife lived close by and looked after her constantly.

As August closed, I suddenly turned to Jamie and said, "We've got to stay near my mother."

My wife looked as if she had been relieved of a great weight. "You are right. We'll figure the rest out later."

But my dear mother died, and life in America no longer added up. If we remained in Connecticut, Harris would soon enroll in the local high school where Laura reported that enormous numbers of boys in black "Goth" trench coats obliterated themselves with marijuana at lunch. After much agonizing, Jamie and I finally summoned the brood together and made our announcement at the end of the school year in 2004: "We are moving back to Ireland because we were happier there. We're selling this house, and that is that."

Chapter 4

Cork had surprises waiting as we pulled back into town. Perhaps two dozen enormous cranes lined our route, some smashing old buildings into rubble, and others building new ones. A little triangle of a gas station had become a four-story office tower; an apartment complex now blocked all view of the iconic spire of Shandon Cathedral, called the "liar's tower" because it had four different clock faces that told four different times. The civic planning was monstrous. But a flotilla of ships sporting merry flags lined the docks, and the town seemed to be bustling.

In a few minutes, we arrived at our old cul de sac. Curtains parted, and Breeda Higgins spilled out onto the street, engulfing us in her motherly arms.

"Welcome home," Breeda exclaimed. *Home.* The word at once moved and scared me. "I knew you'd come back."

"We missed you, and we missed Cork," murmured Jamie.

That much was true, I thought, but the impact of what I had just seen was somehow upsetting. "What is it with all the cranes everywhere we look?" I asked.

"Sure, the whole town is buzzing, what with Cork about to be celebrated as the European Capital of Culture for 2005, don't you know?"

We did. Banners had proclaimed the fact at every major junction. The EU had been showcasing one city or another for two decades with twelve months of hoopla; and, after moving through the biggies like Paris, Madrid, and Brussels, the spotlight had fallen upon Cork.

"They are tearing the place apart to make it ready, and the developers have been told they can't have any cranes around to mar the view once it starts so they are going hell-for-leather now," Breeda said.

Ah, another Irish sleight of hand, I thought.

A petite woman with the vibrant brown eyes of a spirit much younger than her fifty-some years, Breeda gave a little shake to her hips. "There is such fun on those streets, boys and girls. You have picked a great time to come back."

OUR NEIGHBOR WAS PROPHETIC, AT FIRST. The morning Owen returned to his little CBC primary school a dozen boys gathered by the door and chanted his name over and over as if hailing a pint-sized Julius Caesar: "O-wen! O-wen! OW-EN!" At Bandon Grammar, Laura was enveloped in ecstatic hugs.

For Harris we arranged a new private school called Midleton College, its main building a battered pile built for the Anglo-Irish ascendancy in 1696. The place had only forty-five kids in each year—half girls and half boys—and looked after each child closely, even the dreamers and those from afar. It also had twenty acres of playing fields. From his first day Harris revelled in his new world.

Jamie, meanwhile, resumed her work at the Cork Opera House. Its coming line-up included a Shanghai symphony, an Italian opera, and English choral singers; and her step soon quickened with the excitement. The abutting municipal Crawford Gallery of Art had undergone a beautiful renovation and was about to host a display of ancient Celtic hoards of gold. Satellite theatres and galleries across the small, provincial city would boast their own eclectic projects, including the launch of the *Cork Queer Diary*. The town was in a thrall of anticipation at this latest affirmation of the creativity of the little island.

"The moment of newness is upon us," read the official program for the year-long smorgasbord ahead.

Of course, it wasn't long before the town's countless begrudgers began complaining. "Show that to the Cap Cultcherals," said a taxi driver ferrying me home one night as he pointed to a young woman sitting in a gutter with her short-skirted legs out-stretched as she undaintily vomited beside them. "Tell them what we are really capital at—poisoning our young."

"And look at this," he said as we passed a chunk of street that had been freshly unearthed to expose a cavern of mud-encrusted cables and pipes. "They've dug this stretch up five times this year already." Six men in neon yellow jackets idly eyed what lay below as if this ditch led to Mesopotamia.

In any case, there was no looking back. Buyers had materialized for our Connecticut house—and it sold.

The launch of the European Capital of Culture year of 2005 was promised to be "the greatest outdoor celebration in the history of Ireland." Whatever, the early January bash started with a street carnival led by musicians working neither fiddles nor bagpipes but Brazilian samba drums, manned by a crew of New Age travellers in dreadlocks. To this, drag queens danced on stilts. They were followed by indi-viduals dressed up as hairy gorillas, giant spiders, larger ostriches, and longer caterpillars, with blinking-eyed robots shooing them along. In homage to the Irish Antarctic explorers Ernest Shackleton and Tom Crean, men with woolly mastodon beards donned antique parkas covered in fake snow and schussed about the streets on wheeled cross-country skis.

Cork is a New Orleans in more ways than one, a party town awash in festivals for just about everything under the moon—among them cutting-edge film, jazz, chamber music, choral singing, folk ballads, French food, and perhaps tiddlywinks. They all just meld into the general jolliment. Now the town was being instructed to make a statement of itself in an evening *grand finale* by the river. The crime was that you needed tickets.

Tickets?

The one thing that Corkonians—like Irish people in general—most despise is being told what to do. At important sporting events they wave American Confederate flags—not from any love of slavery, since numerous Irish were once themselves sold as slaves by the Vikings—but as icons of the self-styled "Rebel County's" defiance against outside forces, including Dublin. In the middle of any avenue they saunter into traffic, sometimes with a baby in a pram. There they pause to take a call on their mobile phones. Payment for almost any building, cleaning, or maintenance job is demanded in cash so that no central authority can track it. "The People's Republic of Cork," they call it.

Therefore, the locals grew very suspicious about being enjoined to celebrate themselves in a ritual cooked up by unknown forces from the "arts world."

As darkness fell, I myself climbed into the VIP stands for which I had no ticket and attempted to disappear behind an acquaintance who also had no ticket but who was clinging to a politician who didn't need one. The president of Ireland, Mary McAleese, stood two rows ahead. Apparently we were her security detail.

Before us, various bridges over the River Lee were lit up in brilliant green and EU blue and gold, and more than twenty-five thousand spectators braved the chill.

Downstream appeared a mother ship captained by the most celebrated Corkman of that time, the champion hurler Seán Óg hAilpín, who happened to be half-Fijian. Giant video screens up and down the river now amplified this hero's image so that he appeared to be twenty feet tall. To complete the Celtic warrior effect, clouds of primordial smoke billowed from the deck, and "Seán O," as he is called, recoiled his crescent stick and whacked it down upon a burning *sliotar*, the white ball used in the sport that started with bashing skulls around fields. As the missile sailed into the darkness, Seán O's *camán* stick burst into flame.

A DJ on St. Patrick's Bridge blared into a microphone that we were about to witness an ancient rite reborn, the vanquishing of a ghastly river demon by none other than St. Finbarr. With that, a kind of Bunsen burner ignited underneath a filmy heap of white plastic. In the manner of an expanding hot air balloon, and with the help of a series of rigidifying inner rings, the contraption began to fluff into a distinctly conical shape, if wriggling at first in every direction.

"Christ, it's a French tickler!" said somebody behind me.

The phallus was engorging now and had shifted its attention toward the VIP viewing stand.

"They can't even get it up," said somebody else.

"Typical Ireland," said another.

"Maybe it drank too much," responded his wife in a Kerry accent.

But the moment of newness was upon us. The thing had gained impressive heft and was pointing straight at the esteemed President of Ireland, Mary McAleese. I worried that I too was in its line of fire. We both squirmed.

The DJ on the bridge pronounced, "The tails of the serpent are arising," as spotlights trolled further down the River Lee to five smaller barges. Each sported columns of fully inflated ten-foot-high white sheaths, some tipped and listing slightly, the un-tipped variety standing prouder. All were a third the length of the now mountainously erect Big One.

"In the name of Gawd, it's a sea of feckin' condoms," the Kerry woman shrieked.

The King Condom's snout had begun shooting flames. And then fireworks erupted throughout the black sky, tossing hallucinogenic tendrils of color.

There was so much to celebrate. Why, the esteemed *Economist* magazine had just published a survey of 111 countries purporting that Ireland had the best quality of life in the entire world, better than Switzerland at second, and the United States (thirteenth) and the U.K. (twenty-ninth). The clandestine-sounding Economist Intelligence Unit (EIU) said Ireland had become the fourth richest nation in the world in terms of per-capita income; this was quite a change from the 1950s when four hundred thousand citizens fled to foreign shores for work, or even the dark days of the 1980s.

I myself was on a roll, with journalistic assignments mounting. Some of these allowed for close-quarter observations of the happiest country on earth, according to the EIU. Taking the train to Dublin, I visited a big art auction in a gallery called Adam's, across from the central park of St. Stephen's Green. There awaited a crowd of pin-striped bankers and barristers peppered with more humbly dressed if cash-rich builders.

A work by Jack Butler Yeats, brother of the famous poet, came on the block, and nine employees were working telephones to London and New York for absentee bids. In minutes, this painting of 1927 Dublin street traders went to a phone bidder for 245,000 euros— about ten times what it might have fetched a decade earlier.

The Dublin crowd warmed to a string of Irish expressionists. The moneyed classes had recently discovered that, in the breathlessly growing economy of the mid-decade, a fine painting could amortize faster than a prime field. Bidding fired up for an oil-on-board depiction of a peasant lying before a group of black-shawled women carting a corpse away from a thatched cottage.

A Cork friend appeared in the back row and nodded toward a dapper figure in the corner. "That's Champagne Barry. Watch him if he puts on his glasses," said my confidant, Ray Lloyd. "If they're on, he's in." The man in question was certifiably New Irish, a shipping magnate and stallion breeder with properties in London, France, South

Africa, and New York. His shirt looked hand made, his nails manicured.

Ray Lloyd, who sports a giant unkempt beard, pointed to another fellah suddenly thrusting up his paddle. "That's High Stud himself," he said of the rival builder. "Ah sure, he doesn't know the back of a painting from the front of it." High Stud, only recently suited in plaster dust, had made millions in building scores of so-called "holiday cottages" on Ireland's western seaboard. A man of newly bulging pockets, he was one of a legion of get-rich-quick scammers encouraged by laughably easy credit and government tax incentives to build, build anywhere fast without much thought, and blighting the countryside. Tonight High Stud was flush with art fever.

The Adam's auctioneer worked the crowd. The stakes were thiry thousand euros and climbing fast. Suddenly, High Stud stepped behind a human shield of a neighbor so that no one could watch his eyes as his paddle bobbed. But Champagne Barry had donned his glasses now, and auctioneers in his ken knew his intent to top every bid until he doffed them. Gerard Dillon's "Dreamer" was his for forty-two thousand euros. The night's take would be 3.5 million, the highest the Adams Gallery had made in years. Such were the country's glory days.

Chapter 5

Where was Ireland going? That Easter I booked a cottage in a West Cork village named Courtmacsherry for a family holiday and some pondering. Even the drive to "Courtmac" was atmospheric, since you first have to negotiate a stone causeway beside a ruined twelfth-century abbey in a gloomy place called Timoleague.

Afterwards, the road is stitched tight to a narrow bay surrounded by sloping green fields on either side. Even when mist locks in, hundreds of sea birds caw and cavort over the estuary. You are in a separate space now, rare and serene.

The village with its single main street huddles at the water's edge, just a crook of land away from the violence of the Atlantic. For millennia, the cliff-ringed outer bay has beckoned in mariners, and many have run afoul of its treacherous breakers. Over ten thousand shipwrecks wreath Ireland's shores, great numbers of them along this stretch of coast. Close by, in 1917, the ocean liner *Lusitania* was torpedoed by a German submarine, drowning 1,117 and helping to drive the reluctant U.S.A. into World War I. The Courtmacsherry lifeboats were the first on the scene, the local volunteers pulling in whatever survivors they could find.

My family settled into one of the holiday havens that then were mushrooming insanely around Ireland's coastal villages with little to no civic control, this one a twenty-six house terrace built around an asphalt square. The spot used to be called "Siberia" since it is so often blasted by winter winds. Not that long ago, its poor families subsisted by clawing potatoes from the stony soil and earning meager wages from the village's herring plant. The thatched roofs of their hovels were tethered against oblivion by boulders on ropes. That world has vanished, as has all but one of the thirteen shops that once lined the sheltered main street of Courtmacsherry. Gone, too, with the herring are the dozens of fishing boats that formerly moored at the hamlet's pier, and the waterside railway line that served the village until 1960. Still, the community remains close knit and tied to the land and the sea.

As Easter Day approached, Jamie and I took bicycle trips and seaside walks with the kids and skittered Frisbees across gloriously empty strands—scallops of copper shining by the pewter sea. At the pier, we lowered chicken scraps on strings to catch crabs between murky rocks, to Laura's shrieking dismay. Suddenly, a new Irish dream began to grow, and young Owen was more or less its midwife. He sat on my lap and pronounced, "I love it here. The best thing in our lives before was that we were in the country. Now that you're selling our house in America, maybe we should buy one here."

I took a long walk afterwards, contemplating the idea that a bolt-hole in Courtmacsherry might uplift us all. God knows, the vulgarity of the Celtic Tiger had been filling me with growing ill ease, but that seemed to disappear here.

"A small drinking village with a fishing problem," is the motto displayed on the locals' automobile bumper stickers

Early the next morning, I headed out in pursuit of the new fantasy. Above the village lay a new property scheme called "Spruce Grove." These houses were big mothers, stone-clad and three stories tall, and a placard said that they would come with very *en vogue* Aga cookers in the kitchen, and four bedrooms with toilets *en suite*. "En suite" had become a top-selling point across the land, along with the weirdest new object to have found its way to Ireland's shores: a *bidet*. Just what the rosary-rubbing daughters of Christ fifty years earlier would have made of a bidet is anybody's guess. Those who fathomed that the sinful contraptions catered to a never-discussed region of the female anatomy would have hurriedly blessed themselves and fled. Now bidets were a must-have for the newly affluent. To others, though, they were the epitome of GUBU, an acronym for "Grotesque, Unbelievable, Bizarre, and Unprecedented" coined by the writer Connor Cruise O'Brien at the prenatal stage of Ireland's boom.

The price of these new palaces was incredible: seven hundred thousand euros—one million dollars. What had happened to good ol' Siberia?

THE NEXT DAY WAS EASTER SUNDAY, and it was a tricky one. When we arrived for the eleven o'clock Mass at the local church at the nearby crossroads of Barryroe, things did not look right. Everybody was in fleeing mode.

I called out to a man at the front of the pack, "I thought the Mass began at eleven?"

"It did."

"But it is only eleven now and you are all leaving."

"It has gone past twelve, sure. The time changed last night, don't you know?"

I gasped. My personal theology prescribed that I could pile up a million venal sins without much worry, but mortal ones were another matter. And the Catholic Church's terms about missing the Easter Mass of the Resurrection were pretty clear: This was a "mortal sin" and the next stop was Hell.

"Is there any late Mass at all around now?" I implored.

"Try Clonakilty, but you better hurry," the old fellow advised.

The town was about twenty-five minutes away. I hit the gas pedal with a wallop. The car careened over bumps and went airborne several times as I sped toward "Clon," a here-to-now peaceful town of maybe three thousand souls, all of whom I was quite sure knew how to get out of bed on Easter morning, unlike me. I skidded to a halt outside the nineteenth-century cathedral at the end of the main street and shooed the family forward while I implored Mary, full of grace, to let me find a parking place.

Shambling into the church yard a couple of minutes later, I confronted a baffling sight. Maybe a hundred people, nearly all men, stood beneath a loud speaker which was blasting the priest's words onto the steps outside the cathedral. The phalanx was impenetrable. Worse, the consecration of the Eucharist was beginning at this very moment. A tinkling bell signalled the first stage of the transubstantiation, and on Easter, day of salvation, this moment was meant to resonate through the soul. I closed my eyes, praying that the Redeemer would sanctify the lives of my children, who had made it inside the cathedral in the nick of time. But it wasn't the word of God I heard then.

"That wind is going fierce," said a man beside me who looked like he hadn't shaved in a week. "It is an East wind."

I opened one eye, then the other. A second altar bell tolled that the chalice had been exalted higher. Still there was no hush outside.

"The East wind is not as bad as they say. It has its other sides," responded his mangy-coated friend. "It is good for drying the fields, and we need that now."

Had I joined the circle of the damned? The third and final Sanctus bell sounded, but no one was so much as bowing their heads. In fact, fresh stragglers were still joining the ranks outside, and I wondered why this insanely tardy batch didn't just drive around the cathedral once or twice with their car windows open.

"What did that auctioneer say about the guide price of John-Joe's field last night?" said a skinny character in bright blue pants, reaching for a cigarette.

"Ah sure, he'll say anything, that one. And he had a feed of drink on."

What had happened to Ireland's fabled reverence for Jesus and Mary and all the saints? What were these geezers around me actually doing—seeking eternal salvation by standing beneath a squawk box?

The cathedral's doors burst open, and a couple of dozen parishioners scuttled out: The advance guard of the Twenty-Minute Brigade.

Every Catholic of my generation knew that if your timing was nifty, you could slip into the back pews after the Mass got going and wait until the moment the first Communion wafers were proffered to make the rite official. That way your service to the Lord could be done in a third of an hour. Do that at decent intervals, you won't meet the black-eyed fiend with the pitchfork for the next billion years.

I was still working on my theology when young Owen stuck his freckled face between the elbows of two men in overcoats and beckoned me forward. "There is room inside now, Dad," he said as he took my hand and led me into the cathedral, where I wandered down the aisle to take a most imperfect communion.

After Mass we went to a restaurant outside of town called Deasy's, beside which sailboats darted across Clonakilty's inner bay. The food proved to be first rate—starters of fresh mussels and sizzling prawns, followed by succulent lamb and roast potatoes, and then a dessert of ice cream crumble cake.

Owen, enjoying a "feed" of sugary Coca Cola, went brain silly. Secretly slipping out the door, he crawled along the outer walls on all fours. As we were all eye-balling the magical view through the picture window below which he skulked, he suddenly leapt two feet into the air like an exploding frog. With his arms splattered wide, he shouted "BLAH" at the top of his lungs. Somehow, this was so hilarious that Laura, laughing uncontrollably, bribed him to repeat the act before a table of shocked total strangers.

Me, I looked around and thought, "We have gone Irish, each and every one."

JUST WHEN ALL THE MOST WORRISOME THREADS of our family resettlement program—to my mind meaning Jamie and the three kids—seemed to be rewoven into steady, satisfying rhythms in Cork, a loose end developed. And that was me: It's called writer's block. My job became watching the rain, which never seemed to stop. Wrestling with *ennui* and isolation in my garage office, I sought escapes.

Sometimes, I went to the country and sometimes I went to the pub. Alas, my former redoubt of hilarity, the Hi-B had grown stale. The owner Brian O'Donnell had fallen down the stairs with a carton of eggs in one hand that remained intact, but he had not fared as well, suffering a severely broken ankle. His absence created a void and a directionless clientele eased onto the stools.

Around the same time, warm acquaintances began to die, including a baritone singer named Declan. He was part of a collective at a pub called John Henchey's & Sons that materializes every Christmas to street-corner harmonize in wind and rain to raise money for the terminally ill. The choir offered up songs of exultation at Declan's grave, then sad bagpipes filled the air.

At the pub afterwards, my neighbor Pat Lynch came up to me and said, "Nobody does death better than the Irish."

"What do you mean?"

Glasses were clattering, laughter ricocheting.

"Look around. You've got second, even third cousins here, friends of the uncles, the delivery men, and our whole Christmas choir, which sometimes won't even speak to each other for weeks. Then there are the strays."

"Strays?"

"Sure, three or four show up at every funeral in Ireland. They check the newspapers for obituaries, brush their hair and put on a tie. Some only do the church, but most also go to the pub for the 'afters'."

True enough, I spotted several "quare" fellows waving free drink tickets about who looked as if they belonged on bus station benches.

Soon the scene grew so tipsy, it gave me pause. The fact was that as the country grew richer, alcohol abuse skyrocketed. In fact, Ireland soared to second place behind only the Czech Republic in the global sweepstakes of inebriation, leaving even the Russians and Brits in the sawdust.

At the end of 2005, the Republic of Ireland's governmental ombudsman and information commissioner, Emily O'Reilly, gave a speech that began, "Many of us recoil at the vulgar fest that is much of modern Ireland." Then she chronicled a litany of runaway materialism, instant gratification, increasing hooliganism, and excess of every stripe.

"Divorce [illegal in Ireland until 1997] was meant to be for the deeply unhappy, not the mildly bored. . . . Sunday shopping was supposed to be a convenience for the harassed worker, not a new religion," she continued. "Released from the handcuff of mass religious obedience, we are Dionysian in our revelry, in our testing of what we call freedom. . . . Hence the staggering drink consumption, the childlike showing off of helicopters and four-wheel drives and private cinemas, the fetishizing of handbags and high heels."

The boom economy's power brokers insisted there was not much to worry about. Thus, within a few months Seamus O'Donoghue, president of the Vintners Federation of Ireland (VFI), a lobby of six thousand publicans, said:

> We can conceive of no reason why the question of alcohol should be considered in the context of a strategy to deal with the use and abuse of drugs. . . .

> Since earliest times, man has sought and found peace and satisfaction in the alcohol product. . . . The moderate or responsible [consumption] of alcohol contributes enormously to the health of the nation, and to the health of the consumer.

Next, I read that a young Donegal woman had been so elevated by her second pint of Budweiser that she saw a likeness of Jesus Christ floating about in its foamy head: the Irish version of the Shroud of Turin. The epiphany was so vivid that a photograph of it was printed full page in the *Daily Mail*, a British-based tabloid that normally ran photos of young ladies wearing less than a bikini.

Catherine McDermott insisted: "I wasn't drunk. It was only my second beer of the night when Jesus appeared. He wasn't on the head of my Budweiser when I ordered it, but when I gulped some of it he miraculously appeared." She never finished the drink, explaining, "I couldn't swallow Jesus no matter how much I like Budweiser."

My neighbor Pat Lynch scanned the article and chortled, "Thank God she wasn't drinking Guinness, or she would have seen the whole blessed Trinity."

There was a lot of excess then, as the *Irish Times* had recently noted:

> Gardai who searched a Mayo pub at 3:30 a.m. after receiving an anonymous tip-off found nobody inside the pub.

> However, on looking in the publican's attached private quarters, they found eight people, including two bar staff and the publican's daughter, stuffed together in the toilet. . . .

The article quoted the publican's court testimony:

> "I know it sounds funny, eight people in a private bathroom, but there was no party or anything going on. . . ."

Something similar emerged when I brought my visiting brother to a venue that refused to change—a dark bar, the Cork Arms, which was run by a hilarious woman named Patsy. It should have been named the Cork Throats. Philip and I sat down beside a man who was humming loudly to himself and scribbling on his palm.

"The Saints Go Marching In?" I asked.

The stranger nodded and grinned, then abruptly listed right. Before my brother could offer a steadying hand, the hummer fell backwards off his stool. Yet magically he propelled his body laterally through mid air, just as the legendary ancient Irish hero Cúchulainn used to do with what were called triple-salmon leaps. This was Irish diving at its finest. He flapped his arms and knees for extension and managed to land about six feet away from his launching stool, miraculously sailing straight down an open doorway to the top of the steep stairs to the basement lavatory. On the second rung, his head landed with a wicked thump. The ejection-seat force of his arc earned yet further style points, perhaps because his head had affected a drunk's natural resilience of melon softness. In any case, the hummer's head began to bounce off a succession of further steps with a nice rhythm such as a drum major sounds.

My poor younger brother did not comprehend the land's ways and frantically spun about to grab the man's ankles before he could complete his descent. With that, the night's flyer picked himself up, brushed back his hair, and walked out the door.

Somebody else explained, "That's Tim, and he has a drink problem. He marks his palm with a pen for each pint he drinks and tries to stop at thirteen. Tonight, he must have lost his pen."

"Unbelievable!" laughed Philip.

"Maybe," I responded, "but I can't take much more of this vaudeville stuff anymore. I've got to find some quiet place out of town to get the family back together and settle things down because this country is going bananas."

Chapter 6

I reland kept bouncing. Thanks to the mounting wads in their wallets and the advent of cut-rate flights via Ryanair, the Irish had taken to holidaying like there was no tomorrow. By 2006, the little nation logged nearly seven million flights abroad, with about two million to sun-drenched places like Tenerife or the Algarve, Miami Beach, or Thailand. Not bad for a country of four million when you consider that if, say, Americans traveled abroad in equivalent numbers entire Caribbean islands would be sucked dry of their water supplies, deflate, and list into the sea.

Lord knows, the prices of everything had gone through the roof: thirteen euros for a spatula (made in China) that you could buy in the U.S. for a buck and change; eighteen euros—twenty-five dollars, for Christ's sake—for a Dublin cheeseburger and barely warm chips. Hotel rates grew so high, people found it cheaper to holiday in Portugal than Kerry. Yet the developers, egged on by a waterfall of tax incentives, kept building new hotels beside every castle and cliff. Cars cost thousands more than they did almost anywhere else. A scathing phrase took hold: "Rip-Off Ireland."

Still, the restaurants, nightclubs, and pubs stayed full, and swells surfing the crest of the boom kept spending as if price just didn't matter. One of these was a young Dublin property developer named

Donal Caulfield, a former European kick-boxing champion. By the time he started wheeling and dealing at age twenty-eight, Caulfield was driving a Porsche. Four years later he acquired a red Ferrari complemented by a private jet, as he told the *Irish Times.*

> It's not so much about owning the jet. It's about having the money to give you the freedom to do what you want, to say what you want. The more money people have, the more freedom they have, if they have the right psyche. . . . Money is pure and utter freedom.

The pendulum had swung mind-bogglingly far from the former days of want. Almost overnight, private jets and helicopters (called "blades" by the developers) were being snapped up at the highest per-capita acquisition rate in the EU. The excess seemed to know no bounds.

God knows what the martyrs of the Easter Rising in 1916 would have made of the self-indulgence that became the nation's mantra only 90 years later. Nervously watching the stampedes of SUVs that always seemed bent on annihilating everybody who stood in their path, I liked to imagine the consternation that might appear in the flinty eyes of Eamon De Valera had he come back to life for a moment in say, 2006. Ol' Dev was a glowering figure—the idealogue of the revolution; one of the most divisive behind the subsequent fiasco of the Civil War following victory against the Crown in 1921; and, finally back into the fold, the second Taioseach of the land upon which he put his stern and zealous stamp. He was a George Washington with a Transylvanian touch, and to this day no one is quite sure whether he should properly be revered or abhorred.

The fact is that Dev's economic policies helped ruin the aspirations of several generations, being built upon sentimental manifestos envisioning an Ireland pure, archly neutral, and free of outside influence. Once reliant unto themselves, and freed of all trade with the hated British wolf, "the plain people of Ireland" were supposed to reap the stolen promises of their lands and seas and prosper on their own.

According to Dev, a saintly collective of small farmers and their brother tradesmen and shopkeepers would usher in a Celtic Renaissance, and no evil empire need apply. Meanwhile, a benevolent government would look after the downtrodden; and one day the orphaned counties of Northern Ireland would add their weight to the Republic, which would by then be speaking in its resurgent mother tongue. Ah, *Tír na nÓg.*

Naturally, nobody paid those pipe dreams an ounce of credence by the dawn of the Bouncy Castle Era. It was clear as day that the new wealth was streaming in not from the stubborn isolationism of a proud but traumatized new country, but because of Ireland's open palms extended across the seas.

And why not? By mid-century Ireland was a welfare state with a quarter of the population on the dole and the whole scheme funded by endless borrowing. A way forward only emerged with the country's leap into the EEC in 1973—*58 billion* euros eventually to be harvested from that patch, which even in a land of fancy was a magic act. Though the immediate boost was short-lived, a lesson had been learned and it was goodbye Dev and isolationism be damned. To jump start things again, the politicos took to studying the American model for basket-case backwaters like Puerto Rico. In the 1990s they went hats-in-hand to the powerhouses of unrestrained multinational capitalism. You want a tax break? Poof, forget taxes, was more or less the promise. And would you like an interest-free building loan? No problem.

It was rap-tap-tap on the door of Hewlett Packard, Pfizer, Johnson & Johnson, Medtronic, Apple, and Dell, with promises of a young and vital population desperate for work and a red carpet rolled out for anyone who would take a chance on a nation hungry to emerge in the modern world. Thus began the fairy tale of a boom that was never supposed to end.

Voila! By the late 1990s the country had wrestled unemployment down to 5%, and the economy was burgeoning, with surging opportunities for new enterprises and well-paid employment. Ireland set to furiously brooming away all manner of dark spirits from times past. A strange new happy, happy talk was in the air. The bitterness, the distrust, the endemic despair, the famine memories, the haunted certainty of the old people about malevolence being afoot down the lane—all were being tossed into the bin of time. Fairies? British-made Fairy Liquid was what you now used to clean every last stain out of your gleaming modern sink.

So you had the middle class swelling and buying and building, building—installing bidets and Aga cookers!—and thousands of expats coming back in a flood of new hope. You had farmers finding pots of gold at the end of their suddenly hugely marketable fields, coughing up stories of their incredible new wealth every night in the pub. Why, you had plumbers, electricians, and bricklayers pulling in incomes of one hundred thousand euros and buying side properties to fix up and flip on their own. Health spas—health spas!—appeared everywhere in a country so long synonymous with stoic suffering. This was the Celtic Klondike, and in fact gold mines had started in Ireland.

The opportunities seemed to be endless—Mercedes dealerships, custom kitchen fitters, naughty lingerie shops, lap dancing clubs, boutiques offering imported French and English fineries, indoor tennis courts: Latch on to any gaudy new idea and you might just make a killing.

One of the most peculiar new lines of work involved the processing of so-called "asylum seekers" who claimed to have suffered repression in far-off lands and sought refuge amidst Ireland's growing wealth. In 2002, Ireland welcomed nearly twelve thousand of them, speaking everything from Acholi (the language of northern Uganda) to Zulu. A Cork solicitor I knew became a specialist in assisting these new arrivals. A picaresque character, his name was Roger, though he also was known as Sean or "the judge."

One night I found the burly-bearded Roger-Sean at a nearby pub, which was hosting an exhibition of paintings by dozens of Cork artists with the proceeds to be donated to an orphanage in Cambodia.

Curious, I asked Roger what was new.

"Well, I've been dealing with some strange cookies lately," he grinned.

"What do you mean?"

"Yerrah, I had to go to court in Dublin today for a fellow named Thank God Kennedy from rural Nigeria, you would be talking dead poverty there. He thought Ireland was the promised land. But he got into hassles once he arrived."

"Oh?"

"You see, a lot of my people not only have odd names, but also have problems with magical thinking and the voodoo, too. That's what the judges never understand. All they want to hear is the facts and the particulars, but many of my clients don't think that way.

"The judge was keen on establishing the facts of Thank God Kennedy's residence in Ireland and demanded: 'Tell us how and when you first arrived in Ireland.' But that wasn't the right approach. Thank God Kennedy looked at him and said, 'I got turned into an eagle in my village and flew to Ireland.'

"The judge got all twisted, like. 'On what airline?' says he. Thank God Kennedy looked him straight and said, 'No, no, no. I turned into an eagle and flew to Cork airport, but on no airplane, no airplane for me.'"

Roger was by now laughing out-loud at his own preposterous story. "The judge said my case was an insult to his court. He said, 'You don't expect me to believe any of this!'

"I said, 'Your honor, surely you remember that just twenty years ago thousands of Irish people thought they saw that statue of Our Blessed Mother moving and weeping tears in Ballinspittle?'"

Funny stuff and true. With an arms-flying bounce from backyard launching pad, the Gaels were reaching for the skies. Eight decades after a blood-soaked revolution against centuries of repression, you could no longer keep the Irish down. And if old Dev came back to life, he would likely be bouncing, too.

IRELAND'S MOUNTING EXCESS DISTRESSED ME so often that I kept looking for a place apart. The object wasn't money, but peace of mind. Thus, one Friday I twisted up a boreen in West Cork to inspect a dwelling that was said to boast magnificent ocean views. Farm dogs snarled as I parked the car and squished across a bog in the making. Beyond sat the remnants of a classic whitewashed Irish hovel with a rotting blue door that framed an estate agent with bobbed blonde hair. "Lovely to meet you," said she.

Her voice was so trilly English on the phone I first thought her name was "Avaricious" and made her repeat it. "Avril Letitious" was what she seemed to say next. She was quite petite in the flesh and beamed enticingly, despite being caked in mud to her pretty ankles. For some primordial reason, I found this appealing.

"Sorry about that," said Avril, glancing at the oozing and gurgling, which was swallowing my lower extremities by the inch.

"Sorry to be late," I rejoined as a cow in the next field made its noises.

"No, sorry, I was early."

That is how one flirts with the English, by striking up a conversation going backwards.

Avril had a long, delicate neck and pale rosy cheeks. I liked that, and I liked her reedy voice, which was perfect when it was time for just the two of us to play house.

"Won't you come in?" she trilled.

"Sorry, thanks." Er, maybe, no, yes, well, okay, that is if you don't mind, was the meaning.

Beyond waited three adjoining rooms that were each just big enough to hold a ping-pong table with a diminutive Chinese paddler at either end. The first did have a hearth, but this seemed to have been transformed into a service entrance for the mice that had gnawed the rotting curtains left in a heap at its base.

A door to the left was opened. "This is the kitchen," said Avril.

Looking past a battlefield of broken crockery and rusting pots and pans strewn about a filthy linoleum floor with random holes in it, I did see a large ceramic sink. Blue with mould, it looked like a perfect spot for mixing sheep dip.

"Lovely," I mumbled.

Next it was up the stairs, which groaned as if about to collapse. This expedition led to what was benevolently termed "two bedrooms." My six-foot-high head scoured a fresh channel in the cobwebs hanging from the ceiling.

"Look!" commanded Avril. "There is the ocean."

Sure enough, when I lowered my head until it was nearly between my legs, I could indeed peer out through a small window to a wafer of the Atlantic several miles distant.

"That is beautiful," I acknowledged.

We went outside. "This place could be an inspiration with a little work," enthused Avril. "It gets the most brilliant morning sun."

There we go again, I thought, scuttling onto the roof of an adjoining pig sty in order to assess the potential ocean view from an imaginary study there.

"What happened to the owners?" I asked.

"They dropped everything and moved to America."

To America? What on earth was I doing here? After all the striving my ancestors had invested to gain a better life abroad, what possessed me to propel my family in reverse? Why, my own maternal West Cork relations could have owned this hovel a hundred years ago, before they fled to a brighter future.

Nonetheless, I rang Avril the next day and offered ridiculous money for the pig sty and adjoining mess.

"I doubt that is realistic," she sniffed.

Not realistic? My bid was a hundred times higher than the ruin would have fetched when I first came to Ireland in 1973.

I might as well have been waving bank notes from a merry-go-round, what with the ever higher phantom bids that "gazumped" over my phone, as the Irish called that form of price goading wherein rivals were as invisible as the little people and nothing was ever written down. Property fever was at the boil, and people were fairly tossing money at every four walls. "Sorry," I said, bidding adieu to West Cork, a region I loved but that had priced itself out of my world.

In the sleepier region known as East Cork, there lay a tiny cottage up a grassy lane that had the ocean for its front lawn. Okay, it had no plumbing and loose clumps of toxic asbestos insulation dangled from the ceiling. But these were small issues when a vision of infinity lay before one's eyes.

By now, I had this dream-chasing down cold. Ignore the ludicrous, admire the view, then find the local pub to get the scoop. In this particular hamlet, called Guilleen, the job was particularly easy, since there was only one. And it was perfect, with an eccentric owner, photographs of giant locally landed fish on the walls, and a scattering of central-casting locals quaffing their pints.

A fellow with beady eyes approached. "I hear you have been looking at my father's cottage," said he.

Whoa, I thought, it's time for an inside deal, saving thousands. "Yes, it's such a gorgeous spot," I winked.

"Well, you better forget about it right now. We have some family issues. My sister thinks she owns it, but her head has been twisted by an ashram. It's all that feckin' meditation."

"I see," I said, and poof went another fantasy.

BUT THERE WAS GLEE IN THE AIR in the heady peak of the boom. One day Jamie and I walked into Cork after hearing a crescendo of fiddles and flutes resounding from the streets below. And we discovered that every thoroughfare was packed with thousands of people doing the jig to tunes cranked out by heavily amplified bands splayed over eight different stages.

From the massed throng a woman waved to me. This was a friend named Pauline, a normally demure harpsichord teacher, who stopped her spinning just long enough to catch my attention.

"Get a ticket and come dance!" she called.

"Why the ticket?"

"Because we're trying to break the world record for the most people to ever Step Dance at one time, and everybody needs to be counted! We've got about 7,200 and only need a few hundred more!"

"Who's record?" Jamie asked.

"Dublin, Ohio!"

"But I don't dance," I remonstrated.

"Then just bounce along," enjoined Pauline.

And that's what I half-did, like a man impatiently tapping his feet, with my wife spinning circles at my hand.

Chapter 7

After New Year's Day, Jamie invited a few gal friends over one night and discovered that they all wanted to talk about their recent Christmas shopping sprees.

"I just loved New York, the energy and the buzz of it," began one friend named Pamela, who was married to a property developer.

The subject should have been expected since one hundred seventy thousand Irish women, basically one out of every ten adult females, had just made trips to the U.S. to avail themselves of cut-rate American prices, made salivating by the exchange rate. Reports said the lassies had nearly cleaned out Manhattan, purchasing nearly three billion euros worth of presents. There, they stuffed giant suitcases full of designer dresses and Manola Blahnik killer heels, iPods, DVDs, and X-Boxes. Ah, the gravity-defying dears.

"Did you go to the Metropolitan Museum or Carnegie Hall? Ellis Island?" asked Jamie eagerly.

"No time for that," laughed Pam. "We hit the ground running. The first day was Macy's and then the next morning we were off to Woodbury Commons. That place is heaven!"

"But it's also hell!" hooted Mags, knocking back a glass of white wine. "You had to keep your elbows sharp because every aisle was like wall-to-wall Irish. You'd find the Kerry gals stuffing one, the next jammers with Cork gals, and the Dubs. But the deals were massive!"

WINTER TURNED TO SPRING and before we knew it another school year ended with its inevitable sweet melancholy. The jubilation came laden with a special poignancy as Laura graduated from secondary school. Degrees in hand, excited friends hugged each other with shrieks and tears at the sudden recognition that their lives were changing forever.

"I can't believe how beautiful and sad this is at the same time," Laura said to us before a celebration party in our back garden, where yesterday's young girls soon appeared as young women in formal dresses tripping over high heels. Hoisting champagne toasts with their beaux in tuxedos, they nearly underwent an instant metamorphosis, no doubt realizing they were about to scatter to the winds. Would it be Dublin or London, Galway or Edinburgh? Off they went to a hotel ball, to dance away the disappearing innocence of their youth. Yet they shared more confidence for the future than any Irish generation had ever known, without a clue to the heartache ahead.

So this summer Laura was on her way out of our home. And here was Harris waving goodbye as he climbed aboard Ireland's national sail-training ship, the three-masted brigantine the *Asgard II,* voyaging from Scotland to Norway, then to Copenhagen. He was becoming a young man and more than half-Irish himself. In fact, he had by now accumulated a remarkable collection of friends and was savouring Ireland's easy conviviality every day.

Later that summer, Jamie and I packed the protesting boys into the car for an excursion—poor Laura had been invited that week to suffer at a friend's villa in Spain. Our picnic for the boys was at an idyllic spot, but the real scheme had to do with looking for a bolt-hole along the Blackwater, the valley that Bill Griffin had recommended long before. "The Blackwater Valley is Ireland's hidden gem," he'd said. We headed off to a little village called Ballyduff.

At first glance the place looked to be only a crossroads, yet something ineffable hung in the air. This enclave in the far west of County

Waterford sat close to the fabled river through which Atlantic salmon coursed.

Ancient Irish lore reveres the salmon as a mystical being—a keeper of divine knowledge and a mighty explorer, looping its life journey back to holy springs in an endless ritual of rejuvenation. Never stymied, always sailing into the beyond—*salmo salar*, "the leaper," was the supernatural one. Such was the fluidity of the Gaelic imagination that legendary heroes were often depicted as shape shifters who could transform themselves into salmon and leap over mighty trees when cornered, before bursting back into a magical new human form in some other glen.

So here I was trying to remake myself. At first glance, the T-shaped collection of pebble-dashed cottages, pubs, and shops that is sometimes called Ballyduff Upper seemed almost comical, since the county of Waterford boasts another village called Ballyduff Lower, and perhaps another dubbed Ballyduff-In-Between. But turning down the shaft of this T, tranquillity seemed palpable. Marigolds bedecked a pub to the right. Across the street a jumble of rakes and hoes leaned as if on elbows against a hardware shop. Children stood in the road, smacking their hurling sticks against a rock-hard ball called a *sliotar*. The children and not cars owned this pavement, where forty years before there would have been a crossroads of barefoot dancing every Saturday night. Cows lowed from a near field.

Ballyduff's name in Irish, *An Baile Dubh*, means "black village," but this seemed all wrong. Black? The light glowed butter yellow on the cut-stone Catholic church just beyond. Tombstones listed in the yard. A man in rumpled green trousers with a ruddy moon face eyed my car. He had the air of a well-fed cat and lazily raised a hand in greeting.

This simple gesture to a stranger warmed me. When wandering Ireland as a student, I marveled at the easy greetings that arose from every other chink in an Irish hedgerow. This practice stalked my imagination for years, for the simple reason that it was sublime.

Once, every raised hand invited an improvisational conversation that answered no clock. In 1974, it took me an hour to walk through a Donegal crossroads of a dozen houses because of those raised hands. Then the practice seemed to vanish, around the cities anyway. At least here in Ballyduff, I thought with relief, someone remembered how to offer an old-style hello. What a classic eccentric he looked with furry eyebrows arching up to a tousle of white hair. I tipped my steering-wheel finger in acknowledgement, which is how it is done. He half winked in complicity.

"There *is* something magical about this place," I said to Jamie.

"That's your mantra," was her reply.

"I mean, look at this road. It doesn't make any sense," I responded, because it was presently meandering in a slow S-curve to the local bridge. But the twists were avoiding no obstacles since ordinary pasture lay on either side. The car nosed to the Blackwater River, dark as peat from its origins in the distant Kerry mountains. The bridge here was a steel-latticed affair painted red, a vestige of the late nineteenth-century British empire.

On the far side, I saw three things. The first was a former creamery that until a couple of decades back processed the milk of countless local farmers. Now it was locked ghostly tight.

Then from a rise straight ahead loomed a miniature nineteenth-century castle pieced together out of brownstone blocks. It was pretty enough, save for the murderous rifle slits on its twin turrets. The former denizens of this Royal Irish Constabulary barracks had stood ready to shoot any natives who tried insurrection, as almost every generation did in this region since the seventeen century.

To the right of the bridge stood a classic farmstead surrounded by whitewashed stone walls with some kind of machinery muscling iron tentacles above it. A sign announced: *2 Prime Acres for Sale. Development Opportunity!*

"Not that again," moaned Jamie.

The river was wrapped in nothing but pasture, a verdure that rolled up behind us into a quilt of spruce-green woodlands and meadowy hills that ran north toward Tipperary.

"Will you look at all this?" I said to the progeny in the back seat. Their response was a deafening insentience, both teenage boys having plugged their consciousness into some command center in Japan. Sixteen-year-old Harris, back from his Scandinavian voyage with arms stronger and face bronzed, had wires in his ears and was receiving signals.

Owen, newly thirteen, was fidgeting at the buttons of a mobile phone, speaking in text messages. Named after my first paternal forebear to leave County Monaghan in 1844 (a great uncle times five to Owen), he is good-natured when he feels like it. But now he looked up from his electronic rune machine and muttered, "You are never going to find this place, Dad."

Something told me otherwise as we turned right and proceeded beside the river. The road curved under a leafy canopy. Two rabbits watched us pass with a dopey indifference. Lush fields rose left, speckled with cattle destined to become steak dinners in burgeoning Irish markets like Dubai or Libya. (The latter's dictator Moammar al-Gaddafi had supplied free boatloads of machine guns, AK-47s, surface-to-air-missiles, and plastic explosives to the IRA in the 1980s.) A car roared past from the opposite direction, the driver lifting a forefinger of greeting on the fly. Then that silence. A few seconds later another "For Sale" sign emerged, and I pulled tight to a wall that seemed to be propping up the entire pasture.

Across the way sat a peach-colored cottage bordered by roses of vermillion, red, and yellow. Blue and pink hydrangeas frilled the lawn.

A smaller companion cottage, with a little window under the eave, nested beside it, bordered by two pear trees standing sentry off the far corner. One of these was so laden with fruit it listed like a drunk.

"This place is charming," I said to my wife.

"Calm yourself," Jamie exhaled, pushing away the London *Sunday Times*.

"It doesn't look like anyone's at home. I am going to check it out," I announced, opening the car door.

"Dad, don't!" This was Harris waking from the gadget-obsessed teenage wasteland of the back seat. "Don't go there! What if someone's inside? They'll call the Gardai. You are *so* embarrassing!"

I was already crossing the road when a silver SUV wheeled up and reversed into the pebbly driveway ahead. A sixtyish couple clambered out, the long-limbed male scowling and vanishing into the main cottage, the female turning my way with curiosity.

"Sorry, I saw a description of your place in the newspaper and was interested. I didn't mean to intrude," I stammered.

"That's okay," she said and asked whether we might want to see the gardens. "You are very welcome."

Jamie, suddenly interested, emerged and followed with Owen tagging after. Through an archway between the cottages, we shuffled behind the owner Anne Porter. Beyond lay a lawn framed by apple and plum trees. Between gaps in a row of eighty-foot-high cedars, we could see the river, running dark and fast.

Anne steered us to a second garden quadrant divided into many vegetable beds with a conservatory at its base. Lettuce, broccoli, beans, peas, leeks, spinach, carrots, and leafy potatoes arose in tidy rows. A blue shed sat stage right, bordered by enormous gooseberry and blackcurrant bushes.

"Your gardens are amazing," Jamie, avid in such pursuits back in Connecticut, exclaimed.

"They can swallow you for days," Anne responded with a laugh. "But I try to live up to what was done here before." She explained that a Dane with the unlikely name of Hans Christian Andersen had poured himself into the place before she and her husband took ownership, that he had once raised sheep in the fields on either side, which now sprouted a pair of brick bungalows.

We walked through a glade beside the river. Owen was fairly bounding along the steep bank like the boy he still was.

A further strip of lawn funneled to a cleft down the embankment to a shale island in the river. The Blackwater surged by as it made its final run to the broad tidal estuary ten miles downstream that invited in the marauding Vikings. Their Nordic tongue still resonates in the peculiarities of the local accent. In the near distance loomed an ancient Norman castle, battered in 1650 by Cromwell's invading English forces. At my feet, meanwhile, lay perfect riffles for salmon to hold in, a mighty channel through which any spawning fish must course. The place was stunning.

Enchanted, I walked away, turning some stones with a stick. Owen scurried up, inquiring, "What are you looking for Dad?"

"Oh, I don't know. What do you think of all this?"

"It's really, really nice," he beamed.

I touched his shoulder, framing his freckled face against the green valley.

A pair of trumpeter swans wove downriver, white on black water. Their wings made an elemental sound, like the luff of canvas sails filling with wind. Then we hiked up the muddy bank and were invited inside.

The guest cottage was a converted barn, with a spacious bedroom fronted by tall windows eyeing the river through a wreath of climbing white roses. Perhaps we could rent this out?

The next stop was the main cottage with twin glass doors to a dining room with vaulted ceilings. Two double-windows framed the river. Everywhere I turned I was entranced.

A small kitchen off this room opened to a lair-like living room, with a woodstove tucked into its hearth. Seated beside a nice fire, Murray Porter, the man of the house, rose to offer a handshake.

A pair of large bedrooms sat left and right, one boasting a framed needlepoint canvas that said "*Laura*"—our daughter's name.

We sat down to tea. Sip, sip, chat, chat. Murray, a professor of psychology with a droll wit, picked our brains. In the end, a properly played fish will come to its handler. I knew I was that fish, perversely admiring the net.

As dusk gathered, we bid goodbye and found Harris still glued to the back seat of our car, firing off text messages.

"Listen, Dad. I was texting Fuller." He was talking about a close friend from his secondary school.

"Oh?"

"That field with all the horses in it, I think that's Fuller's and that I have been here before. He lives just up the hill. I think that most of this land here belongs to his family."

I scanned the hill, contemplating.

"We should buy this place," insisted Harris, who hadn't even deigned to get out of the car.

I paused and saw many things: my boys learning to cast flies at my hand while having a friend with a farm waiting across the way; Jamie gardening to her content; Laura coming home from university to a room with her name already on it; and myself coming to terms with the madly shape-shifting country of Ireland.

Then I did the math. And I calculated the math of breaking children's hearts with false promises.

"It's just a dream, and we can't afford it." I pressed the throttle hard along obscure roads twisting back to Cork as darkness fell.

Chapter 8

The problem with adopted countries is that their bureaucracies are even more horrible than the ones you left behind. By now, Jamie and I had jumped through most every hoop the Irish government could throw at us. We had become tax-payers, home-owners, rubbish bin tag-holders, and, after a tortuous process bulked up by fifty-two pages of supporting paperwork, co-nuptial citizens of the Republic of Ireland—the latter thanks to my wife's closer ancestral connections via her Roscommon ancestry. But one issue still lurked.

I was still motoring away on an American driver's license, having cruised Ireland at will for something like five years. I wasn't the only wayfarer in Limbo since four hundred and fifty thousand Irish motorists, *one out of every four*, were tooling around on a Learner's Permit which forbids them to go anywhere without a fully licensed driver in the next seat. That stipulation is universally ignored.

Nonetheless, I eventually sought the sunlight of legality by facing the hurdle thousands avoid—the Irish driving test. Sure, I'd passed the American version at age sixteen and figured I'd sat rather ably behind the wheel of all manner of vehicles for approaching three quarters of a million miles since—including dump trucks for transporting steaming hot manure from an upstate New York bovine insemination center.

The Irish authorities do not see any relevance to their roads in time spent on American highways. To gain legal status you must undergo an indigenous half hour of torture, whose curious, very un-Irish cardinal rule is that no talking is allowed.

I greeted my driving tester cheerily and attempted to tell him about the fullness of my experience, including that summer trucking the manure of freshly masturbated bulls. Con, who had sagging jowls and dull eyes, silently shuffled some papers.

"Look, I've been living in Ireland for years and driving for almost four decades," I pressed as we walked to the "car park."

"Could you open your bonnet?" Con rejoined.

I got the hood open.

"Identify the brake fluid," commanded he.

"Jeez, I'm not sure. My mechanic handles that."

Out thrust a clipboard, and a displeased check mark was registered. We got in the car, Con and I. "Execute a left turn out of the car park and then proceed to the junction, and then turn left again."

I did what I was told. A friend who had spent nine years driving a taxi in the bedlam of New York failed his first Irish driving test, but revealed the secret to success. "Act like your head extends from a string. At every intersection bob it right and left, look at each mirror, and then do it all over again while craning your jaw as if you are an utter moron. They like that," smiled Brian.

So there I was at the first intersection, craning this way and that in ridiculously exaggerated style. Then I made perhaps the eight-millionth turn of my life. Out thrust the clipboard, and Con gave me another bad mark. The fecker.

We came to a roundabout, through which motorists were doing a furious loopty-loop from five entry points. Me, I eyed the mess cautiously, bobbing my head back and forth like a perfect Mortimer Snerd. Con glared.

Things got worse further on. "Reverse observantly around the entire length of the turn into this cul de sac, keeping within eighteen inches of the kerb for approximately eighty meters. You will not be penalized for time expended and may re-initiate the exercise at any point," the robot next enjoined. I had never encountered any driving situation like this in my life but I tried—clumsily.

The inevitable bad news was delivered at Con's desk. According to him, I wasn't remotely ready to drive on the Irish roads I'd been whistling over for the last half decade. Con thought I had showed excessive hesitation by looking too hard into my mirrors and not driving *fast* enough.

I needed a shoulder to lean on. So I sought out a witty friend named Peter Harding, who was presently refurbishing a pub intended to become a Cork citadel of rhythm and blues. Peter, at age fifty-five, was pursuing his own dream. Before he opened the place, I had found him standing on a tottering stool behind the aged bar, declaring that he would renovate it himself and in a matter of days. Cables from previous generations of electricity were lassoed around his head, which was so white-haired anyway that he resembled a light bulb. As he yanked at another wire, a blizzard of rat droppings cascaded down from the ceiling.

"Peter, I'm going nuts here," I said as I sidled up another day to join his initial customer base of zero.

"Join the club," he chortled with his typical manic laughter. His several brothers insisted that his personality wasn't merely split but required advanced long division to decipher. Hilarious, impulsive, wildly gregarious, and brooding—you never knew which Peter you might meet.

"I just failed my driving test."

"How many cars did you hit?" he smirked.

"It wasn't that. The guy said I was too hesitant. I was trying to be extra cautious to make him happy, but he didn't like that at all."

"Maybe he was a keen observer," said Peter. "Maybe he had your number. Maybe you *are* getting too hesitant. Okay, you came over here with the family on the great dare, and that was mighty, sure. But then you started singing songs about finding some place in the country and this and that, and between the jigs and the reels you got cold feet. Look around. The Paddies are buying up the Algarve and Croatia, and apartment blocks in Berlin. They see something they want, and they go for it. Why don't you pursue your supposed dream?"

The truth of Peter Harding's words stung. There was a lot I wasn't following through on lately. I talked about fishing without doing much of it. I talked about going off on distant excursions to Donegal and Belfast, but never hitched up my horse. I talked about starting a regional magazine but pulled back. Then I found the cottage in Ballyduff, and what did I do but hesitate anew, just like the driving tester had observed.

"I thought the hotdog franchise was your most brilliant idea, really," my friend needled. "You'd look great pushing a cart in a mustard-stained white coat."

OF COURSE, JAMIE AND I HAD OTHER THINGS ON OUR PLATE. First, we had to settle our sons back into another year of school—with Owen joining his brother at Midleton. Meanwhile, Laura was about to depart for Trinity College in Dublin, the same institution I had briefly attended more than thirty years before. Jamie packed the car with everything a doting mother could think of—pillow cases and frying pans, a twelve-pack of tuna fish and a George Foreman lean, mean grilling machine—and off we went at the end of September. Laura, by now an eighteen-year-old red-headed beauty, was percolating with excitement. Gaining acceptance to Trinity, the most highly regarded university in Ireland, is no small feat.

After a few hours drive, Jamie and I arrived in Dublin on a golden afternoon. One could see a capital city come of age. Cranes swung over dozens of flashy buildings arising along the River Liffey; and smart restaurants and galleries dotted every turn from the city centre to the tree-lined Georgian boulevards that led to Laura's new digs.

The outlying "halls," as they are called, were a pleasing collection of new six-story towers of red brick and glass that was softened by trim lawns dotted with fountains and copper-leafed trees. The scene was alive with hope, with young students clustering on the grass with their guitars, books, and beers. The Beatles song "All You Need is Love" spilled out from some window. Jamie and I shouldered Laura's stuff up to her suite, then hugged her.

"You are so lucky, Laura, it makes me happy, not sad," said Jamie with eyes moist. "For the first time in thirty years, I wish I were eighteen myself."

Our firstborn had left us for good.

THINGS FELT UNSETTLED WHEN WE WENT BACK TO CORK. Just a few years earlier, an amphitheater of green hills was our view. Now rows of brutally identical block houses rose toward barren business parks. At the base of one slope, the greenswards of a convent that had run out of nuns had been filled in with expensive apartments in a development named "Eden." A rising twenty-story tower of putative posh called "The Elysian" now dominated the once low-slung little city. Historic buildings in every quarter were being knocked into rubble. It looked as if the town was undergoing a missile attack. With rents skyrocketing, quirky, generations-old local businesses were giving way to antiseptic foreign chain stores.

Yet with prosperity came the fabulous new university art museum and music college, and an admirable remake of the county hall. On the back lanes, new cafes with outdoor tables enlivened this humming little city of but a quarter of a million. Cork's ambience was changing fast.

That night I had a powerful dream. I was standing knee-high in the Blackwater River behind the cottage in Ballyduff, casting a fly line into swirling rapids. Suddenly, a massive salmon leapt high, spun in mid-air with a flash, and its left eye locked with mine. Then it knifed back into the current and was gone.

Curious, I phoned the estate agent selling Marston Cottage in Ballyduff, teeth gritted for the usual "gazumping" of phantom bidders.

"There are no current offers on that property," said Tim Heggarty. "Also, the asking price has just been reduced by twenty thousand euros."

Reduced? This was unheard of. Was the Celtic Tiger on its last legs? The next weekend, Jamie and I headed toward the Blackwater with our newly acquired springer spaniel, a black and white rescue dog named Rudy. As we drew close, the river's sweeping turns below the ruined castle at Mocollop (*magh-cholpach*—plain of the cattle) seemed at once gloomier and more mesmerizing than before. The Vikings had christened Waterford (originally *Vedrafjord*—or weather haven) during their ninth-century invasions. Then came the Anglo-Normans and later English; Waterford's castles, abbeys, and prehistoric monuments encapsulated all the anguished cycles of Irish history. Yet the river looked untroubled now. Fuchsia danced a red riot in the hedgerows.

The moment we opened the car's doors to Marston Cottage, Rudy shot out and whirled through perhaps six revolutions of joy. Then he disappeared with his back legs bounding like a deer's.

"The dog's made his choice," Jamie laughed.

Murray and Anne showed us about very carefully this time. After looking around, we decided to explore the gorse-spiked uplands that once comprised an ancient kingdom curiously known as the Barony of Iffa and Offa. Beyond lay a range of dark and lonely 2,500-foot-high mountains, weathered over eons into the shapes of massive domes and giant arched breasts. Their names of Knockmealdown, Knocknagnau, Knockalougha, and Knockghmullion translate quaintly—variously, hill of the honey fort, whortleberry, pig, and leprechaun.

"Iffa and Offa"—was this the story of my recent life? The wind whistled as Jamie and I looked down over the vast green expanse of the Blackwater Valley. From this height, the mighty river resembled nothing so much as a brushstroke of the divine.

Further down the valley, the Blackwater spreads into a half-mile-wide estuary below a small town called Cappoquin, where the British reportedly once hand-cuffed together a score of pike-wielding insurrectionists into pairs and threw them into the river's murky depths. Wreathed with undulating hills, the lower Blackwater was so majestic, English landlords likened their vistas to those of the sweetest courses of the Danube or Rhine. This was the hidden Ireland, home to Sir Walter Raleigh and Edmund Spencer.

We came to the pretty village of Lismore, where the Duke of Devonshire's massive Gothic castle creates a magical tableau above the river. But nearly as impressive to me was the local butcher's shop, named Charles McGrath & Sons. Inside, three stout brothers, each around sixty and cinctured in blue-striped aprons and white cloaks, were busy sharpening knives or trimming steaks on an oaken block whose middle had gone concave from generations of hewing. A sign on the wall explained that almost everything the McGrath brothers sold, the lambs and the cows, was raised on their own two nearby farms and carved up fresh before dawn.

When we tried to pay for some T-bones the oldest brother said, "Give it to the missus," and pointed to a confessional-like window in a wainscoted wall at the back. An old wooden box with a half-dozen compartments housed her various gradations of change. The place defied time. It also closed the deal, seducing us to believe a sanctuary had been found at last. Next stop: Marston Cottage.

Chapter 9

S ome of the most beautiful rich country ever seen," the English
novelist William Thackeray said of the Blackwater Valley in 1842.
Standing outside Lismore, the traveler Walter Fraser observed
a few years earlier: "Nothing can surpass in richness and beauty, the
view from the bridge, when, at evening, the deep woods and the grey
castle, and the still river, are left in shade, while the sun streaming
up the valley gilds all the softer slopes and swells that lie opposite."

Our first afternoon in Ballyduff, the light was actually brilliant. I
walked the grounds, counting fourteen plant species already in blos-
som, even though it was not yet the first of February, or *Imbolc*, the
start of spring in the ancient Celtic calendar. Back in the cottage,
my wife was testing out wall hangings, while the boys flopped from
bed to bed and bickered about who deserved which. Jamie sang over
the top of them and her rising cadence filled our little home. Once
again, I was touched by her resilience.

Happy talk. Talk about things you'd like to do. You got to have a
dream. And now we had one.

Exploring the study in the guest cottage, I came to a curious
bureau. Its first drawer held finely pointed pencils and paper pads,
the next a crisp American two-dollar bill, then an array of watercolor
brushes. As I eased the drawer closed, I had a hunch that Murray the

psychologist had carefully selected each of these items as talismans of good will.

Suddenly, another presence chilled the room, and there lurked one of the ugliest cats I had ever seen. It was oatmeal-colored with rheumy eyes and a rash of ginger pinprick spots around its mouth. The animal's back was hunched and its spirit was menacing, as if the thing was declaring itself the rightful owner of our new house.

"Get out of here!" I shouted, only then remembering that Anne said she'd been feeding the feral animal that inhabited the garage. "It's called 'Cat,'" she'd said.

OUTSIDE, I OPENED THE BLUE GARDEN SHED within which innumerable tools hung on the walls—drawing hoes and Dutch hoes, rakes, cultivators, spades, shovels, pickaxes and pitchforks, loppers, clippers, fertilizer spreaders, pesticide sprayers, acetylene torches, and even aerating sandals for whatever weird purpose they served. Below these sat five different watering cans. There were sacks of lime, compost elixirs, and slug pellets; potions for staving off potato blight, black spot, and mildew; dried food for roses, roots, and tomatoes; pesticide misters, bags of bone meal, Epsom salts, and further brews arcane to me. A high shelf also held trowels, dibbers, secateurs, and various other implements that looked suitable for medieval torture chambers. The bottom shelves were packed with balls of string, skewering stakes, netting to protect berries from marauding birds, soil acidity test kits, packets of German-made plant wire *(Pflanzendraht),* work gloves, knee pads, ear muffs, safety glasses, seedling trays, cloches, and clay pots. This was quite an armamentarium.

The shed's potting counter bore compartments filled with seed packets for flowers, but also cabbage, leeks, Brussels sprouts, "early purple" broccoli, golden celery, cucumbers, carrots, running beans, climbing beans, dwarf beans, fennel, and tomatoes. The lettuce selection was a cornucopia unto itself: Little Gem, Avon Defiance, Paris

White, Corsair, and Devil's Tongue. How did humans, but yesterday subsisting on mauled animals, figure out how to grow an ever more dainty panoply of lettuces with such sweet names? The shed, piquant with the aroma of stored onions, felt like a sanctuary of all the knowledge I had never learned.

Gazing from its window, I sagged into a moment's despair. Below lay twelve separate vegetable beds. What crop belonged in each? At which weeks in spring should these magical seeds, these implosions of life, be planted? Just beyond loomed the greenhouse. Beside it rose a plum tree, with rows of dormant elderberries, gooseberries, blackberries, strawberries, and raspberries—all in need of pruning. All very intimidating.

On our lawn, Jamie and the boys were shouting and tossing a Frisbee. As if from nowhere, Harris's lanky friend Kenneth Fuller appeared from his parents' nearby farm. The sailing disc elicited whoops of laughter as it darted over leaping grasps. Lunging for a sally from Harris, I nearly fell head over heels.

Jamie turned my way, laughing. "You'd better start exercising now!"

Dusk thickened, and a three-quarter moon began to rise. A dozen black starlings burst aloft from a row of conifers. A pause, and now another hundred or so of their mates followed. Thousands more starlings soared down the valley in wave after wave. I hollered for Jamie and the boys to come see.

"What call can they possibly be answering?" wondered my wife.

"Maybe they're like the salmon," Owen observed. "Maybe it's magnetic."

Harris, so close to nature as a boy in the Connecticut woods, watched wide-eyed.

I prayed that I had done right by us all, that I had found the key to contentment in this radically changing Ireland.

Early the next morning, I walked down the road and came to a neighbor's bright modern bungalow that was so tidy it made me stop.

Under low stone walls stood hundreds of daffodils in full bloom. The house and its walkways were bordered by neatly demarcated ornamental beds that showed not a trace of weed, no dead growth, from the last season. The whole place whispered of readiness for spring.

As I took in the Blackwater's twisting expanse, the property's owner called hello from behind a hedge. A shortish, handsome man of about sixty, he had sparkling blue eyes and silvery hair.

"A fine morning," he hailed.

"Lovely," I rejoined.

"Did ye just move in down below?" I am quite certain he said, but after that, verbal confusion infiltrated. We stood less than a mile from the border with Cork County, the talk zone so long familiar to me. But I couldn't understand half of what was being said.

"Isyesettl'?" he asked, or something approximate. The peculiar intonations of the West Waterford accent, which extends familiar single-vowel sounds into double-vowel elongations—called "diphthongs" by linguists—are strangely compacted and almost garbled, like three-hundred year-old west-country English mixed with ancient Gaelic rhythms. The visitor can be overcome with the impression of encountering an entire populace who have just been implanted with false teeth.

Meanwhile, my new friend was struggling too.

"I'm David," I began.

"Darragh, is it?"

"David."

"Danagh?"

"David. And you're?"

"Seamie."

A blank pause. Were we supposed to point at our lips and move to sign language?

"Seamus, was it?" I persisted, because that was a name I well knew.

"Seamie."

Eventually, we grew more comfortable with each other's speech, and I told Seamie Flynn that I found his gardens to be stunning. In fact, his entire property seemed to have a prism-like quality that drew in extraordinary concentrations of sun. Obviously, he was a master at coaxing buds to life and it was apparent that I could learn much from this man.

The talk turned to the river. "Do much fishing yourself?"

"Well, I like it, but I only know trout really," I admitted.

"Yer better off. Salmon fishing takes forever and I've no patience for it. But there are nice trout down there, David. I'll show you come spring."

Seamie, a Waterford hurling champion and lorry driver in his younger days, would not let me depart without bequeathing a satchel of cooking apples.

I drove into the village of Ballyduff. The hardware shop there had caught my eye. Here against the wall lolled spades, pickaxes, rakes, sledges, and ladders, as if the idea of thievery had not yet occurred to this shop's owner.

I needed picture hooks. So I walked into this Dickensian store, cavernous, cluttered, and dark, with its implements scattered in wild disorder. Clamps for relieving sheep of their testicles sat near containers of purgatives and worming powders. Another precinct offered rows of paint cans vying with coils of drainage pipe and a goodly selection of foul weather gear, which more or less carried on with the idea of fluids. To the side were toasters, space heaters, lamp shades, and pictures of Jesus.

What I wanted to purchase was so embarrassingly close to nothing, but the man behind the counter had his gaze fixed upon me. Though in his late sixties, he was still tall and lean, with brown eyes that were almost boyishly radiant. His thatch of white hair was swept in at least four directions at once—right in the front, left in the middle, up on one side, down on the other. His chiselled face sloped down over taut cheek bones to a firm chin, but it communicated ease.

"WHAT can we do for you today, SIR?" the man clasped his hands and asked eagerly. His head tilted close as his eyes met mine.

"I was looking for some picture hooks," I said meekly.

"I'm sorry," the hardware man said, swiveling his right ear closer. "I sowree," was the way this sounded.

"Hooks for hanging pictures. Picture hooks." Here my fingers described a big frame-like square in thin air.

"Pictchah hukes!" said the shop owner, rapping his knuckles in recognition upon the counter.

Grasping my confusion, one of the other shoppers whispered. "Pad has no hearing in his left ear. It happened as a boy, and he hasn't much hearing in the right either. He's trying to read your lips."

Suddenly, I heard a lot of things myself, beginning with the resonance of a magnificently unhurried human being embracing my presence at first sight. "Just a couple of picture hooks, that's all," I repeated more loudly.

"Here you are now," said Pad, handing a packet over. "Are these all right?"

Now his eyes met mine, and he said, "You bought Murray's place, didn't you?"

Nod.

Pad thrust out his hand. "Well, there will be no charge. We hope you will be happy here."

I shook his warmly and felt like I had met in Pad Flynn an Ireland I had craved from the start.

Chapter 10

Thanks to my encounters along the Blackwater, I wanted to share my sense of rejuvenation with Cork friends. So I stopped at my neighbor Ray Lloyd's, only doors down the terrace in our cul de sac. A stranger would have thought nobody lived there since the grass on Lloyd's front lawn was over a foot high and across the middle of it lay his single garden artifact, a wooden ladder that had not moved an inch in seven years.

A rap on the weathered red door provoked some rummaging sounds in the hallway, followed by a voice, hoarse and suspicious, demanding to know who was at hand.

"The guards," I said.

"I'm already detained," he said, opening the door just wide enough to reveal the tip of an SS dagger. This was an item from the varied military collections of Ray, a solicitor who doesn't actually practice law, and a bookseller who doesn't actually sell books, but rather stacks them—along with Samurai swords, rare prints and fine paintings—under tables, up and down hallways, and in his back shed, where they rot.

"Already deranged," I responded as he let me in. This morning Ray's head was topped by a blue Napoleonic tri-cornered plumed officer's hat. Lately, Ray was going for the Tolstoy look, with his whitening beard running amuck in all directions, just like his lawn.

His plaid shirt was terminally wrinkled. A crumpled daffodil drooped from the left lapel of his tweed jacket, which sported an enormous black ink stain below the side pocket, the one in which he kept scribbles of his last evening's ideas. Ray was not wearing shoes, but he was grinning as happily as a boy showing off his new Christmas toys.

"Well, you might as well come in," my neighbor said as loud voices guffawed from the back room. "We're having a beard convention. You can be Robert E. Lee."

I followed him between heaps of unpaid bills and crumpled newspapers, spent whiskey bottles, a mangled toaster, and two boxes of newly arrived eighteenth century first-editions of a philosophical nature. Several wires snaked dangerously from broken lamps. Ray did not believe in throwing things away, nor could he easily, since he refused to pay to have his rubbish collected, and instead skulked around in the wee hours to stuff his take-out food remainders into more upstanding citizens' bins.

In his kitchen, the painter Bill Griffin, the artist for whom I had bartended in the cathedral, stood laughing with another friend named Tom Harding. A lifelong seafarer and older brother of Publican Peter, Tom kept his personal beard short and neatly trimmed. Around his feet lay several mouse traps sans cheese, since our host Ray didn't know how to bait them. Between these a stray black cat slurped at a plate.

"If it isn't the Smith Brothers," I said, referring to a collection of bearded faces that once sported over an American box of cough drops, iconic in its day.

Lloyd twittered, "Would you like an espresso? I've just purchased a new machine."

Sure enough, a gleaming black and chromium coffee maker sat on the counter to the right of the sink. Oddly, two nearly identical coffee machines occupied the facing counter top.

"Yes, thanks. But why three espresso machines?"

"Well, you know, I like a strong cup," began Ray. "So I bought one of these a while ago," he said, pointing to a severely dented coffee maker which was bordered by two identical toasters. "It produced great stuff all right, but these yokes are fierce complicated. I mean making heavy bomb water for Hitler would be easier, and it got broken one night. So I had to buy another. Then I lost the instructions for that one. But I was nosing around the pawn shop, and there was another one at half the price, and it was in its original box. Fucking brilliant, what! Jesus when you think of it, haven't the Irish gone a little mad for coffee? Now there are forty or fifty coffee shops every where you go."

The black cat continued with his slurping. A box of at least a half dozen broken toasters sat amidst a pile of junk outside the window.

A bizarrely out-of-synch demitasse was passed my way. "God, this tastes like battery acid," I said, putting it down. "Look I've just come back from the cottage in Ballyduff. "

"Ballyduff? *An Baile Dubh,*" responded Ray, who is a fluent Irish speaker. "That's near Lisfinney Castle, right and isn't that so? You know that one of our greatest patriots came from there."

"Pray tell," groaned Tom, whose voice fairly booms. The stray cat jumped back at the sound of it.

Lloyd ignored him. "Well, his name was Jasper Pyne, and he got himself elected to the House of Commons during the Land Wars. He was a right beaut, but a little off."

"Like yourself," said Bill Griffin.

"He was a Protestant landlord but hated tyranny. And he came with a castle on the River Bride, which flows into the Blackwater not far from your Ballyduff. Well the Crown threatened to arrest Jasper. So he fled back to his castle, which had this high tower, which he had packed with provisions in case of trouble. The Royal Irish Constabulary came after him, but he scurried up the ladder and locked the trap door. Then he shouted down to his neighbors to spread the word."

"Yes?" said Griffin, scowling.

"Next thing you know Jasper was attracting big crowds for speeches he would give from his tower, sometimes from a huge bucket on a rope. He got five thousand people to march in from Tallow behind the town band, and in the commotion afterwards, which included a stampede, Jasper escaped."

"How do you know all this, Ray?" demanded skeptical Tom.

"Because of something I just read, look here," said Lloyd. He waved to his dining room table covered with a hundred or more stained and crumpled documents.

"I got trapped in a castle once myself," started Tom, who had recently enrolled in university at age sixty-three. Sensing a good story, I moved closer.

"We had landed in Istanbul the day before and a few of us had gone on the piss, okay the mother of all piss ups. Some things happened, all right? Like, the first mate disappeared.

"The next thing I knew I was found sleeping on the cobblestones in the courtyard of the Topkapi palace at four in the morning, the most secure castle in Turkey and the place where they keep the crown jewels. A lot of soldiers were shouting at me in the darkness."

"Home at last!" laughed Bill Griffin.

"They asked me who I was," salty Tom continued. "So I said, 'Well I'm Tom Harding,' and I signed something in Turkish and fell asleep. The next thing I knew they said I'd confessed to a plot to rob the crown jewels and that I'd secreted myself in the afternoon behind the iron gates and the moats so that I could pillage the most revered treasures of Turkey. I said this could not be true since I knew perfectly well I had been in a fight with some assholes on a street below the castle around two a.m. I had a Turkish friend who was wearing my best suit, my sartorial suit, my beautiful suit, and he tore the knees off my beautiful suit when I threw him over the hedge. Therefore, I said, I couldn't have been secreted in the castle in the afternoon."

Ray's newest espresso machine responded with a belch. The black cat inched forward.

"So the interrogator said, 'Well how did you get in? This is an ancient fortress, and it was designed to be impregnable. I said, 'I don't know how I got in, I just wanted a fucking nap and *I don't know.*'"

I was thinking Ray's kitchen was as fertile as any field in Ballyduff, and that there was no place I would rather be than in mad, talk-talking Ireland.

"Anyway, they put me in solitary confinement," continued Tom. "They would bring in all these soldiers with some stupid lawyers and spies in the middle, and they all squatted on the floor while eating their lunch. They would just watch me like a chimp in the zoo. The police chief spoke good English, and he explained that in Islamic society at that time they believed people with beards were either mad-men or holy men, and they were trying to figure out which I was."

Now Tom was concentrating his formidable energy upon studying ancient civilizations, while battling modernity in his spare time. For him the dark forces of the moment were personified by one of the latest property development schemes along the Cork coast, this led by a cringingly-named group called "XCES Projects."

Curious, I asked Tom if he would like a lift back to the harbor town of Kinsale where he lived, a journey of eighteen miles.

"When?"

"Now."

"That would be great. I'll show you what XCES Projects is all about."

On we went. At the crest of the last hill in our path there lay a serpentine estuary with its surrounding headlands fanning out into the Atlantic—a postcard view. The brightly colored houses of Kinsale glittered by the harbor at the bottom of the slope, where up to a hundred English ships of sail once provisioned every day in this protected anchorage before heading off to the Americas. The place is storied.

In 1601, a fateful turning point in Irish history unfolded just outside Kinsale, when six thousand Ulster men under the chieftain Hugh O'Neill capped a sixteen-day march with a headlong assault on a massed British army. As Tom explained, the northern Irish tribes assumed that they would be joined by an equal force of Spaniards who had seized the then-walled town a couple of months earlier. Due to farcical miscommunications, the Iberians missed the battle, and the Irish were slaughtered wholesale.

The English subsequently enjoyed a very good run in Kinsale, until merchant ships of sail inevitably vanished, and the town languished. But in time the harbor's vistas beckoned in new blood, and in the 1970s and 80s the place began to thrive again.

We rounded a wicked bend beside Tom's favorite pub, The Spaniard. Built in 1659, it was named for Juan de Aguila, the commander of the sixty-four hundred troops who did not show up for the title bout for the future of Ireland. "See these houses right here? They're nothing much, but they go for over a million each," Tom harrumphed.

"This spot is called the Cape of No Hope," he continued.

"Why is that?"

"Because everybody founders at this bend and goes into The Spaniard and time stops. You have an entire corner of fishermen, mariners, and sailors in there, and a ninety-three-year-old fellow who was once shipwrecked on the Skeleton Coast of Namibia, and came back to Kinsale with his pockets full of rough diamonds that had washed up on the strand. But his mother threw them out!"

At the end of a lane barely wide enough for two-way traffic lay a headland of shimmering fields undulating toward the Atlantic. Then a rutted boreen dipped toward a sheltered bay. "This is Ballymacus," said Tom, "the place where we spent every summer of our childhood. My father, who couldn't keep two shillings in the same pocket, would hire a car for the big day in June to bring us seven kids here, and we would all burst out singing as we got near. The place was so magical, it was like time stopped."

We parked the car. A fresh wind was bending the small trees bordering the lane and tossing white caps across the sea.

Tom waved an arm over the scene and began speaking of a great plague overwhelming Ireland. "Just before us now, above the cove, the hoors plan to build their hotel, and above that on this hill here," he pointed to the left, "will be two-hundred-fifty holiday homes, every one more or less the same. Then over that way will be the equestrian centre and the conference hall and beyond that the golf course."

We descended a grassy path with hawthorns budding on either side. Birds trilled in the hedges, there was no other sound.

"Well, here we are standing on what will be a massive parking lot," Tom hissed, with his eyes burning. "That's why I am taking these feckers to the High Court."

That he soon did, and he became known as one of the more remarkable, if lonely protestors in Ireland—a single, half-broke figure of defiance against the break-neck progress on all sides.

Chapter II

At least we had found refuge ourselves—a parallel Irish universe perhaps. With spring approaching, I was drawn at every free moment to the cottage in Ballyduff, and was consumed with the alchemy of making it our own. The greenhouse seemed like a good place to start.

I circled the construction a couple of times, noting the moss-covered glass panes. Next, I began to discern a gallery of secret faces in the mold. These turned out to be those of Cork friends like the beard-brothers Bill Griffin and Ray Lloyd, the various Hardings and the rest. These rogues cried out for a scrub, and at last the tedious work ahead had some appeal.

Owen wandered by. He had been splitting logs with Harris beneath the copse of towering cedars and was looking for an excuse to stop. "Dad, the way you are cleaning those panes is kind of funny. Why are you skipping the manky ones?"

"Because they have faces of friends in them and need special treatment."

"Whump!" sounded the axe. Harris was still thundering into blocks of wood behind us.

"I don't see any faces," Owen scowled.

"Well, look harder. See, here's a fellow we call "the Bird" who's always grinning. He needs a little shave," I said as I lathered the bottom of a particularly encrusted pane and began to wipe it clean from the bottom up.

"Sometimes I don't know about you, Dad."

"I think I'll leave his eyes for a while. There's a nice smile about them, don't you think?"

Owen laughed. "You're a little crazy, but you know, I see it."

"Good, now get rid of them," I said, sticking my son with the job.

I was idling happily when Jamie called out from the main cottage. "We have a visitor!"

Jamie is an excitable creature. When a black bear showed up one morning on our Connecticut lawn, she cried out so loudly that the beast twice her size spun off in terror in the general direction of Canada. She now exhibited a newly curious demeanour.

In fact, Jamie was fairly strutting to keep up with an extraordinarily tall man in blue overalls who had the loose-limbed, floppy gait of the straw-stuffed Scarecrow in *The Wizard of Oz*. The visitor had flying wisps of hair and inordinately roving eyes, like some strange inspector from the Department of Ultimate Irish Curiosity.

"This is Fergal," said Jamie as they came to a stop.

Hands were shaken, and his proffered one was strong, though he was rail-thin.

"Ah, it's so magical here. The scent of those cedars—it all comes back!" Fergal enthused as mist began to bathe the air.

"Fergal says he was brought up here, that his sister owned the cottage for decades," said Jamie.

"Yes, yes—right! It was a fine place to grow up. Ah, it's looking very well!"

"Why thank you, Fergal."

"But I wanted to warn you about the cows," the farmer said in a near whisper.

"The cows?"

"Yes, yes, the cows. You see them over there across the river? Well, they won't be any bother for a while all right, since the Blackwater is so high now. But if it gets low as it will get low in the summer, they might come across. And they would bring trouble with them at that, you can be sure. These gardens are so lovely but if they got in they could ruin everything and that would be a shame and a very destructive thing. I have seen it happen."

"What should we do?" a worried Jamie inquired.

"You want to mind those cows there very carefully. You might think of putting up a fence to protect your gardens."

Fergal's angular face now tautened, his lips stretched wide enough to reveal a keyboard of clenched teeth. I examined the three-hundred feet of river frontage that had become ours, contemplating an impossible feat of engineering, a bovine Maginot Line. "A considerable fence would be required, wouldn't you think?"

"No, no. Small gates at the right spots on the bank, that's all. But of course they won't help you with the rabbits. Rabbits are another issue," Fergal said, his eyes chewing over our multiple vegetable beds, all presently clotted with weeds.

"The rabbits have become very bad here. You might say they are out of control. Their numbers were low when people used to shoot them for stew, and fine eating it was, and we were wrong to stop enjoying it. But then they got the myxomatosis, making them go all blind and stupid. Some say it can't get into humans, but you hear different as well. In any case Irish people won't eat rabbits anymore. Except, true as I am standing here, they pass them off as chicken nuggets in that fancy restaurant over by Tallow. And the one up the main street, well they're grilling horsemeat in there and calling it steak and charging to the top of the sky. You would want to watch out for Irish restaurants and just about everything else around now, if you don't mind my saying so."

"Thank you, Fergal."

"One other thing. You have nice neighbors here, but a couple of them are not quite what they seem, so you might want to be careful there as well. They might not dress like lords and ladies but a few have so much land they are worth millions. Don't underestimate your neighbors. The ones who shave the least might know the most."

"Would you have time for a cup of tea?" I asked.

"Sorry, I'd love to but I have to look after my cows." And off Fergal went upon legs that seemed to have no joints.

THE NEXT DAY A COUPLE OF HARRIS'S SEVENTEEN-YEAR-OLD FRIENDS were dropped off by one of their mothers. I left them alone and sat down to some weeding beside a garden bed. After a while I glanced up into the trees. The sights there proved to be fairly shocking. A pair of Crested Doves were scuffling up and down on each other like there was no tomorrow and squawking merrily, avian porno-style. Meanwhile bees were doing things with flowers that seemed a tad too self-stimulating. Mother Nature was beginning to look downright frisky.

In the meadow across the road about forty heifers were glaring at our dog Rudy. After some feeble barks, the born coward began skulking away.

I turned aside to examine a freshly budding hydrangea. From behind it sounded a most ethereal fluttering. What, did this place come with fairies?

The mystery was revealed in a spiked bush, for here was a gorgeous moth beating its black-and-gold-spotted wings into a frenzy as it appeared to suck nectar from a thorn. But wait a minute, thorns don't exactly issue ambrosia and nectar, do they? And aren't moths supposed to cavort at night? Perplexing was the scene. I moved to within inches and still the petticoats did not stop fluttering. Suddenly, it became apparent that the moth was impaled on a thorn, furiously beating its wings in an attempt to reverse free. How strange. I found a twig and nudged the insect clear, and off it darted. How wondrous. I was seeing things clearly now. And I thought: this was the point of it all. The point of Ballyduff, the point of moving to Ireland was newness.

Shouting sounded from back by the river. I followed the rumpus to find Harris and his friends digging a hole in a sand deposit at the Blackwater's bend—a four-foot deep and infinitely pointless hole. The dirt-caked seventeen-year-olds were traveling back in time to their younger selves.

The days lengthened, and as my infatuation with Ballyduff grew the pleasures of simpler living becoming manifold. Jamie and I would walk with the dog along the river road, admiring the vistas and often stopping to chat with our neighbor, Seamie. Things would go wrong, and then right. One time the boiler stopped working, so I called on Pad Flynn in his eclectic hardware shop

He leaned eye-to-eye and asked, "What is the problem?"

I explained that our heating system had just failed, and he said, "Let's have a look!"

Off we veered across the red bridge and turned down the road to Marston Cottage. Off with the boiler's frame and in with a whisk of his long fingers and *voila* the warmth machine rumbled to life. I offered Pad some money, but he pointedly looked away toward the river.

Pressing my hand, he said, "There's magic here. I hope it is all that for you."

It was.

Neighbors brought us flowers, plants, food—a renewal of life in small unlabelled packages.

In the early evenings, Jamie and I would stop by our favorite pub in the village, Maura Lindsey's, for a quiet pint. Always this born-lady now in her seventies would inquire about our day and introduce us to a new customer—the veterinary surgeon, the salmon ghillie, the English roofer who ran the local restaurant, a plasterer fond of reciting scurrilous poems backward. A few of the older customers might huddle in the corner, keeping their suspicious distance, but most people extended easy welcomes.

None did so more emphatically than Pad Flynn, in whose hardware shop I would learn all manner of things—for example about the discrete fundraising that allowed local people to take the most infirm citizens of Ballyduff to the Marian shrine of Lourdes in southern France each spring. Sometimes the giving in these parts, which was invariably led by Pad Flynn, was more practical. A local woman who was nearly incapacitated by multiple sclerosis had her husband fall to his death off a ladder. Soon three villagers pledged to pedal their bicycles all the way to Dublin and back in one day— an aching round-trip course of two hundred and fifty miles—if their neighbors would pitch in some contribution for every mile conquered. Nearly fifteen thousand euros was the result. "This is what Ballyduff is about!" Pad proclaimed.

Pad often unselfconsciously held my hand for the first few seconds of his stories, as he was wont to do with one and all. Invariably, the conversation would start with gentle solicitations, "Are you well? Do you need anything?"

I was trying to pay for a ball of twine once but found him uninterested.

"Another time."

"But I must get some things from the yard as well."

"John will look after you there," Pad smiled. I would leave his hardware shop feeling like I was departing a secret chapel. Of course, the man had once studied to become a priest, and his older brother was the head of a revered order based in Rome. Another had fled Ireland to work at Universal Studios in L.A., while the local brother "Ownie" was busy raising a thoroughbred that was destined to soon win the Cheltenham Gold Cup in the U.K.—the famous steeplechase race on St. Patrick's Day.

Pad's "yard" was a separate world across the way. It consisted of an old school house and adjoining garage with a paved lot. These confines held all manner of the bigger things that keeps the countryside functioning—fencing and posts; sand and cement; sacks of feed, fertilizer, poison, and coal; stacks of lumber, plaster board, iron gates, and stone blocks; cattle troughs and irrigation hoses and sheets of corrugated tin. The best thing about this enclave was that it was presided over by the king of Irish nonchalance, John Flynn (no relation to his same-named employer).

John was ruddy-faced and stout as a Cornishman, with deep blue eyes that bore a constant glow. He was always dressed in a pair of baggy trousers held up by thick suspenders over a tattered work shirt. After a lifetime of raising cattle, he had sold off most of his herd and settled in to the hardware shop's yard, thereby advancing his mastery of the art of perpetual relaxation.

"How are you keeping?" John offered.

"Very well—and yourself?"

Here he rubbed his hands together. They, like his round face and thick neck, were weathered by decades of exposure to the elements. "There could be but little to complain about on such a fine day," offered John.

I explained that I might need some fencing to keep away pestilential rabbits.

"It's a magic ray gun you might be wanting," chuckled John. "Do you mind my asking where you come from originally?"

Connecticut, he was told.

Then he related his love for vintage tractors, especially those from America, and the fact that they lifted families like his out of poverty. "I am sorely pushed about one of those old mules at the moment. I feed her and house her but she'll barely tick over which is not good when there is an all-Ireland fair coming on soon."

Just then, a flatbed trailer truck arrived at the mouth of the yard, its boomingly voiced driver calling for John to get a push on with his forklift. I left them to it.

THE NEXT AFTERNOON BROUGHT A MAJOR LOCAL EVENT—"The Long Puck." The astonishingly athletic game of hurling was Ballyduff's passion. This community of but a few hundred souls often won hurling-mad Waterford's junior intra-county championship against far larger towns, while producing some of the sport's greatest legends. The problem was there was no hurling in late March, leaving the populace bereft.

The idea of a "long puck" was therefore conceived—a competition to see who could prove best at whacking the sport's rock-hard balls up and down the length of a four-mile triangular course of narrow roads. People of all ages gathered to watch. Eventually, we circled up to the finish line, just before a barn-like new building with a corrugated roof. The inside was startling for a small village, revealing a gleaming new basketball court, plus a separate wing of squash courts and new locker rooms.

"Every thing you see here was built by local volunteers," Pad Flynn explained. "People brought their trucks and their backhoes, and their dedication. Sometimes there would be forty people working here, all on their own time and for no money. They gave more than two hundred thousand euros out of their own pockets to get this built," he beamed.

Pad pointed me toward a builder who on weekends tutors young people in traditional Irish music and dance in the community hall and is a driving force behind the village's nationally renowned local theater. "Tom and his friends teach two hundred kids a year for not a penny. He is a remarkable fellow."

"I don't know about that," Tom Hyland shrugged modestly.

By now, I was sold on Ballyduff. As far as I could tell, an enlightened spirit reigned over our new community, a tranquility that emanated from the verdant valley with its ever-renewing river. The Celtic Tiger seemed to have left this place unscathed.

Chapter 12

I was keen to reach out from Ballyduff, to come to deeper terms with this island that had become our home. But where to start? Perhaps remote Donegal, or anguished Belfast, finally enjoying some semblance of peace? No, I ultimately decided that what had drawn me to this country in the first place was more compelling than any physical points on the compass—namely, the extravagant visions of its writers.

What did all these world-celebrated writers, from Swift to Yeats and beyond, share in common? At heart, the whole bunch were determined to mark their little island as one of the most extraordinary places on earth, the motherland of eccentricity and dream, subversion and surprise. Just consider: Ireland has but half the population of Belgium, little architecture to write home about, few good painters, generally wretched food, and skies that can be dreary all day. So why do seven million foreigners bother to come here every year? To live out their inner fictions, was my answer. For Ireland enjoys a mythological status that is out of all proportion to everything about it save its silver tongue.

There was one man left alive who had pumped up the Irish imaginings of half the world. This was J.P. Donleavy, the author of *The Ginger Man*, a hilarious and ribald tale of misspent youth in a thoroughly anarchic and alcoholic post-war Dublin. That book was as iconic to my generation as *The Catcher in the Rye* or *Catch 22* and eventually sold fifty million copies. Celebrating indolence and inanity, sacrilege and debauchery with an equal swagger, *The Ginger Man*, first published in Paris in 1955, was of course banned in Ireland itself until 1971. Reading it put a hex on me. Wouldn't it be curious, I surmised, to meet its author and find out what he made of the latest turnings of this culture?

The New York-born Joseph Patrick Donleavy, who had first arrived in Dublin at the end of World War II with little more than a defiant beard, over-large ego, and a veteran's free-education stipend, was now eighty-two and a virtual recluse. Sequestered in an ancient twenty-five room country house in County Westmeath, he was said to entertain few visitors. Nonetheless, I decided he should make room for one more.

I had dispatched a brief epistle mentioning that I had been friends with his daughter and son while at Trinity College, Dublin. Waiting for a response, I scrambled to find his later works and discovered that almost all except *The Ginger Man* had gone out of print, even *The Onion Eaters* (1971), a comic masterpiece about life in an Irish castle of the absurd. What did this mean? Was it that Donleavy's fictional world had gone anachronistic? Or that his tales described a country that the young Irish had no interest in?

One late April day I eagerly set out to meet him. At the border of Tipperary, the new motorway from Cork to Dublin vanished into the main streets of dull townships. One offered a crossroads pointing to Ballyporeen, the ancestral village of Ronald Reagan, fortieth president of the United States. Its main pub was carted off—lock, stock and barrel—to re-emerge in Simi Valley, California as a centerpiece of "The Gipper's" sixty-million-dollar presidential library. I wondered whether Reagan would have appreciated the charming con-man of a character resembling his presidential self in *The Destinies of Darcy*

Dancer, Gentleman, who happened to be variously named Rashers Ronald or, when manipulating his most supreme swindles, the Earl of Ronald Ronald?

As I drove north, the Galtee Mountains lay to the left with not much else to see for miles and miles afterward. At last I came to Portlaoise, a town of fifteen thousand located about forty miles east of Dublin that is best known for its massive prison, over which a great tri-colored Irish flag billows. Even from a distance, this is a certain tip-off to a major concentration of criminals, because Irish country towns rarely display the national banner unless they happen to hold a gaol. County flags festoon every fifth car antenna on the weekends of any important hurling match, but the Irish national flag is far more prominent on the New Jersey shore than in its birthplace. Perhaps, I thought, my ancestral race prefers to think of itself as a collection of provincial tribes defying collective identity.

The national flag's three striped colors are meant to keep everybody happy. The green stripe signifies Gaeldom, followed by a white one to extol neutrality, and vermillion in recognition of the Anglo-Irish descendents of William of Orange. It was William who put the final boot into the country in the 1690 Battle of the Boyne, and who is celebrated to this day in drum-booming Protestant "Orange Day" summer parades all over Northern Ireland.

The second Portlaoise roundabout brings one up close to the prison's thirty-foot walls, whose height had been extended to keep mind-bending drugs away from Irish felons. Those fellows in their numbered jump suits have a knack for enlisting friends from the outside to heave-ho the stuff into their confines via ingenious conveyances. Tennis balls stuffed with heroin were a big item for while. Then the wardens stretched protective wire netting over the inmates' exercise yard, making it look as if the lads were perambulating underneath a massive pergola, pondering their next game of cricket. The friends of the felons came up with the brilliant solution of loading their narcotics into light bulbs, such missiles being delicate enough to explode upon contact with the overhead netting behind the barriers. The impact sets the convicts to scurrying about with tongues outstretched, like dogs leaping for tossed biscuits.

The walls in places like the Portlaoise prison were made higher still, and yet a shocking number of inmates remained stoned out of their minds. How? It became apparent that the convicts now seemed to be receiving blizzards of postcards of thatched cottages and foals in fields and other visions not normally associated with rapists, gangsters, and murderers; and moreover, many of these postcards seemed to be inordinately thick. This was because two cards were being glued into one in order to provide an inner sanctuary for stashes of heroin and cocaine.

I now found myself being herded forward by a posse of five SUVs, two on each side and one to the rear. Each was driven by a woman in her late thirties or early forties, and four of them were blonde. The longer and larger the SUV, the more alluring was the driver. Ergo, I thought: Females with horsepower controlled the throttle of the Celtic Tiger. Travel books about Ireland leave out a lot of important facts like that.

The way out of town produced one further curiosity and this was Lilliput. At the end of a new motorway that appeared in the middle of nowhere, there suddenly appeared a sign pointing toward this mythological destination based upon a kingdom of mischievous tiny people from *Gulliver's Travels*. The author of that eighteenth-century epic, Jonathan Swift, possibly the most cutting satirist in history, hailed from the vicinity, which now has a lakeside resort named after him.

Finally, I came to a T-junction at the main street of Mullingar, just beside the Fat Cats Brasserie and a barber shop named Top Class which abutted an emporium called Suspense Lingerie. A shop called Way Out Passion waited breathlessly across the broad avenue. Pendulous antique lamps hung off above many a hallowed-looking pub and older haberdashery. A magnificent twin-turreted and domed Romanesque cathedral glowed luminously at the top of a gentle incline.

Below it were shops named Polski Sklep and Dobreo Bo Polski, the latter's minor signage announcing that it too was a Sklep, in service of the ubiquitous Polish. Finally, the Greville Arms Hotel appeared, its yellowish facade rather time-worn. This hostelry quickly revealed itself to be a bastion of old style, Irish cordiality. The ginger-haired desk clerk remembered my name from the morning's phone call and did not so much as ask for a credit card to secure my room. "Ah sure, you can give it to us in the morning," he said.

The dining room bore the name of the James Joyce Restaurant and a fridge inside the door was crested with a plastic sign denoting it as the James Joyce Wine Cooler. Nice of you to remember him, I thought while climbing the stairs and confronting a plaque pointing toward the Nora Barnacle Suite, named after the yielding-before-marriage and therefore eternal-damnation-risking eventual wife of the famous author.

A cavernous, darkly-wooded nineteenth-century Irish fantasia of a Gothic castle's entertainment hall waited. Its effect was morbid, with portraits of fusty long-dead squires spying down from multiple dark nooks. Across the way, a silvery old gent sat within a spotlighted glass box that nearly ran to the ceiling. Even more perplexing, your man was serenely reading a book in this humidor.

And who was the fella examining his page in such supreme repose—some *eejit* of an Irish eccentric, possibly waiting for a bus? Riveted, I moved closer and suddenly realized: The guy was none other than James Joyce, the icon of the twentieth-century novel. The wax figure was astonishingly life-like, right down to every last contour of the long angular face, with thick glasses over cool grey eyes, aquiline nose, jutting chin, and thin lips. This was High Mortician Art, as good as it gets, convincing right down to the tailoring of Mr.

Joyce's blue tweed suit, gently buttoned over a white silk shirt and striped silver tie. The impact was stupefying until the accompanying plaque revealed that cast had been had been lifted off Joyce's plaster death mask by the town undertaker, one Leo Daly, in 1982. But no explanation was offered about the extraordinarily realistic fine grey hair that swept discretely back from the top of his subject's mien. Had one of Mr. Daly's lesser stiffs been scalped?

Dispute if you like whether *Ulysses* or *A Portrait of the Artist As A Young Man* number among the greatest novels ever written. But there is no question that the man who brought Joyce back to life forever more in the Greville Arms—where the author stayed a couple of times—was the Michelangelo of his ghoulish trade, and a possible visionary. Think: Why does every single cadaver in the world have to be displayed prone with hands clasped together at the waist? Why can't Irish wakes feature the occasional construction worker in overalls leaning over his beloved shovel, or pin-striped barristers propped up behind a BMW steering wheel?

After stowing my bag, I retired to the downstairs James Joyce Bar. Ordering a drink, I noticed that a procession of staff behind the counter were each outfitted in teal blue shirts bearing little caricatures of the angular face of Joyce on their breasts, his thin lips seeming to widen lasciviously when displayed over feminine appendages. The head bartender was a thoughtful-looking man in his late thirties named Des.

So I asked, "Do you like Joyce yourself then?"

"To be honest, I haven't read him," said Des, who had soulful brown eyes and sandy hair that was prematurely greying.

"Well, he looks to be comfortable up above. But there is actually another famous author still living just outside town, J.P. Donleavy. Do you know him?"

"No, but I am not from here. I'm from Cavan." Des, whose voice was whisper-soft, said. "I don't have much time for books. The

Discovery and History channels, that's as far as I go. My life is work, family, more work, then sleep, with no time for anything else." He was perhaps speaking to the pulse of modern Ireland.

Des explained that his six-year-old son was "mildly autistic," requiring enormous effort and expense for his care, and that his wife had to leave their home at seven a.m. each morning to reach her Dublin secretarial job by nine o'clock, and did not make it back until seven-thirty p.m., all in order to help pay for intensive therapy for their young boy. None of this would have been imaginable a few years earlier.

Dinner time arrived and it was on to a fashionable nearby restaurant, Oscar's. Four Eastern European beauties served the food, each lovelier than the next. I tried to get the attention of a Liz Hurley look-alike, dark and shapely.

"Zorry, sir, I am very zorry, but I only do the dezzert," this Polish eyeful apologized. Duly chastised, I bid a blonde Eva Herzigova to deliver the starters. A diminutive type delivered the Italian wine. Now it was time for "the mains" which produced a fresh crisis, since the house hamburger in Oscar's hit a new high of twenty euros or thirty-three dollars, which in a provincial town of the same size in the U.S. would feed burgers to a family of six. A leggy approximation of Petra Nemcova stood by as I attempted to order the alternative: duck.

"Dick?"

Well, now Petra, I thought, the humor in here is pretty rich. But I restrained myself from peeking at whatever she had just written —or drawn—on her pad, and merely repeated, this time more firmly, "duck."

"Ah, zee dook!" Petra giggled.

The morning broke cold and wet, but nonetheless offered a kaleidoscope of fresh images of the Old Ireland banging against the New. I huddled into a leather banquette in the James Joyce Restaurant. And lo, a plump, jolly all-Irish brunette appeared, displaying a smothering,

mothering eagerness to please. "It's a nice morning for sitting over the coffee with a bit of a read, and don't let me be bothering you," the lassie said, hovering impatiently.

Outside, after breakfast, there strode a pedestrian in her thirties, with a mop of professionally frizzled jet black hair and a wiggling carriage. Her ample bosoms were spilling from a frilly low-cut and clingy black lace bustier, and her jeans were skin-tight. She was nearly stumbling forward on her black high heeled boots, transparently freezing from the exposure—one of the popular dress codes to emerge during the boom.

The gal's most remarkable feature was that all her displayed flesh glowed. In fact, she was orange. The world still likes to think of young Irish maidens traipsing about with mist-softened rosy cheeks and pale alabaster hues decorating their freckled forearms. But at the height of the boom, the Colleens were taking annual holidays to the beaches of Tenerife or Majorca and coveting the umber sexiness bestowed upon the swarthier races. So prone to turning lobster red, the Colleens wanted that hot, tawny look bad. Beauty parlours in the most remote backwaters now teemed with pale lassies paying large to change their hue with sun lamps and ointments with names like Beyond Bronze, St. Tropez, Sun Shimmer, Egypt Wonder and Summer Skin.

Abruptly, an armoured car came to a stop before a rather battered-looking branch office of the Bank of Ireland across the street, with its paint flaking in sclerotic strips. I'd heard rumors that Irish banks had stopped all renovations, owing to some ill wind they had detected. This morning's breezes were now certainly hitting gale force as six soldiers in camouflage fatigues stepped out of their armored vehicle with automatic weapons drawn, owing to the IRA's recent penchant for preying on vulnerable money transfers in the Republic to fund their mayhem in the North.

No mind. A collection of perhaps twenty-five shouting school boys in grey sweaters and woolen trousers suddenly burst down the street with glee. Two showed the copper hues of Pakistan or India, one the dark skin of Africa, and several looked wan and threadbare as if they had just alighted from some downtrodden village in Eastern Europe. Citizens of the new Ireland, they were all one.

So what would J.P. Donleavy say about all this?

Chapter 13

L evington Park, J.P. Donleavy's 170-acre estate, lies sequestered behind a quarter mile of lofty stone walls that line a back road outside of Mullingar. Its high green gate, boarded by twin cottages in disrepair, held this peculiar warning sign:

> Mad Bull,
> High-voltage Fencing,
> Wolfhounds.
> No Entry without Notification.

The day had grown blustery and dark as I drove through a park land sporting hoary old oaks and green expanses in which daffodils shivered. Ahead rose the great house, an imposing two-storied, cut-stone pile built in 1748, with twenty twelve-paned windows at its front, out of any one of which could now be gazing the most famous living novelist in Ireland. But wait, I next noticed that all their inside wooden shutters were drawn closed, and the closer I inspected Levington Park the more forlorn and almost uninhabited it looked. The place was so brooding, it was easy to picture the writer penning these recent words about his greatest book, *The Ginger Man*, on just such a miserable day as this:

> But come here and I will tell you. Of a further word I have to say. Out here in the windy, wet remoteness of the west. Where

the dead are left to be under their anonymous stones. . . . And
who would no longer have to wonder about the stars. Or who
would know or care. That I had set out one June near the sea
in County Wicklow, Ireland. To write a splendid book no one
would ever forget.

Standing on the Doric-columned porch, I rang the bell and listened
to silence. A goodly retinue of servants had maintained this residence
for generations, a few still employed after Donleavy and his second
wife, an American named Mary Wilson, purchased Levington Park
in 1972. It seemed that these figures had all vanished, just like the
eccentric half-crocked butlers, bumbling kitchen maids, and crafty
stable hands who populated his later novels.

In a minute, Donleavy's assistant, Virginia McGillicuddy, opened
the massive door and beckoned me into the high-ceilinged front hall,
offering laments about the weather. "Well, you can relax now. J.P. will
meet you in a moment in the kitchen."

Oh yes? Not a soul was visible in the adjoining rooms, so where,
I wondered, did he work?

"His office is quite far away actually," Virginia, sleek and denim-
jacketed, smiled as if hearing my unspoken question. "Sometimes we
don't see each other all week."

The back hallway faced a grassy inner courtyard framed by further
wings of this substantial house. Crescent horse stalls along its rear wall
would have once harbored many steeds, including those Donleavy's
ex-wife retained for her fox hunts. But this former actress had long
since run off with a genuine lord who presided over a forty thousand
acre English estate. At one time, the closets had been stuffed with
riding boots.

A log fire crackled in the spacious kitchen where a kettle was
whistling on the stove. Above a dresser ran twin racks of mostly
empty and dust-coated wine and champagne bottles like reminders
of nights vanished—the room felt frozen in an age past. Stacks of old

newspapers sat indifferently upon various corners of the bare wooden floor, baring revelations from months or perhaps years earlier. While waiting, I occupied myself by picturing Donleavy writing at the pine table before me, perhaps penning right here his testament to the solitary slipping and sliding that comes with the writer's territory:

> Here in
> This hinterland
> Lonely sad and black
> There's a midnight skater
> Figure eighting
> And that's
> A fact

Suddenly, from high in a far corner, an overhead speaker erupted with the voice of the author himself—the accent strangely English-sounding for a born New Yorker who had spent most of his adult life in Ireland. "Ah Vahginia, there was a call in from Lown-dun just now," the thing squawked. "Kawn you ring Damian, please?"

The effect was akin to hearing the Great and Powerful Oz hollering forth from behind his curtains. It slightly intimidated me as I waited, tapping my scuffed brown shoes on the bare floor. A notoriously natty dresser in the past, Donleavy was said to have greeted visitors in bespoke tweed suits with a debonair ascot or crisply knotted tie at his neck. Moreover, he was on record as *despising* brown shoes.

But the laird of Levington Park put me at ease upon arriving. Slighter than I had imagined, his face had an owlish look, the eyes deep-set and pensive behind his glasses and framed by hair and beard gone largely white and thin. Once something of a dandy, his own attire could not have been more casual—track pants with a collarless top under a fleece vest that for some reason had its buttonholes festooned with paper clips. The only hint of affectation arose from that voice, deep and mellifluent, but with its odd, off-putting whiff of the Anglo-Irish country squire.

"Did you stay locally?" the famous author asked solicitously.

"Yes, with James Joyce in the Greville Arms," I said.

"Ah yes," Donleavy chuckled. "I believe that's one of the most extraordinary hotel decorations in the world." He added that Joyce had stayed in his very own house, back when his civil servant father was briefly bivouacked within its walls in 1901. "But I'm afraid people on his trail out here just get me."

He told me about a fresh comedic tale in progress called *The Dog on the 17th Floor*. Set in New York City, that story concerns an extravagant jetsetter who has her boyfriend mind her prized pet to disastrous effects, since the canine follows a bouncing ball out a penthouse window left ajar. He added that he was also busy painting a fresh series of sketches and watercolors, in preparation for an imminent exhibition at a Dublin art gallery.

"There seems to be a small demand of people interested in acquiring my pictures," he said humbly. That locution was in itself interesting since Donleavy's first goal was to be an artist, back while living in a stone cottage by the sea south of Dublin with his young English first wife, the beautiful Valerie Heron. "That's quite important, selling a couple of my drawings. It's like having cattle, you sell a few cattle and things proceed."

He knew something about that subject, having raised prized Herefords here since buying Levington Park on sight in 1972, an impulse made possible by the spectacular success of *The Ginger Man*. Back then he had kept three flats in London, an apartment in New York, and one in Zurich, until becoming enamored with country house living in Ireland.

"I was re-married, so I came down here and there were a couple of children around," he said, clearly referring to his own offspring, but with a head-scratching circuitousness. "Plus I had two more children," here he paused and trailed a larger riddle with what would prove to be deep and deliberate opacity, "who were the children of the woman

I was involved with [his second wife]. So I have been here ever since. To find a house like this one with its conveniences and everything is practically impossible, and maybe it's the only example of a really comfortable country house in Ireland, because they are all either cold and gloomy or overwhelming."

He was still writing daily, but at a leisurely pace, he said. The details grew odd, although perhaps revealing for the author of a funny late-1990s novella titled *The Lady Who Liked Clean Restrooms.*

"I gravitate from my room upstairs where I actually sleep but it is like a study as well. The wonderful thing about this house is that there are ten bathrooms. And this has been of tremendous importance to me. So one might stay in one's room for a period of time and get to work there. And now I will find that I go down to the library which is below and I will sit down and write."

Had Donleavy gone as eccentric as one of his own marvelously dotty characters? Meeting him was a privilege, but plumbing talk wasn't what had beckoned me. So I redirected the conversation toward a subject known to be dear to him—boxing. "Do you still work out on a punching bag?"

"Yes indeed," my host instantly brightened. As a young writer about bohemian post-war Dublin, Donleavy enjoyed a reputation as a fearsome pugilist, taking on bullies and jumping to the defense of cornered chums. Outside Davy Byrne's pub one night, he pummelled his former friend Brendan Behan, the picaresque, prison-educated author of *Borstal Boy* and *The Quare Fellow.* A lot of people didn't mind, since the object of his ire had by then come to be regarded as a bathetic poet of the barrooms, and the epitome of the buffoon-for-hire or "stage Irish" personality when reeling with drink.

Fifty years later, Donleavy's eyes glinted as he rose from his chair. "Shall we see my left hook, just for a demonstration?" Here, Donleavy began raising a flurry of uppercuts into thin air. "You can't even see it, but it's a punch that goes all the way around, just like that," he said while unleashing a fresh chop toward the ceiling. He turned with boyish self-delight. "I still throw, I guess, one of the fastest punches in the business."

Quite a boast for an octogenarian, but then no one ever accused Donleavy of underestimating himself.

"Who was faster, you or Gainor Crist?" I asked, referring to the hilariously off-the-rails American expatriate, by turns chivalrous gentleman and sleeve-tugging ne'er-do well, who was the real-life inspiration for Sebastian Dangerfield, the protagonist of *The Ginger Man*. With savoir faire intact even when penniless, the high-mannered Ohio native was a dandy with a twist. He prized courtesy, but could suddenly flatten those he thought brutes, especially if they happened to intimate that he was effete, or interfered with his binges. One Dangerfield/Crist episode in *The Ginger Man* went this grammar-defying way:

'. . . Hear me, I'm drunk and I'm going to level this kip, level
it to the ground, and anyone who doesn't want his neck
broken get out.'
    The whiskey bottle whistled past the bartender's head,
splattering in a mass of glass and gin. Dangerfield drank off the
whiskey in a gulp and a man up behind him with a stout bottle which he broke on Dangerfield's head, stout dripping over
his ears and down his face, reflectively licking it from around
his mouth. . . . Sebastian over the bar standing on it. Selecting
a bottle of brandy for further reference. Three brave figures . . .
and one man's hand reached out to grab him . . . and he
jumped phoof on Dangerfield's shoulders and was flipped
neatly on his arse five paces down the street.

As I recounted such scenes, Donleavy chuckled. "Crist was very deceptive. His behavior was normally so gentlemanly, it was hard to imagine him throwing a fist at you, but ah he could, and he could look after himself." Long after his mysterious death on Tenerife at the age of forty-two, Gainor Crist clearly remained Donleavy's muse.

This aesthete saturated with the Rabelaisian spirit of an earlier Dublin out-scored Brendan Behan's theatrical debauchery by his greater savoir faire. *The Ginger Man* featured a thinly disguised meeting of the two characters:

> A man, his hair congealed by stout and human grease, a red chest blazing from his black coat, stumpy fists rotating around his rocky skull, plunged into the room of tortured souls with a flood of song.
>
> > *Did your mother come from Jesus*
> > *With her hair as white as snow*
> > *And the greatest pair of titties*
> > *The world did ever know.*
>
> Mary tugged at Sebastian.
> 'Who's that? It's a shocking song he's singing.'
> '. . . His uncle wrote the national anthem. . . .'

The young J.P. Donleavy was out to grab the world by its collar and shout that Ireland is not what you think, but is so priest-ridden and repressed that it incites, no, encourages outright depravity. "You see, we would go into this underground world called the Catacombs just to get away, and my, the things to be seen—drunkenness and fornication at every turn," Donleavy chuckled.

Students everywhere seized upon the book, translated into forty languages, as an anthem of rebellion, and Donleavy's fame grew. Inevitably, Mick Jagger became a fan and showed up uninvited for a book party in Levington Park in 1973 with his wife Bianca turning heads with a diaphanous see-through blouse. Appalled at their vanity, Donleavy fled up the stairs.

Now, the author spoke of someone with equivalent star power in the person of the Hollywood actor Johnny Depp. He had become so enthralled by *The Ginger Man* that he had recently flown from California to New York for a meeting about acquiring film rights. "I simply have to describe that he did fly to see me in New York from

California and I am not sure that he didn't take on a whole aircraft to fly himself. We had a couple of meetings, it was good fun. . . ."

I mentioned that *The Onion Eaters* with its time-warped Charnel Castle was perhaps his tour-de-force. That tale features an indolent protagonist gifted with three testicles—a descendent of Clementine of the Three Glands, whose heraldic arms sported three onions, a benediction to the bizarre anatomy of all males in the clan. The story features demented geologists who gouge up the great house's front hallway, black mamba snakes, bizarre sexual episodes involving roller skates, and a Major MacFugger who gallops out of the sunset of the Anglo-Irish gentry tooting on his fox-hunt horn about insurgents lurking in the hedgerows, saying:

> 'Clementine. To us. Two last princes of the west. I thought you
> lot were all finished down over there at the Charnel. But by
> God we join forces tonight. Our flags will fly together into
> battle. Are you with me.'
>
> 'Well yes I think so.'
>
> 'Think so. That's no answer for a Clementine with the
> three grapes dangling from his vine. These ruddy upstarts have
> got to be put in their place. Back down where they belong.
> Nobody is going to dislodge this Macfugger without a fight I
> can bloody well tell you. One of my grooms will make a good
> sergeant major Three of the gardeners can man a mortar, in
> this kind of terrain it's a ruddy must.'

There's another dose of your real Ireland: Donleavy, scornful of the IRA, seemed to declare that a madhouse that obeys no rules and makes little sense was game for pitiless satire. The author stared appreciatively at me with each plot twist I recounted.

"I had forgotten about that book," he murmured. "Was it difficult getting a copy of that?" Suddenly, a slightly lost quality winged down into Donleavy's time-weathered eyes.

I ladled on more questions about the whirl of life this house had known, and the class distinctions that he had observed, back when he consorted with the Anglo-Irish gentry whose distinctive hauteur has since largely vanished. Their shenanigans and high airs became further grist for his comic mill.

Donleavy described a certain friend's behavior at a party once held in the next room. "I remember that my former neighbor Randall Dunsany, who was Lord Dunsany, every time he heard someone speaking with a heavy Irish accent, he would move away. This amazed me. . . . Then I was in the [Royal] Hibernian Hotel," he began, referring to a once-elite Dublin hostelry, "when they had a big open reception area and I was sitting there minding my own business. It was a great meeting place in those days. Suddenly a lady came across not too belligerently but making her presence known as she came across the sitting room, and she pointed at my tie as I sat there. She bellowed, "*Suhr!* You are wearing my racing colors!" Donleavy was laughing out loud now at the recollection of his absurd scolding or whatever in the name of Anglo-Irish eccentricity it was.

"Across the lounge was Randall Dunsany who began to laugh uncontrollably. I crossed over to Dunsany and I said, 'Randall, you seem to be highly amused by what happened over there. And by the way, why aren't you wearing your monocle?' I got this wonderful response, which was, 'I am not going to wear my *monocle* when you've got a *butler* in one of your books wearing one!'"

Lord Dunsany was referring to the bizarre butler Crooks of the Darcy Dancer trilogy, forever tipsillated after raiding the wine cellars of the dilapidated great house of Andromeda Park, and often listing so badly when serving dinner that his monocle would fall into a guest's soup tureen:

> . . . Crooks . . . with his whiskey smelling breath sprouted polysyllabic at me.
>
> 'Good lord my god who hath made my legs weak and toes pained, beseech you deliver us from fornication, and all the other deadly sin and from all the deceits of the world, the flesh and the devil.'

'Is that you Crooks.'

'Yes.'

'Are you speaking to me Crooks.'

'I speak to my God first before I shall speak to any earthly master . . .

Crooks slippered footsteps shuffled off down the hall into the darkness. And it always rather amazed and alarmed me at how unconcernedly he would, without being summoned, march at any old time . . . his voice mumbling as he went.

'O this house, this house . . .'

We talked about the fox hunting scenes in several of his novels, featuring prodigious drinking, riders cracking whips at each other's behinds, and dalliances in the odd field. "Did any of this happen here?" I asked.

Donleavy's response was clipped. "This county is nothing but horses. They did hunt here with my second wife. She was just obsessed with horses." There he stopped. Only later, would I find out why.

The quiet that ruled this house now brooded in stark contrast to the huge levity that it had once known. I asked whether he entertained company any more.

Donleavy paused meditatively. "Not a great deal. The odd people might come by, but not often."

I reeled off the names of various luminaries who had graced Levington Park's doors, the authors, the artists, and the earls. Did such like still call to him? "Most of them have died," Donleavy said wistfully, adding that those who hadn't had moved elsewhere. "Indeed, I often think—my god what a sensible thing it is that none of these people have stayed here. They've gone to other places. Of course I came back here strictly for the income tax business," he said, referring to the tax-free status the Irish government conferred upon many artists and writers for a long while (and now in jeopardy).

I asked Donleavy what he thought of modern Dublin, the city he had so gloriously celebrated. His answers were consistently vague. "I used to patrol Dublin with some fascination and a degree of horror. I loved going out and just exploring. I walked and wandered everywhere and sometimes for miles, it used to be a great thing of mine in the afternoons, even to go to places where you might run into trouble, in the slums and along the quays. But it's just a place now that has suddenly Europeanized and has a world reputation, so it's like a tourist town. I don't think one cares about Dublin particularly."

"Are you saying that the romance has gone out of Ireland?" I asked.

"Pretty much so. Ireland has inevitably become like one of the modern states of Europe. The simple fact is that people don't have the leisure time that the generation did before. They don't have the room to be eccentric because there is far more competition for earning a living."

I thought of the strange cast of characters who haunted my life in Cork, the more colorful citizens of Ballyduff, and the eccentrics I met every time I visited Dublin. Didn't Donleavy see positive changes as well?

Well, yes, J.P. allowed. "This is still a pretty good life in Ireland, things are permissive enough now that most people can enjoy themselves. There's no more of that church business, there's no more of the censoriousness and sexual problems. They've removed all the restrictive matters. So this is an open country in effect now and probably ideal."

As all must, the famous bard had gone old—if in admirable fashion—in his lonely castle of which he now offered a tour. The front drawing rooms were stately with ancient marble fireplaces and eighteen-foot-high corniced ceilings. But mildew was on the creep and the paint on the walls sadly faded. Curious paintings, many by the author himself, looked out from their frames, and various nooks held pottery with whimsical creatures doodled upon it. The latter were the work of Donleavy's daughter Karen, now living more than five thousand miles away in Idaho.

A door opened to a thirty-foot long salon, and at its end stood a grand piano, whispering of nights past. We paused to look at various portraits holding their many memories, then stepped outside to the beginning of an arbor way that my host said James Joyce had once depicted in *Stephen Hero*.

Donleavy's sizeable office had walls thick with books, mostly his own in various editions and languages. The middle of the floor was a Giant's Causeway of file boxes of his correspondence, notes, and various manuscript drafts, all being carefully catalogued for eventual historicl purposes. Upon Donleavy's desk lay a copy of his autobiographical work *The History of the Ginger Man*, a tale-within-a-tale that chronicles along the way the bitterness he still nurses about a Parisian publisher first releasing his masterpiece in a "dirty book" series.

A broad stairway led to an enormous upper hallway. Many framed pictures listed against its baseboards, bound for Donleavy's imminent art exhibition in Dublin. The nearest was a watercolor of a graveyard with neglected tombstones slumping sadly, but with the sky above as cheerful as a pet day in May. Its title was, "Breathing the Sunlight before the Darkness Should Come."

I was impressed.

Donleavy offered a tour of a succession of bedrooms, most boasting antique four-posted beds. He pointed to a great wooden tub off one of them and remarked, "They each have bathrooms, you see!"

They have what? That this celebrated oracle of Ireland kept harkening back to this pedestrian topic was troubling. But what did I have any right to expect? J.P. Donleavy had kindly welcomed me into his life, and this was a gift indeed.

At the stoop, the aged writer extended his hand warmly and I thanked him for the world of pleasure I had found in his works.

"To make the innocent stars dance in consternation," he'd written once.

THERE WAS A LOT TO THINK ABOUT AS I DROVE AWAY. That a cultural hemorrhaging had befallen Ireland, as my host observed, was patently obvious and distressing.

By a crossroads to the north there sat a blocky pub named The Shebeen. It didn't look like much, but I parked and went in to ponder things over a jar.

The farming crowd was in strapping form, staring at race horses whipping across a television screen and shouting, "C'mon ye worthless fucks!"

Waiting to be served, I thought of Donleavy's words from years ago: "I sometimes look around and think every other person in Ireland is half-mad."

The young publican fussed along the counter before working up the nerve to ask, "You're not a local, no?" As if he didn't know.

"Ah but I am. I live in the basement across the street," I almost said.

My pint was poured country slow, giving me ten minutes with which to observe him right back. What my wandering gaze espied on a shelf behind the bar was a wrist-thick wad of vermillion fifty-euro notes and a companion pack of aquamarine twenties. Your publican got busy peeling off top layers and dispensing a fifty here and a twenty there to the shouters at the TV, then accepting notes in return that customers seemed to bequeath back with an impressive generosity. Likely, money was being raised for a good cause, and the bar owner wouldn't even think of serving as the bookmaker of this crossroads. Now would he?

After dinner at a pub down the road, I booked into a room at a country house called Mornington Park, which came with another long driveway. Conversation with the owner would wait until breakfast the next morning, served to me by my lonesome at the end of a twelve-foot-long walnut dining room table.

"So what did J.P. have to say yesterday?" asked my host while serving coffee and an initial caddy of toast. Dressed in a pink I-don't-give-a-damn cardigan, Warwick O'Hara had a princely charm. He was a towering figure of six-foot-three with extra altitude provided by a spectacular mane of white hair.

"Well, the conversation wavered some, but it was all very interesting to me," I said as a silver breakfast tray made its tip-toed way through the great room.

Warwick rubbed his hands together and said meditatively, "We enjoyed some mighty nights with J.P. in our time, especially after the hunt." He brandished a stentorian voice that evidenced considerable breeding since Mornington Park, with its high-walled gardens, disused stable block, and pretty fields, had been his family's stronghold for the last 160 years. "But Donleavy's place has gone very quiet, didn't you find?"

It was hard not to like Warwick, except for the fact his toast was piling up. I had an old habit of counting it when staying in such family-portraiture-ridden places, because each slice represented extra cash to be dispensed with the final goodbyes. Warwick's first toast caddy bore four slices of soda bread. Fine and fair and four times ten would be just around standard B&B rates. But wait a minute. Here toddled forth my host with a fresh caddy boasting, count 'em, six sections of the white pan. Has anyone ever eaten ten pieces of toast?

"Warwick, I think this will suit me," I said.

For a moment, he looked hurt.

But yon Warwick was an amiable man. So he told me stories, bouquets of stories about the hunt parties at J.P. Donleavy's. Just when I was chuckling into another slice of toast, the door opened and in rolled the heavy artillery, his brown-haired wife Anne in a wheel chair. Her manner was so no-nonsense, I warmed to her instantly. Though multiple sclerosis had impeded her mobility, the lady of the house was sharp as a tack and wanted to know all about my visit with the couple's old friend.

"God, we used to have so much fun with J.P. back in the old days riding at the hunt and drinking half the night. I used to help prepare the dinners, and they were huge affairs," Anne O'Hara recalled with a laugh. "One thing that happened is that we would bring our groom over there, who was very good, but Mick had a small fondness for the drink. There would be rivers of it on hand at J.P.'s with a fat keg of Guinness left unguarded by the front door. Mick would say to me, 'Would you look after me missus?' with a tip of the forelock. Ah sure, I would bring him his pints, but I will never forget the time J.P. found Mick steadying the reins of twin stallions by the door with one hand somehow holding his pint without a drop spilled. Donleavy found this so hilarious he wrote the scene into one of his books."

Dishabillé was often noted, according to Anne O'Hara, with couples who didn't belong together careening up the driveway half-dressed on certain mornings. But the most provocative feature, which I had heard from others, was that twin lords of the Guinness brewing family, the brothers Kieran and Finn, grew to like the ambience so much they would decamp in their turns for days on end in the dual gate lodges at the entrance of Levington Park. Eventually, Mary Wilson-Price left the famous writer for Finn Guinness, with whom the former actress now raises champion thoroughbreds in a great English estate. This revelation explained a few of Donleavy's circumlocutions, and one of his little poems:

> When you find a friend
> Who is good and true,
> Fuck him
> Before he fucks you.

Though written decades ago, it sounded like a paradigm for some of the worst excesses of the Celtic Tiger.

Chapter 14

A new road on a new day, and my eyes fairly jumped at the sight of a triumphal Roman arch in the middle of an apparent cow pasture. Why, there's a man working on a nearby stone wall. I rolled down the car window, asking in the hemming-and-hawing Irish style, "Sorry there, I was wondering would you have any idea at all what's the story with that arch over there?"

"Oh that," he laughed, leaning on his shovel. "That's the entrance to a big house which is a quare sort of place."

"How so?"

"Well, they have opera festivals in there and tea parties in their gardens, which are said to be full of sculptures of spiders and frogs and such."

And J.P. Donleavy said the eccentricity had gone out of Ireland?

I was winding my way into County Meath, seeking a collection of Neolithic tombs at a place called Loughcrew. The next turn into a dale between steep hills brought me to their fringe. The afternoon light had gone luminous, so for a moment euphoria reigned. But when I opened the car door the wind nearly blew it off its hinges. This was a gale with a Biblical vengeance and felt strong enough to scatter my limbs back to the Barony of Iffa and Offa.

Were the graves of ancient chieftains worth the risk of turning oneself into a human kite? I decided to give it a go. So, bent forward from the waist, I trudged up the nearest hill, with no one else in sight. Recently, a Swiss aerialist in a wing-suit had dropped himself out of an airplane fifteen thousand feet over the Aran Islands and then pointed his head toward eleven-miles-distant Galway City. Wouldn't you know it, but a commercial prop plane showed up in his airspace, aiming for the same destination. They gave each other room to move on. But guess who dropped down on the local runway first?

Herr Üli Gegenschatz, nicknamed "Sputnik," could have made it to the Matterhorn in one gust if he followed my path up this green, green lonely hill. My eyes were not only tearing before the violence of the wind, they were being driven back into my skull, which made it difficult to see, even if my feet were still on the ground. Slowly, I inched toward the crest. Oh here were some sheep. Hello, sheep. They scurried. And revealed that they had been scratching their backsides on a scattering of standing stones stuck upright into this hallowed soil by god knows whom and when. I dared lift an arm and my jacket billowed so violently I nearly became Sputnik II. Strangely invigorated, I climbed higher, ever higher into the cyclone.

At the crest, I met eternity. From up here, one could see forever, vast lakes shimmering with incandescence, folds of hills and mountains beyond washed in bewildering shades of green and umber, magenta and pale blue. I was sure I could see clear to Monaghan, county of my ancestors, and maybe Mayo and Donegal. And what was that beyond, that glowing isle at the edge of the horizon? Was it *Tír na nÓg*, where the hero Oisín went to live forever? Or was it just Iceland? Up here, the imagination went celestial. I was half frozen but so very glad to be alive.

For company, I had the long, long dead. The summit was crowned with stone circles and three to four thousand-year-old burial cairns. One was about thirty feet high and a hundred feet in circumference and perhaps contained three million rocks. Discrete signs indicated that this hill had formerly been called *Sliabh na Calli,* "the hill of the witch," since a legend explained that the stones had all been dropped to earth by a supernatural witch. In fact, a massive flat-topped, rune-inscribed boulder at the back of the main cairn was still known as "the hag's chair." On this hill and the next two loomed forty of these eerie testaments to an age now unfathomable. Looking toward so-called Carbane West, the eye met further mounds gloaming at its crest, obviously intended to be visible from every reach of the horizon.

Short of witch work, how did they get there? What super-human effort went into hauling these untold tons of boulders, pebbles, and rocks to such heights? What gods did the ancients murmur to as they ascended these hills? What blood sacrifices were enacted where I stood? No one knows.

With the wind pummeling my eyes, I sidled around the largest cairn. The prehistoric tombs of nearby Newgrange are world famous and visited by incessant throngs, but this evening only the sheep and myself seemed to be aware of Loughcrew's existence. Yet some forma-tions here were over five thousand years old, which would make this one of the oldest burial grounds in the world. The effect was akin to stumbling upon the heights of Machu Picchu or the temples of Angkor Wat without another human being within miles.

I found the entrance way to a passage tomb, reputed to be the final resting place of a high king and celebrated poet named Ollam Fodhla who lived around 1300–1350 BC., about the time of Tutankhamen. Ingress to the central cruciform chamber was blocked by a small gate with a padlock on a thin chain—such was the only security, other than the sheep watching me. Both sides of the cairn's passageway were flanked by tall slabs feathered and cross-hatched with prehistoric runes and whorls, some repeating mystical numerical slash patterns—the tomb exuded magic. And well it might, for not too long ago, modern researchers discovered that this cairn had been precisely aligned to embrace the first rays of the winter solstice. The dawn when the sun dangles at its lowest rising of the year, the swing point in the annual pendulum of death and rebirth, was the only moment when its rays streaked all the way through the cairn's spidery dark passageway to the innermost chamber. There they fell upon the bones of the high king. Just standing beside his ancient tomb I felt as small as a blade of grass—and as exalted.

THE NEXT DAY TOOK ME TO THE HILL OF TARA, just a couple of dozen miles deeper into County Meath. Ancient chieftains from across Ireland convened at this fabled spot to coronate and honor kings like Ollam Fodhla. So many Neolithic monuments, burial chambers, and defensive earthworks ring the hill and surrounding valley that the area is considered a cradle of ancient Celtic civilization. Now a massive motorway, the M3, was pushing through their midst. To make way for it, numerous hallowed nearby archaeological sites were being bulldozed and paved over, with their various artifacts and even ancient skeletons carted off to oblivion in Dublin warehouses.

Historians howled that this was rank cultural vandalism, but the government's chief archeologist had a gobsmackingly different take. "It could be argued that the M3 will be a monument of major significance in the future," Brian Duffy proposed. Then he twisted his spade of anti-reason a mite deeper by saying, "The existence of a cultural, historic, archaeological landscape in the vicinity of the Hill of Tara is not an issue. Indeed, as we live on an island that has been occupied by man for ten thousand years, it can be argued that the whole country is a cultural landscape." Ergo, altering the motorway's route might set a precedent that could arrest development across the entire nation. And that was one thing the government absolutely did not want.

For a long time the populace paid little heed. But eventually, luminaries like the Nobel-prize-winning poet Seamus Heaney cried out that the project epitomized the wanton heedlessness of the Celtic Tiger era. "I think it literally desecrates an area—the word means to de-sacralize," Heaney said, warning that the destruction "will be a signal that the priorities on these islands have changed. The Tiger is now lashing its tail and smashing its way through the harp."

The chief executive of the World Monument Fund in the U.K., Jonathan Foyle, weighed in grandiloquently on the BBC, saying, "[It] actually reminds one of the Bamiyan Buddhas [ancient massive cliff face sculptures in Afghanistan] which were destroyed by the Taliban in 2001, against international uproar."

But people in the mushrooming Dublin feeder towns of County Meath had been long clamouring for a new motorway to speed their agonizing commute to the boomtown capital. The government's planners decided upon the straightest route, the one just under the lee of Tara. What they did not foresee was the mobilization of a ragtag band of hippies, anarchists, and greens determined to obstruct every inch forward. They, I thought, might offer another interesting perspective on current affairs.

The afternoon was soul-bleak—damp and bone-chilling. From the crest of the Hill of Tara, the view over the Skyrne Valley proved to be pretty enough as it was salted with several distant castle keeps. But the green slopes around them looked almost ashen in the grim light. Shivering with the cold, I entered the visitor center for a cup of tea. The adjoining shop offered the usual kitsch—garish tweed caps, shamrock-themed ties, and leprechaun dolls. But beyond the tin whistles and mass-produced "Claddagh" good-luck rings lay a zone of greater curiosity: the bookshelves. These sported dozens of quasi-mystical works with names like *Ancient Tara Lessons, In the Grove of the Druids, Celebrating Wiccah, Thirteen Lessons for Facing the Divine*, and *Walking the Mist*. Apparently, if you bought one of these, you'd find your inner moon goddess or have a whale of a time at the solstice.

I flipped through a more high-brow anthology and found these lines from the nineteenth-century poet George Russell:

> The majesty of fallen gods, the beauty,
> The fire beneath their eyes.

They huddle at night within low clay-built cabins;
And, to themselves unknown,
They carry with them diadem and sceptre
And move from throne to throne.

Duly warned, I ascended the rise out back in search of the ancients. The place at first offered all the fascination of an abandoned golf course. You found your way around it via a series of demure signs stuck on little posts, and these might as well have said "Thirteenth Green," or "Seventeenth Tee." There were no monumental sculptures or murals to connect modern man to his ancient past, a neglectfulness that seemed fitting in lonely Loughcrew, but inadequate here. I climbed through a moat-like ditch to the top of a grassy plateau that had once boasted "the fort of the synods," a sort of three thousand-year-old parliament in the rough, Valhalla-style. To the west lay the Boyne Valley, where the Protestant Ascendancy was cemented in the epic 1690 battle between William of Orange and the deposed Catholic king of England, Scotland, and Ireland, James II—the latter supported by thousands of locals rising against a massed British expeditionary force. After the slaughter was done, James fled to exile in the warmth of France, thereby earning the sobriquet *Seamus a chaca* or "James the shit."

I came to another mound surrounded by another moat-like ditch. Germans in anoraks were scrutinizing its details with burrowing avidity, as if anticipating an in-depth examination at the conclusion of their latest holiday. The top of this earthwork, which once held a banquet hall for the High Kings, sported four Americans wearing baseball caps and bewilderingly unseasonable shorts. William Butler Yeats had penned a much different vision of this scene, reading:

King Eochiad ran
Toward peopled Tara, nor stood to draw his breath
Until he came before the painted wall,
The posts of polished yew, circled with bronze,
Of the great door . . .

Nor door, nor mouth, nor slipper made a noise,
Nor on the ancient beaten paths, that wound
From well-side or from plough-land, was there noise . . .

Taking a less nostalgic view of coronation rituals was the chronicler Giraldus Cambremsis or Gerald of Wales (c. 1146–1223), clearly no admirer of the Irish:

There is in the northern and farther part of Ulster . . . a certain people which is accustomed to appoint its king with a rite altogether outlandish and abominable. When the whole people of that land has been gathered together in one place, a white mare is brought forward into the middle of the assembly. He who is to be inaugurated, not as a chief, but as a beast, not as a king but as an outlaw, has bestial intercourse with her before all, professing himself to be a beast also. The mare is then killed immediately, cut up in pieces, and boiled in water. A bath is prepared for the man afterwards in the same water. He sits in the bath surrounded by all his people, and all, he and they, eat of the meat of the mare which is brought to them... When this unrighteous rite has been carried out, his kingship and dominion have been conferred.

I next happened upon "the stone of destiny." Another legend says rivals for high kingship had to rub it for divination when seeking the supreme ruler's throne. If supernatural voices could be heard crying the length of the valley afterwards, you got the job. Touching the stone, I heard nothing but the shrieking of the wind. A little further, a deep, human-dug ravine had served as a showy promenade for the comings and goings of great chieftains and potential High Kings. Now it led me down the hill toward an encampment of the Celtic Tiger's drop outs, the true object of my visit.

At the edge of a lower field, a man draped in a woolen blanket strode forward like an extra from *Braveheart*. "A miserable day," I started.

"It will pass," pronounced the maybe forty-year-old, who had but a crop of stubble upon his head, with a distinctly English accent—a

Manchester accent, to be precise. We talked, and he pointed into the near distance. "Look past the fourth field there. That's where they're building a fifty-three-acre interchange that will spit out noise and smog night and day. It's an atrocity."

Then he cut the conversation short, saying, "Look, you should walk down to the vigil teepee if you want to find out more."

The camp, which lay on a slope below the next bend, seemed eerily vacant at first, although a central twenty-foot-high teepee was indeed coughing puffs of smoke through its top opening, as if some Cherokees were off on a hunt. Around it were ten or so more conventional tents and tarpaulin-covered shanties with wood-pallet floors. These were crammed with sleeping bags and storage trunks and various pails, pots, bins, mugs, rugs, and jugs. The compound also featured a stage encircled by massive, totem-pole-like upright logs.

A man with a ginger pony tail emerged from the surrounding wood. "I'm just poking around, and I was wondering what this platform is about?" I started.

He muttered vaguely about "group celebrations" before the stage's bonfires—these in fact sometimes featured mass chanting led by robed druids and witches. A nearby tree's branches were festooned with bird feathers, patches of cloth, panes of stained glass, and "Sioux dream catcher" talismans of bright yarn. I asked the fellow, named Derek, about this.

"It's an aura tree," he explained, "but I'm not sure what goes on with it because I've just sort of moved back here myself."

"Where have you been?"

"Well," he said, "I was camping the last seven months at our stronghold at Rath Lugh down the road. Rath Lugh was an ancient fort defending Tara."

That site had hit the headlines when a protestor named Lisa "Squeak" Feeney locked herself for three days in a hastily-dug tunnel under the earth-moving machinery's latest attack, more or less challenging their drivers to risk killing her if they proceeded. Dozens of so-called "eco-warriors" from across Ireland and Britain had lived in huts and tree houses at Rath Lugh for up to two years. Occasionally they threw themselves before approaching excavators, or chained themselves to their fenders.

"Squeak is gone from Rath Lugh. Everybody is," Derek said mournfully. He explained that just the day before the police had evicted his whole lot. "I'm in a very intense state still, to be honest with you," he confessed. "We were rolling up our tarpaulins when this security guard started standing on them and taunting us. He had his hard hat knocking into my chest, just daring a response, but most of us just really, really insist on non-violent direct action and are completely pacifist. So we walked away."

Here on the Hill of Tara, the nearby wigwams were called "benders" since they employed bent saplings to support their tarpaulins. The scene was half primitive and half not. The group washed in nearby rivers but also improvised technology to suit their more modern needs, including maintenance of a website called "Pixie Net."

"How do you do that without electricity?" I asked.

Derek's explained, "Well, I put together a bicycle-powered generator that I peddle and that stores enough energy to allow us to go on the internet. We have a wind-powered generator as well. But why don't you come into the vigil teepee and meet some of the others? There's been a fire burning there without stop since the summer solstice of 2006."

The flap was opened to a smoky world in which counter-culturists of various ages were sitting on stools and even an old sofa drawn close to a central fire. Bongo drums and guitars lay about.

A young, auburn-haired woman with a checkered scarf wrapped around her head, Palestinian-style, began speaking of their cause. "Someone has to fight this madness," said Fiona, "and we all have a passion to protect Tara here."

An Englishman with vacant, stoned eyes spoke up, saying he had been involved with eco-warrioring for nine years. Then a woman named Denise introduced herself. "I come from about only ten miles further north, which used to be another world from Dublin. But my village has been turned into suburbia and you can see right there that there's no planning going on in this country, that it's all about instant money. It's a fucking privilege to live here instead!"

Denise had been a potter and photographer before enrolling in a Dublin architectural degree course, then dropped out to join the Tara protest for a year. "I came to the camp mostly to learn about my own heritage as I want to be a teacher before I'm done. And I will tell you, I learn stuff every day. The point is that the desecration of our national heritage is worse now than anything the British ever did to us. We fought hundreds of years for our independence, and now we're throwing all tradition away in pursuit of ugly, rampant consumerism."

I hungered to see what was happening in the valley, and Denise offered to be my guide. After a short drive, we came to the ever-forward-moving path of the M3, and it was a swath of obliteration at least a thousand feet wide. Just beyond the mess, a castle keep that once housed a king called "Blind Cormac," looked pitifully irrelevant.

Next, we arrived at the wooded Rath Lugh site at which scores of protestors had camped until the previous afternoon. "God almighty!" cried Denise, pointing at a high, spiked fence that had been erected overnight. "They said we were preventing public access to a national monument. But judge for yourself who's preventing access now."

The hillock behind the fence wasn't exactly inspiring—just a thicket in which no relic of the past could be discerned. A security guard for the Spanish construction firm building the M3 was sitting in a car across the road.

"We got rid of the ecos yesterday," he said in a crude Dublin accent. "They was squatting in there saying they was trying to save the hill, that dere's a monument in there or something. It's supposed to be about our ancestors and that."

"Why the fence?"

"Just to let the people who was in dere know that they're not allowed back."

Further on, four giant diggers were gnawing into the earth. "Until March, there was a complex of fifteen or sixteen soutterains here," Denise said, referring to the underground tunnels ancient Celts dug as escape routes from their fortifications. "They were never even explored or catalogued, but they're all gone now."

So it went—a passage tomb here, the barely visible remains of an ancient celestial observatory there, a pagan burial ground from which twenty seven skeletons arranged in a star pattern around a central urn had just been removed—perhaps a score of archeological sites were being bulldozed. Beside the site of the first-century observatory called Lismullin, another armada of earthmovers and dump trucks was stirring clouds of black dust. Meanwhile, two white SUVs slowly traversed the approach road, their drivers clearly watching us. "That's the security, don't stop," Denise warned. "This lot can be rough."

Several boxy orange steel dumpsters, or "skips," squatted left. "They're full of our stuff!" cried my guide. The "stuff" consisted of worthless-looking plastic tarpaulins, wooden pallets, soaked sleeping bags, and ratty blankets. Ahead, two wildly-haired men were gesticulating before a pack of security guards—fellow eco-warriors.

These people were not exactly my type, but their passion and self-sacrifice were impressive. In any case, a couple of months later their issue became moot. Denise and company would be scattered to the winds by a government grown fed up with digger-diving and vigil teepees and hooked on the idea of development at any cost. The highway pushed on and the ancient mysteries of the Hill of Tara complex could now only be witnessed to an incessant background thrum of vehicular progress.

Chapter 15

Back in Ballyduff, my problems were simpler: beans. I had tried jump-starting them in the greenhouse but got not a sprout. Seamie Flynn came over to have a look. "But why wouldn't you just set them in the ground?" he asked, shaking his head. "That's all I do. The danger of frost is gone."

We walked the gardens, where irises and tulips were blooming and the peonies had pushed forth inches of new growth this very morning. Yet the vegetable beds looked forlorn. "What's in those?" Seamie asked.

"Well, that one's supposed to be lettuce." The only visible crop was weeds. "Nothing seems to be coming up."

Seamie scowled. "Have you put down any slug pellets?"

"Any what?"

"The slugs and snails can swallow an entire garden here before it even starts. You want to get some pellets fast."

I nodded gratefully, while feeling four years old.

So it went—Ireland old and new kept doing a Kerry dance with our lives. My son Owen and I called to Seamie's with two wheel barrows to collect manure for our unsown beds. The sight of his flower-bordered vegetable plots, now bursting with all manner of seedlings, was humbling. He lived only a shout away, and yet his garden was weeks ahead of ours. But it was a lift to watch Owen's eyes widen to this horticultural paradise, the fruit trees and vegetable plantings all manicured to perfection, the tendrils of clematis unfolding showy flowers from his cottage's walls.

After spreading the manure, we drove to the village for supplies. The aged owners of the bereft little shop-cum-post office across from Pad Flynn's had just locked their business up for good, so we went to the one at the corner. Now, I learned that this was for sale, too. It was very hard to put one's finger upon any part of Ireland that would stay put.

FOR THE TIME BEING, I had other matters to attend. One concerned a feeling of unfinished business with J.P. Donleavy, whose thoughts about this country's transformations had struck me as being so opaque. So I made arrangements to attend his art exhibition at the Molesworth Gallery in Dublin.

The train pulled in punctually, allowing time for a late afternoon visit to the famous Horseshoe Bar in the elegant Shelbourne Hotel off St. Stephen's Green—a favorite haunt of Donleavy in his day. With high corniced ceilings and shapely vases of cut flowers by the door, the maroon-walled public rooms are meant to exude elegance. However, many of the people scattered around the truly horseshoe-shaped bar and surrounding banquettes seemed to be loudly talking of only one thing—money. Curiously, the few native Irish demurely modulated their voices so that they sounded vaguely English, and one of them even referred to an acquaintance as "this chap."

Meanwhile, the actual English softened all their cut-glass accents into an approximation of an Irish country lilt. "Ah sure, we had a rake of drink on last night," said one Canary Wharf type, making me do a double-take. But then again, money talks: The Irish had accounted for almost a quarter of all foreign investment into British property in 2006. Then, the often rags-to-riches property magnates from Dublin and the back of beyond were outbidding Saudi princes and Wall Street syndicates for prime slices of the new financial districts by the Thames, and icons of London's former citadels of power—among them prized hotels like Claridge's, the Connaught, the Savoy, and even the Conservative Party's headquarters.

Me, I was just sipping in the Shelbourne Bar when a particularly dashing fellow, surely an aristocrat, fingered toward a waiter with a discrete hauteur. Around fifty, your man was quite distinguished, with a close-cropped salt-and-pepper beard, a tailor-made blue suit and a suave yellow cravat with a matching hanky fluffing from his breast pocket. God, I love the Englishman who remains unrepentantly upper-class, I thought. But of course the mysterious toff soon revealed a cringe-making Long Island accent. The puzzles of cultural identity—and what remained distinctly Irish—were not going to be solved here.

The time came for J.P. Donleavy's art opening, so I headed down Kildare Street toward Leinster House, the seat of the national government. A pair of policemen there seemed to have nothing better to do than to inspect me from head to foot, which unnerved me enough that I stopped for a sartorial self-review in front of the house in which Bram Stoker had written *Dracula* in 1897. Oh, oh. Once again, my brown shoes looked so scruffy that I nipped into a shop to fetch some polish.

One couldn't possibly saunter into a premier cultural event looking shabby, could one? I used some notebook paper to squish the goop onto my footwear while on the street, even as streams of passing gentlemen in pinstriped suits turned in consternation. The result did not exactly make me look fit for acceptance in the *Hermetic Order of the Golden Dawn*, a secret society of which the horror-stricken Bram Stoker and his Celtic-dreaming friend William Butler Yeats were founding members.

But here I was at the door of The Molesworth Gallery—the

adjoining entrance to which still holds the mystical emblems of a former Grand Lodge of the Freemasons. Ah, the capital so fair! The buzz from the exhibition was giddy and so too were the outrageously red pants of the man who put the show together, Damian Matthews. And there was Donleavy's assistant, Miss McGillicuddy, trilling warm introductions right and left. Behind clusters of lissome young ladies in black shifts and grand dames in shawls stood the author, looking as if he had just shed a decade. Now back to country squire form in a tweed suit with an elegant silk tie, he was being interviewed by a national television crew.

His paintings ran along wall after wall. Mostly watercolors, they revealed all the delicious whimsy and wit of his writing. Some were little more than cartoons, but the best, like *The Flowering Planets* (1985) or *In The Moon Machine* (1994) were as beguiling and playful as the work of the German modernist Paul Klee. The captions were, well, funny: among them, the clown face *Hey I'm Here Where's The Party*; a misshapen antediluvian fish in *My Mother Is An Intellectual;* or strange figures by a minimalist graveyard, *The Inhabitants Communicating the News of the Presence of Terrestrials.*

The artist and novelist came over to bid hello. "It is so nice that you could make my little show." Soon, a panoply of characters introduced themselves—Dublin artists, a political cartoonist with a handlebar moustache, a British screenwriter, a Florida collector of fine art. Laughter was shared, wine was quaffed, and a recording of Donleavy's stilted voice bizarrely echoed down the stairs. Then suddenly all was done, and I was left alone upon a spring night in Dublin with nowhere to go.

In and out of bookshops, I wandered and then crossed the cobbled three-hundred-fifty year-old courtyard of Trinity College which I had once often trod as a student, and where my daughter Laura now did the same. Alas, she was out of town. So I shuffled back up Grafton Street with its glitzy shop fronts that were once unassuming, before this little commercial thoroughfare temporarily became—incredibly—the sixth-most-expensive piece of commercial real estate in the world.

At least Stephen's Green hadn't recognizably changed from its tranquil state of oasis, its bowery walks leading to verdant lawns. Here, Joyce's Stephen Dedalus wandered with a youth's yearning in *A Portrait of the Artist as a Young Man*. Prodigious beds of tulips touted their lurid colorations towards the setting sun, their harlequin's orange and harlot's rouge, their chemise yellow and punk rocker's purple. Then, as if upon hearing some secret signal, they all simultaneously began to retreat sadly back into themselves, like parasols folding up for the night. The ducks, as always, indolently patrolled the pond, scrapping after bread that children and lovers from the benches tossed. A deranged and disheveled figure shrieked from a copse, "You've gone mad with your SUVs! You're all going to hell!" What would a park be without doomsayers in its trees?

At dusk, I exited Stephen's Green and crossed the street to the sidewalk before the Shelbourne Hotel. Suddenly a short man with a shag of black hair stopped in his tracks and beheld me with beaming eyes, his lips catching at one side. "I know you!" the interlocutor pronounced.

He had an amiable smile and dipped his shoulders in greeting, first the right one and then the left, like a pilot saying hello with his wings at a country air show. The accent was maybe midlands British. But who in God's name was he? He looked the ringer for the late actor Dudley Moore, but this man, with a sweet-looking woman attached to his arm, was alive, seemingly with all the liquidity Dublin offered.

"You were at J.P.'s exhibition," he correctly observed. A few more words and we were back in the Horseshoe Bar, exchanging pints and life stories. Colin and his wife Leslie were passionate readers of every word Donleavy had ever written. "We fell in love with each other even as we loved the books more and more." Teenage sweethearts who had held together for decades, they lived ordinary lives in Essex, while starting from humble backgrounds. Yet, they shared such a thirst for knowledge that they both completed university when in their fifties and gave each other not flowers every week, but books. No fake accents with these two. But they each held a fantasy that is entertained around the world, which is that one of the most exhilarating opportunities life offers is to get drunk in Ireland, perhaps even in literary company. And let the chips fall where they may.

Leslie tottered off to bed. Colin and I decided to wend our way up Baggot Street to J.P. Donleavy's private dinner party at the United Arts Club, among whose founding members was W. B. Yeats. We addressed the locked door on the Georgian brownstone's stoop with gusto and were ushered to the inner sanctum. At the end of another horseshoe-table configuration Donleavy stood before about twenty diners completing a speech which had to do with the comic inspiration to be found in Ireland. As Damian of the red pants poured us wine and proffered a parfait, this soon resurrected its hydra head.

Virginia McGillicuddy's name came up, so I asked a man with a thin little moustache about how someone so-called could have such a posh English accent. "Well, because she was married to the lord of McGillicuddy Reeks. He owned the whole bloody Kerry mountain range and was called *The McGillicuddy!*" he roared through rabbit teeth.

J.P. Donleavy drifted out of the room on the arm of a lady wearing a cashmere sweater and red beret atop a long mane of silver hair—the owner of the Loughcrew manor with its folly of a Roman arch and sculptures of rabbits and toads.

We remnants went upstairs to the members-only tavern to discover its apparent *Hermetic Order of the Golden Barfly*. At its tables were scattered a still life of bearded and bosomy characters such as Breughel might have painted into place four hundred years ago. They certainly looked frozen in time, hands dangling idly before an impressive array of glasses. Then someone bellowed from the back counter and the artfully arranged grouping by the entrance resumed jawing as if pursuing a game of musical chairs. Colin and I plunked ourselves down beside them and began chatting with a lady of cleavage. This was a bad choice, for she belonged to a nearby mustachioed gentleman in a bow tie and white three-piece suit who had a snarl buried in his beard. He was a perfectly absurd Irish eccentric playing the sneeringly superior retired English major in the very manner J.P. Donleavy whistled into being in his later books. "You actually reside in Ireland, do you?"

"Yes, for some time," I said.

"Quite," he sneered as if he was stirring old tea with fresh contempt. "Somehow fitting."

"What?"

"I mean you would, with that beard? It must have started somewhere, what do you say? Perhaps in the Rocky Mountains with a mule standing by the ol' campfire? After a hearty massacre of the pesky redskins? Can you cook a proper flap jack, like Paul Bunyan?" The man was so beside himself, he was cackling.

This carry-on was par for a certain type of Irish late-night conversational course as practised by the Messer: When in doubt about any contrary point of view or un-introduced personage appearing in your midst at 1 a.m., try to obliterate the new interlocutor with a fusillade of insults—that's the Messer's brief.

I muttered something back, only to discern that Major Tut Tut's eyes were roving below my knees.

"Did you buy those brown shoes in America?" he snorted.

Revenge proved unnecessary, for the paragon of high Anglo-Irish breeding had reached his personal tipping point. Triumphantly, Major Tut Tut hoisted his substantial glass of red wine toward his insult-brewing lips, but before the docking-in-space could be completed, he abruptly cocked his neck to the right with such a vehement smirk that he somehow spectacularly missed his target. Then the entire contents of his *omphalae* waterfalled down the lengths of his impeccably white suit. The effect was delightful. Huge crimson blotches welted at his elbows, midriff, and knees, while a puddle dribbled and grew into a slack little pond between his assuredly black—and not brown—shoes.

The chortling bartender raced over and dumped a blizzard of salt upon Major Tut Tut. But there was some secret ingredient in the wool of this finest of Dublin suits that the salt catalyzed into a sartorial form of an anaphylaxic reaction. To my astonishment, the man began to sprout stalagmites. This created the effect of a wooly mammoth emerging from the depths of encrusted time.

"Bollocks!" he cried, pointing at me. "Look what you made me do!"

AFTER A HOTEL BREAKFAST I STROLLED TO AN ART GALLERY. Then it was back to Baggot Street, a close little thoroughfare running towards the posh neighborhood of Ballsbridge where barristers live in multi-million-euro redbrick houses and a piece of commercial real estate had recently sold for fifty-three million euros per acre—one of the highest prices ever realized in the world (and one that would soon leave that developer bankrupt). I once knew the stretch as a place where young couples desperately squeezed each other on door stoops before hurtling onto the last double-decker buses of the night. The street now sported a place called the Harvest Moon with a sign beckoning "Have a Lovely Day Every Day," which was quite an injunction for a country that used to revel in its misery.

I went on to my favorite bar in Dublin—Grogan's. This is located on an obscure South William street patrolled by rival dueling Sikhs in their turbans, one tall, one short, but both bearing restaurant menus and waving passersby toward their doors. Grogan's in contrast offers toasted ham, cheese, and onion sandwiches, nothing else. In Grogan's one falls under the care of a gentle white-bearded publican named Tommy Smith, who holds an honored position in the national poetry society.

Tommy needs be droll since the bar, which is lined with its patrons' paintings, is curious, being divided by its own Berlin Wall. In the front you have the horse-bettors, spongers, artists, thespians, and writers. A swinging door leads to the still murkier back "lounge" where unrepentant trade unionists mutter conspiratorially about subjects from past times. As a rule, the two sides never mix, never speak, and barely nod. When tilting forward to receive drink, they can momentarily glimpse each other from either side of the dividing line and technically belong to the same race. But so do the North and South Koreans who have been scowling across the DMZ at each other for the last sixty years. Ah, forever tribal Ireland, I thought, settling in.

This afternoon I was hailed by an old acquaintance with a scarf about his neck, an actor who entertains me by describing the worst films ever made, within all of which he claims to have made appearances. I told Vincent Smith I had seen J.P. Donleavy the night before.

"*The Ginger Man* was a great book," he said, then got local as Irish people always do, painting identity by pub. "But I didn't think too much of the company he kept in McDaid's."

"The biggest bunch of bowsies and losers who ever lived," snorted Tommy Smith. "Literary Dublin? You wouldn't allow your dog in the company of those eejits!"

Vincent said he delivered newspapers to the supposed greats of Irish writing hunkered on their McDaid's stools. "I used to go in there to sell the papers, I'd be about ten years of age. The barman used to give me glasses of minerals. I'd sit there, and Patrick Kavanagh would want to take a newspaper for nothing and so would Brendan Behan. The first time I ever met Brendan he was painting a pub up the road, and they wouldn't serve him. So he asked me to mind the ladder for him since he was going down to McDaid's. The ladder was there the next day."

Did he know J.P. Donleavy's hero Gainor Crist?

"I met him. He was a fucking lunatic, he was. One time I saw him in there with his feet normal like on the ground. The next thing I know was he jumped. I don't know how he did it, but he elevated himself in one go from the floor onto the top of the bar and was standing there twice my size."

"Gainor Crist was a gentleman," interrupted Tommy. "See here—we have his picture behind the bar."

Out came a small black-and-white portrait of the hero of *The Ginger Man*, his dark eyes plaintive and feline in their knowing, his features handsome in the way the Germans call *raffinert*, his suit nicely cut. The effect was altogether haunting, seeing as this man was said to have mysteriously fallen into the sea off Tenerife while young, although his body was never found. Donleavy himself told me that, visiting Dublin years later, he had the spooky sensation that Crist materialized before him, only to disappear into a crowd.

But this was now. At the base of this near daguerreotype, this tiny epiphany, a scribbled message read: "A small secular shrine to the memory of Gainor Stephen Crist, ghost of The Ginger Man."

"Flip it over," said Tommy.

There I read: "This is the ginger man's only memorial. Hang it where boozers booze. Affix firmly to wall. I couldn't find Paddy O'Brien or any other ghost in McDaid's, so it has to be Grogan's. Mac."

"Where did you get this?" I asked Tommy

"From Mac, a man who used to come here. He found it in London, he lived in London."

"I see," I said. I did, I had. In these last few weeks I felt I had traveled as far as one could into the spirit of *The Ginger Man*, the fable of Ireland that so many had once loved. The ending to that book was a lonely beckoning:

> God's mercy
> On the wild
> Ginger man.

Donleavy had known Ireland brilliantly. But now, it seemed, I knew it better than he. It was time to move on. He wasn't on the wild anymore—I was.

Chapter 16

Gainor Crist almighty, but things would not stay put. The delirious housing market finally began to sputter, and a great hissing sound of deflating bouncy castles could be heard across the land. Alarm at the skyrocketing costs of everything stirred a nationwide ill ease, with the excesses of so-called "Rip-Off Ireland" repeatedly skewered on the airwaves and grumbled about on the street. Here and there, multinational corporations began closing down their Irish plants, saying it was cheaper to do business in Poland or the Far East. Was the fairy tale about to end?

To whet the continuing mania for property speculation, the builders and bankers turned to emerging markets like Slovenia and Slovakia. The newspapers touted "foreign property fairs" and small investors pumped savings sight-unseen into Irish-built apartments from Budapest to Montenegro as well as buy-to-let syndicates in Berlin or New York—anywhere but overpriced Ireland. Not to worry, the banks' economists kept saying, the economy was simply undergoing a correction. At worst a "soft landing" lay ahead.

A general election was in progress, affording much diversion, if little oratory. Mainstream Irish politicians prefer to circulate door-to-door like Jehovah's Witnesses, and festoon thousands of lamp posts with their pictures, slapped above a safe slogan. In the spring of 2007, the long-ruling and property-developer-backed party of Fianna Fáil ("soldiers of destiny") dished forth a stupendously banal one—"Protect Our Prosperity."

Fianna Fáil had plenty of reasons to divert the public's attention, particularly when the Taoiseach or prime minister Bertie Ahern began to morph into a figure of ridicule. With his bull-dog face and determinedly beaming eyes, Bertie was no beauty, and his suits were so often rumpled and ill-fitting that they looked like hand-me-downs. But his unpretentious, homespun ways had won him much affection, partly because the far more stylish prime minister of the 1980s, Charlie Haughey—under whom he cut his political teeth—had been a swindler on par with the worst crooks of Tammany Hall in nineteenth-century New York. Bertie, in contrast, came across as a hard-working pragmatist, who had helped lay the groundwork for the country's vaunted economic miracle and was a key contributor to the gradual triumph of peace in the troubled North.

The problem was that a tribunal from the country's High Court had begun looking into his murky personal finances. Their remit was to investigate whether a major property developer had bribed him in order to win a go-ahead for a vast Dublin County shopping mall.

The headlines focused on a string of cash payments that had mysteriously drifted Bertie Ahern's way when he was minister of finance. Though trained as an accountant, he said he could neither remember nor trace their provenance since he never kept a personal bank account in the 1990s when he was first presiding over the nation's booming economy.

"You were minister of finance, and you didn't have a single bank account and kept no personal financial records?" asked the dumb-founded judges.

"No, I kept my money in cash in a safe in my office," explained the Barney Rubble-faced Bertie. Guffaws and phlegm-flying coughs echoed though the Four Courts, Dublin's citadel of jurisprudence, but the electorate's response was initially muted, since vast numbers of transactions were completed throughout the boom years with no receipt. One of Bertie's wads of cash had materialized in an unmarked envelope from an Irish property developer based in England, who was suspected of currying favors for a get-rich-quick Dublin casino scheme.

This, the Taoiseach clarified, was but a "dig out" from "a close personal friend."

"A dig out?" snorted the judges in their horse-hair wigs.

The Taoiseach explained that, while a humble cabinet minister, he was weathering a painful separation and often sleeping in near homeless fashion in his Fianna Fáil regional party office. Sympathetic friends therefore gathered "dig outs" and friendly little loans which he termed "whip-arounds" so that he could buy a certain house, which happened to be owned by the boyo from Manchester. Also, he dimly recalled making big winnings on a certain race horse, its name forgotten.

The testimony was dumbfounding, but the populace mostly sighed and looked away, complacently reasoning that the amounts in question seemed small and, sure, all politicians were a bit crooked, weren't they? That Irish complacent attitude seemed to lie behind much of what was spiraling out of control on all sides now. But for the time being, Bertie Ahern dodged the bullet, and his party scrambled together enough votes to forge a new coalition government. The seas were getting rough, but the endangered little boat of Ireland sailed on, like St. Brendan's coracle.

VISITS TO THE VILLAGE OF BALLYDUFF brought frequent inquiries about the progress of our garden. In Maura Lindsey's pub or the shop, the question was always the same. "How go the beans?"

"Desolation row," was my response.

"Maybe it's the slugs," suggested John Flynn beside the hardware store, as he lolled on a wall. "They'll eat everything in sight."

"I think I've got half a million, John."

I had grown to know something of this subject, and that it was at once seminal and vaginal, and grotesque. Every night, legions of these hermaphrodites crawl through the country's vegetable beds, exuding trails of mucus upon which to glide and fornicate. Their coatings grow more repulsive when one understands how inimitably well equipped the slug is for procreation, coming each and every one with both a prick and a twat. Some evenings both ends of same self-meet in congress. When Amour is afoot, they curl together with a friend, push some mucus out of one orifice, ingest a squirt from another's, and make a dozen to a hundred more of themselves before you can say Bob's your uncle. In fact, they do it with Bob the uncle, too.

Every slug comes with a schlong and some can expand theirs to five times their bodies' length, which in human terms would mean thirty-feet long. These are apparently succulent, since passersby frequently bite their neighbor's off. This stops nothing, since some little sluggy is always digesting sufficient seedlings to manufacture another battering ram. They are insatiable. In fact, the great grey slugs like to maneuver down slime trails they distend from branches so as to meet for orgasms in mid-air.

Every non-arid country has its slugs, but no northern one boasts more than Ireland, with up to a quarter of a million of these fornicators inhabiting each half-acre of the island's damp, fecund ground. The fiendish part is that each little streak of slime comes with up to twenty-five thousand teeth. In the course of a growing season, a lone slug can devour one and a half pounds of plant material, which works out to nearly forty-five hundred tons per acre, and that amounts to a lot of beans. They got all mine.

With summer approaching, the first weekly renters of our cottages began to arrive, among them opinionated Americans. "You don't need those horrible pellets, which can kill the birds, just lay out some strips of brass around your beds," chided one know-it-all Californian. Right. Somehow, various vegetables prospered, and the peas, those most prehensile of all vegetables, extended their astonishingly feeling tendrils into netting and climbed high.

The days offered their revelations. A prodigious hawthorn became wreathed in thousands of delicate white flowers, and around these bees swarmed in stupendous numbers. I warmed to the fantasy that I was getting lost in the most secret of worlds, *the present*. And—what now—the tree began to snow. The morning was mild, yet a blizzard of white flakes fell around the hawthorn, and many of these seemed to possess some hidden means of locomotion that allowed them to dart and veer in whatever direction they chose. Curious, I grabbed one as it shuttled past and saw that these were seed pods of miraculous design. Each came with a superstructure of minute webbed ribs narrowing ineffably at the tail, with the latter tufted with silken strands tipped by their barely visible packets of future life.

Alas, my own attempts to imitate nature's wizardry by tying trout and salmon flies seemed unspeakably crude in comparison. Our guest cottage had an oaken former library cabinet crammed with oddities shipped over from America—elk, squirrel, possum, and muskrat tails; ostrich, guinea hen, and peacock feathers; and strange humanoid cock-ups with names like Zonker Strips, marabou, chenille; and let us not forget the Krystal Flash Wow Wow. Out of such ephemera, I had once created countless lures. Now, I grabbed a rod and flicked a grayish fly to a recurring dimple in an otherwise still point of water. Bang came a take. Yikes, what I reeled in was so small, it was a laugh. But the brown trout writhed with life as I released the hook and set it free. Again I cast and more small fish came to me.

That night I stopped in Maura Lindsey's pub and began to describe my funny trophies to Connie Corcoran, a master ghillie who had landed thousands of prodigious salmon from the Blackwater.

"Oh they were massive! Every bit of six inches!" I enthused.

"Right monsters so!" Connie chortled.

When the conversation paused, an affable bartender named Bridey delivered some news that fell with a hammer's thud. "I don't mean to alarm you, but Maura has decided to close up next week."

My heart sank. Paranoia was so widespread about the country's draconian new drunk-driving laws—which included random breath-testing at seven a.m. to see if you had too much the night before—along with dismay over the cost of drink, that the rural pubs were dying right and left. The arch anti-smoking laws contributed to the exodus of customers from that bastion of cheer in the world's mind, the Irish pub. The loss of this particular one—Maura Lindsey's—felt like a last straw. "Please tell me you are joking!" I protested.

"I am afraid not," said Bridey.

Nightmares come in multiples. It was Thursday and Jamie and the boys would be arriving the next morning. I worked until the light began to fade, which by now was after ten p.m. That's when the door first opens to Tobin's, the most ancient of the four pubs in Ballyduff. Behind that hole-in-the-wall's bar, a pair of aged bachelor brothers shuffle as slowly as they please since the place has been in their family for more than one hundred and fifty years. Ritchie and Denny Tobin exchange few words, because their tavern is a place for murmuring when the spirit dictates—or saying nothing at all. The place is as unhurried a venue as can still be found in Ireland, a sipper's refuge with not even a radio to interfere with the tick-ticking of the clock. Countrymen gather upon the battered stools to talk, when they chose to, of the weather, the news, the price of lambs and cows.

Tonight, however, a man named Martin was getting himself into a lather. "How many cows are being milked up now compared to fifteen years ago?" he asked in response to a question no one asked. "Who's around now to calve a cow even?"

All heads lowered like a congregation stoically settling into pews. "You don't need to pay a vet like to take a calf off a cow. You put your hand in yourself." Martin was growing florid. "Isn't that so, Ritchie?"

The publican gazed toward the window, murmuring. "Very true, yeah."

Martin continued with his soliloquy. "There's a pile of good men gone like, because they couldn't make it pay."

Ritchie, then eighty-five, added, "Think of Seanie Barry with his hundreds of cows, gone altogether." His voice obliquely trailed off, "All gone."

Martin raised a hand toward providence. "And they'll never be a cow back on them places like. To get a good fellow to milk a cow now, he's not there."

"No," Ritchie agreed dolefully.

"You can't get a responsible man like that anymore, a man who's going to give you the twenty-four hours."

This was rural Ireland, still pure and true, I thought. But would I ever belong to it, especially when it sometimes appeared to be singing its own death knell?

"Yeah," Ritchie said. He and his kid brother Denny, eighty-one, manage only a couple of cows now themselves, but often go to the weekly cattle mart in just over the Cork border in Fermoy, just to keep an eye on the action.

Martin was not done with his dirge. "Think of David Aglesby. He was so manly, he milked five hundred cows."

Ritchie looked sceptical.

"That would be morning and evening," Martin conceded.

An older fellow with thick white eyebrows weighed in. "David Murphy came to Balhstrom the back end of the year, and he took in fifty calves from September on and two hundred fifty from February on. David Murphy was over there, and you would get nights out of him, wouldn't ye?"

To my relief, this funereal conversation finally ceased.

Clearly, Tobin's was no flash Dublin pub. Its rhythms had been worked out over generations, and a newcomer only started a fresh conversation in here very carefully. But keep quiet long enough in such a citadel of the old, watchful Irish culture and your turn will inevitably come—at least when the general levity sets in. Sure enough, the premises eventually grew more animated, and a stick of a man leaned close, wanting to know what part of America I was from. He was so thin his blue suit hung limply from his bony shoulders, but Kevin, as he introduced himself, touched my wrist with an easy affability. He was once a star on the London stage, he claimed, and I half believed it because he had élan, and also because little Ballyduff boasts a remarkable community theatre which has launched many professional careers. The next thing I knew Kevin burst into singing "Oklahoma" to an accompaniment of nothing but his own dancing feet.

"Brilliant," said I, raising my glass.

Now closing time approached and with it came a stampede of conversation, uninhibited at last. A farmer who tended cattle by the river asked after my health. "Are ye liking it here in Ballyduff?" inquired John.

I confessed that I was depressed about Maura Lindsey's closing.

"We all are, because there's huge sadness in that," he agreed soulfully. "But there is even worse news tonight."

"Christ, what's that?"

"Pad Flynn is shutting down the hardware shop next month. The heart of this village is after being broken."

I nearly choked on my pint. Goodbye Oklahoma, goodbye mad Kevin, and Ritchie with your pastoral ways, I whispered under my breath as I shambled out under a watery moon. I felt like I was losing my footing and not from the drink but from a nagging worry in my heart. Was everything that I revered about Ireland disappearing before my eyes?

THE NEXT MORNING I WALKED DOWN to the hardware shop's yard. The driver Ritchie was loading the shop's delivery truck that had called for decades to every farm in this jewelled stretch of the Blackwater. It hurt to think he was now embarking on one of his last runs. There was ruddy faced John sitting ample on a wall, John of girth, John of sun.

"How are you, John?"

The smile, the come-here-to me-smile, as wide as a street. The slow shift of his head to take in the clouds by their turn and then me, as if all was of a piece. "A grand day now," he said, with his hands on his suspenders.

"John, I am so sorry to hear Pad is closing," I fairly gushed, wondering why I felt so desperate, when it was not my job being lost, but his.

"I am a bit shattered, to be honest," nodded John.

I said, "John, but you will have all the world's freedom ahead. The lassies should look out."

His eyes did the obligatory twinkle, but the hurt in them was plain to see. "I'll farm a little, all right. But I will miss seeing people all day."

"Is there anything good to come of it?"

"I don't know," said John, looking very sad.

And I was nearly fighting back tears myself. This was the most disturbing sign yet of the imminent collapse of the Irish boom.

WHAT EXACTLY WAS ENDURING, I kept wondering. Suddenly, it was made known that a local man named Seamus Kelly had taken to the bogs to answer the same question, knowing the acids in peat tannin can preserve things for thousands of years. At first, Seamus started digging into prehistory for the trunks of seven-to-nine thousand year-old oaks and yews in order to make fanciful furniture. Then he began using his hoary finds to create totemic sculptures, a number of which were currently on display in galleries in Kerry and Dublin. Lately he had begun excavating the skeletons of mammoth-like giant elk from oh, thirteen or fifteen thousand years ago. Well, that's permanence worth looking into, I thought.

A soft rain was falling when I knocked on the door of Seamus's remote studio, a stone farmhouse in which he had been raised in the middle of County Waterford. A low gate pushed open, and a pair of Springer Spaniels leapt excitedly. Piles of branches and tree trunks lay strewn around an overgrown lawn. From out back came bird cries, cacophonous and weird.

Round-faced and droll, Seamus came to the door to greet me.

"What's with that mad screeching?" I asked.

"Those are my pheasants. I keep pheasants, which leads me to my second pre-occupation, which is fighting magpies and other flying vermin," he said, pointing to a tree where a newly deceased black bird sprawled head down from a crotch in its branches. How very Hitchcock, I thought. "I have to spend a lot of time shooting crows and magpies because they won't stop attacking the young pheasants," he nonchalantly explained.

We had some tea, then trekked on to his favorite bog, a bleak expanse beneath a bowl of low hills. Over these dark clouds scuttled—the scene was lonely but serene. Very carefully, I slogged behind him into a world of sponge. As each footfall landed, you heard a slurp—and this was the driest outer edge of an inland sea of sinking ground. In another minute, your entire leg risked disappearing with the wrong step.

Meanwhile, the mist grew so thick you could lick it off your lips.

"All of this would have been a lake thousands of years back, a lake where the giant deer came down here to drink and feed long before there was a single person about," observed Seamus, pointing out a barely discernable route through his revered world of muck.

The great elk, or "giant deer," flourished in Ireland more prolifically than almost anywhere else in Europe. They were celebrated in ancient odes since they stood taller than the greatest moose—prodigious engines of rutting and destruction from eons past.

As we progressed, nearly every footfall sunk deeper through the decaying organic matter, down, down into time. Traversing a turgid channel, we came to a pit about twelve feet long and eight feet deep. Its bottom was rank with peat-stained water, primordial and black.

"That is one of my sites," Seamus said before what looked very much like a hole to nowhere, or perhaps a latrine. "Mind yourself by the edge. You wouldn't want to fall in there, I can tell you."

"It looks like you'd never get out if you did," I responded.

"You could be right," Seamus chuckled. "But that's where I found my first giant deer. I was just poking about, looking for bog oak with a friend when it was dry last summer. We work with the spade to a certain depth, and then I probe with my iron rod to see if there's anything below."

"But this bog is so enormous. Why did you choose to dig right here?" I interrupted.

"That's the thing—you never know. You just have to follow your intuition. We were digging away blind like, when bingo, there was a funny touch to the end of the probe that made me know there was something unusual down below."

This did not seem like the most sophisticated of techniques, and I almost wondered whether he was putting me on. But no, Seamus insisted it was all a matter of touch. "It can be hard to penetrate far enough with the probe because of all the shattered rock you find at a certain depth, back from when the Ice Age came in. But yerrah, it was a fine evening, and I knew I had felt something strange so I pressed on. At first I thought it was a piece of wood—maybe a section of bog oak—but then I said to myself, 'It's too deep to be wood,' which would come from a later time than the giant deer. So I kept at it."

The landowner had given Seamus free reign to dig in this soupy ground. So nobody paid any mind when he rushed back the next morning to continue his excavation. But before night fell again, he had unearthed one of the most stunningly preserved thirteen thousand year-old great elk skeletons to be discovered in Ireland. Seamus has been digging for the giant deer ever since.

"I couldn't believe the sight of that first yoke. I mean, to just stand there with it was like stepping into another world," he said as we moved onto another trench. Here, he had unearthed the remains of not one but two ancient elk.

"The thing is," Seamus responded, "nobody has a clue about all this, not even the biggest archeologists in Ireland. Ah, I have had a bunch of them down here to watch me work, and had experts radio-carbon date my finds. Why, when you listen to them likes nattering, it's clear they don't know a whole lot more than I do myself. Did the Ice Age drive the giant deer down to this lake? Did they just get trapped in the mud? No one knows."

He said he had yet to explore most of even this single bog. "The thing about this work is you never know what you'll find or where or when, if you find a single thing. So you dig and you dig and then you dig some more." He confided that a man in Florida had given him some extra motivation to keep at it, claiming he might pay seventy thousand dollars for a perfect specimen.

"What's perfect?" I asked.

"How long is a piece of string?" he laughed.

Later, we headed back into his tin-roofed barn. Piles of nine thousand year-old bog oak hulked beside a lathe just inside the door. These petrified gunmetal grey trunks and branches were crackled and burled with time.

The better stuff lay deeper in the shed—a sprawling mortuary of antlers, vertebrae and leg bones of great elks that would have trumpeted ten or fifteen thousand years earlier from every next field. Medieval kings and queens used to pay small fortunes to bring such heraldic specimens back from Ireland to adorn their distant castles. And now some of the finest specimens in the world were waiting for my inspection inside a tin shed in a forgotten part of County Waterford.

Hoisting one enormous skull from a shadowy corner, Seamus's eyes gleamed. "Do you see the heft of this? It's like an anvil! Imagine him charging you at thirty miles an hour, with his rack of antlers stretching twelve feet wide! You would run away in terror!"

I groaned as I tried to lift the same rack over my head. "How could any neck have handled such a weight?" I gasped, since great elk antlers run to ninety pounds.

"You haven't felt the vertebrae yet," clucked Seamus. He soon showed me these exquisitely interlocking jet-black structures, four inches thick, and as smooth as the most exquisite modern machine burnishing could render.

Inside the cottage, Seamus showed me some of his sculptural work, which mixed great elk rib bones with hoary bog oak, yew, and elm, to create images of ancient Celtic warriors or of twisting river tributaries. One piece in progress was intended to be thirty feet tall.

More tea, and now Seamus displayed photographs of a three thousand year-old human being who had been unearthed from a County Cavan bog. Evidently he'd been tortured to death as an offering to ancient Celtic gods. His leathery skin was almost ghoulishly intact, the hair still curled above his head. The guy was only four feet tall.

"The father of us all?" I offered, and Seamus chuckled.

"There are quare things to be found in Ireland yet," said he. And in fact, that little phrase at that moment renewed my faith.

Chapter 17

Our daughter's first year at Trinity College had come to a close. Collecting her in Dublin, I found Laura sagging a bit on a sofa within her dormitory suite. Her blue eyes looked sad under her mane of strawberry-blonde hair.

"How are you Laura?" I asked gently.

"Tired. The final exams were really hard."

What did I know? Laura had been run through the grinder of the top tier of an educational system that sought world-class status but could be mercilessly stern and even pedantic.

"I think I may have failed German. Two-thirds of the kids in my course think they failed."

Out on the lawns, students were lolling about in the sun. Others were busy loading gear into their parents' cars. Me, I was fretting that the challenges of raising a family in an adopted country never stopped.

"Well, you can relax for a while now because we're going to spend a night or two in Ballyduff before going to Cork," I said nonetheless.

The boys, for their part, were doing fine. Owen, turning fourteen, had become passionate about rowing sculls and sleek four-man boats with his Lee River club in Cork. Harris landed some part-time work that put change in his pocket, while Jamie kept savouring the creative buzz about the Cork Opera House. Ballyduff being rented out for much of the summer, they were all about to head back for a holiday in the U.S. without me, since I was preparing for another Irish pilgrimage.

I OPTED TO HEAD OFF TOWARD DONEGAL, the most remote and reputedly unspoiled county in the country. On my last visit there in 1985, it felt like a place that danced to its own time. Had it also suffered merciless change? Or had I indulged a nostalgic vision of the county from the start? Perhaps, this journey would help me solve some personal questions about what remained right and true within Ireland.

My first stop was the pretty County Mayo town of Westport, where a cousin named John Hurst now lived. With him I shared the legacy of my maternal grandfather who had literally ridden off on a pair of Palominos with his dumbfounded bride to mine silver in the Yucatan when young, later heading north to sell the earliest John Deere tractors in Canada. Instead of wealth, he apparently passed on a wandering gene to his grandson John, my cousin, who spent decades teaching in the Far East and never returned to the U.S. Then, he became caught up in his own Irish dream, uncannily parallel to my own. After a decade of summering in County Mayo, John bought a local used book shop and took up permanent residence.

I found him in a venerable Westport pub called Matt Molloy's— owned by a member of the internationally renowned band, The Chieftains. Thin, rangy, and white-haired, John was trading barbs with a laughing crowd at the corner of the bar, as if he had lived in Ireland for decades. What, was he stealing my act?

"Christ, you look alike, you act alike, and you even sound alike," chuckled a barrister from Northern Ireland who had ditched a lucrative career to take up folk singing and live the Mayo life. "I feel sorry for you both."

John's partner, Tricia, a Hungarian raised in Australia, joined us for dinner at a restaurant across the street. "So what are you hoping to find in Donegal?" John asked.

"Interesting people mainly," I said. "A stroll into the past perhaps."

"Well, did I ever tell you how we got here?" began the cousin. "It had to do with a white witch. About fifteen years ago I got interested in a property advertised in the *International Herald Tribune*. It described an old cottage with beautiful views over a lake in the mountains in Donegal and it sounded wonderful. It was by a village named Church Hill, and Jane Crane the witch lived there."

I gawped, since I had pencilled in that obscure crossroads as a certain destination for my present journey, Church Hill having been my lodestar when traversing Donegal in 1974. The turf smoke lazing in the mist, the banter with farmers idling on muddy lanes, the yelp of sheep dogs expertly rounding flocks by the nearby lake, the head-spinning stories that went on over pints—that place had put a trance on me. I took a room above the pub for two nights, to better explore the surroundings. "Church Hill grabbed me on sight. I want to see what has happened to it now," I told John.

"Well, that's weird," he responded. "Because I flew all the way from Singapore to Ireland in 1994 and went straight to Church Hill. Jane's place there was pretty enticing, and we hit it off. That she was a white witch didn't bother me because she was a hoot. The problem was that her place needed a lot of work."

My cousin sipped at his coffee. "Anyway, I ended up driving to Westport and finding our cottage. But Jane and I stayed in touch ever since. I'm telling you she is unique. You ought to meet her."

The next morning John Hurst and I took a drive. A back road lifted to the crest of a rise that bestowed distant views of the island-peppered expanse of Clew Bay. It was rimmed by weathered mountains that came with a near pyramid rising through the clouds, a mountain both majestic and brooding. This was Croagh Patrick, upon whose peak the patron saint of Ireland had an encounter with God that changed

Ireland forever—and, through his disciples, helped rekindle the light of Christianity throughout Europe.

"Stunning, isn't it?" said John as we stopped and stared.

I drove on alone to the holy mount. Forty thousand people had climbed Croagh Patrick's punishing, stony ascent for a mass on the summit the previous Sunday, many of them barefoot, since that is the tradition of veneration there. Maybe Irish Catholicism has vitality yet, I thought after learning this. Today, many visitors milled about at the holy mountain's base, including bus loads of Bavarians sporting yellow t-shirts emblazoned with images of uplifted forefingers forming some emblem of exaltation. At the base stood a bronze sculpture of a famine ship pointing in the general direction of North America—and haunting was this vision. Bug-eyed skeletons were stretched out helter-skelter above the deck, clinging at each other's hands as if knowing their lives were dangling before imminent death. Ravens stalked the yardarms, waiting to feed on them.

"Every time I see this I nearly cry," my cousin had said.

GETTING TO DONEGAL IS NOT EASY. Two days driving is the routine. So I pushed up the coast, bypassing Sligo town and only stopped briefly at the Drumcliff graveyard of William Butler Yeats because he told everybody not to, with his tombstone injunction commanding, "Cast a cold eye/ On life, on death./ Horseman, pass by." Though the road roars just beside it, the place holds some interest, lying as it does under the lee of the sphinx-shaped mountain of Ben Bulben. But there is a grating banality to the scene, beginning with the cement parking lot that runs intrusively to within two feet of an ancient Celtic high cross, its scroll work rendered barely-intelligible by a millennium of wind and rain. A close look showed weathered carvings of Adam and Eve, Cain and Abel, Daniel and the lions, and further anguish of the damned playing out beneath a figure of the crucified Christ.

Yeats's grave—in which the wrong skeleton may have been

implanted after the poet was attempted to be dug up from the south of France—lay beside the pretty protestant church out back. Tourists shuffled around it for a camera click-click at the grave, followed by a duck into the Drumcliff Tea and Craft Shop.

Only in the chapel did one true pilgrim become manifest. He wore a white sailor's cap and stood in the third pew dementedly proclaiming verses from the Book of Hebrews in a distinctive Derry accent. The congregation consisted of just him, plus me.

Horseman, pass by. Pass by the Yeats Tavern, pass by the Yeats Pub, pass by the Yeats Restaurant, and the next thing you know a sign points to a small peninsula named Mullaghmore, which is another place etched in history. Here above gull-screaming cliffs lies one of the most storybook castles in Ireland, a magnificent, multi-turreted affair called Classiebawn with panoramic views to distant islands and back to the eyeful of Ben Bulben. At the end of its mile-long drive, Lord Mountbatten used to idle every summer, a vaunted presence in that he was a grandson of Queen Victoria, former Commander of Allied Forces in Southeast Asia during World War II, the Admiral of the British Fleet, last Viceroy of India, First Sea Lord, and Earl of Burma.

People like Joe McGowan, a local historian with whom I had talked, said he got on so splendidly with the locals that he didn't bother with much personal security. What a mistake. On a late August Monday in 1979, Mountbatten set off in his yacht the *Shadow V* to look after some lobster traps with his two young grandsons, his daughter Patricia, her husband, and her mother-in-law Lady Doreen Brabourne, plus a local sixteen year-old deckhand. It was a fluff of a day.

But the "Troubles" were frenzied in Northern Ireland that year, and the Provisional IRA wanted to make a statement the British would never forget. In the seventy-nine-year-old Mountbatten, they believed they'd found the perfect target. No sooner had the *Shadow V* set to sea than a remote-controlled bomb in its hold exploded, killing

Mountbatten and his grandson Nicholas, fourteen; Lady Doreen; and the local lad. The rest were just maimed.

Mountbatten's last voyage started in the harbor at Mullaghmore, picture-pretty still since it is sheltered by cut-stone sea walls. Children in wet suits now splashed about near bobbing boats; vacationing adults sat on picnic tables watching from over lunch. Forgetfulness ruled. I couldn't square it and went into the hotel, needing to find someone to paint time's truth. Working the front desk was a stocky local woman who related her own troubled memories:

"Mountbatten loved this place, and he was well liked, I can tell you," she said. "He had no problems here, none at all. If anything he was a friend of the Irish cause. Everyone knew that, but the IRA didn't care. It was outsiders they brought in to do what occurred."

I inquired whether people resented having the subject raised.

"No, it's not that," sighed the clerk, squeezing her eyes closed. "We wish that it had never happened."

CROSSING INTO DONEGAL, even the sunlight seems different, scrubbed and cool in high summer as if it were an early April day. Soon one confronts the rugged mountains which backbone the county and fling vast swaths of shadow under their lees. The sense of expanding space stirs the feeling of entering a place apart—Ireland's Wyoming. As the road beyond Donegal town moves up the coast the terrain grows elemental—wave and rock, heather and mountain—and purifying.

At Killybegs, the largest fishing port in Ireland, dozens of trawlers were unloading their catch; beyond, refrigerator trucks panted gasoline before a vast processing plant. Many would be heading off to Spain and Portugal, by way of a ferry to Wales and a dash to the Channel Tunnel at Dover. Others would stop in Dublin, London, or Paris. The modest four- and five-man fishing boats at the docks mostly bore Irish names, but these were dwarfed by a number of massive factory ships flying Spanish colors; several of them were flagships of a locally hated conglomerate called Pesca Nova. Fishermen on Ireland's west coast are still embittered that the country handed over rights to one of its greatest natural assets, the produce of its seas, to foreign fleets to gain access in 1973 to what was then called the European Economic Community. In short, things are not what they seem in apparently bucolic old Donegal.

Traveling alone, I was free—free and able to let impulse guide me. Someone said an obscure village further on, called Kilcar, had pubs in which fiddlers and singers gathered many nights. The picture was enticing, because I also hoped to meet there one of the most inspired vocalists in Ireland, a Donegal woman with a voice like falling water and the flaxen hair of an angel. Mairéad Ní Mhaonaigh had learned ancient ballads, in Irish, at her father's knee in a thatch-roofed cottage near the sea, and was said to live somewhere near.

Mairéad was the lead singer and fiddler with the celebrated Irish traditional music band, Altan, whom Jamie and I had seen years earlier. Their music made the heart soar, and equally impressive was the adoration Mairéad obviously shared with her young husband, a flute player named Frankie Kennedy. But Frankie contracted brain cancer and died. And now, no matter how long I pottered about, my meeting with Mairéad, sought by emails, did not seem destined to occur.

So I drove on to a more remote village called Teelin, a settlement inscribed against a narrow, sheltered bay. Booking a bed and breakfast, I began to explore. Through rugged terrain beside the Slieve League *(Sliabh Liag)* mountain I nosed the car until the road blurted out onto cliffs above the sea. At points they drop like a shriek over a thousand feet into the Atlantic, making them among the most vertiginous in Europe. The road at their crest is barely wider than a car and has no protective girders, *nada*.

Being a chicken, I therefore opted to continue on foot. Now the world went Shangri La. Sheep scurried at my side, seagulls wheeled and cried, and the gently setting sun cast ribbons of silver over the vast bay curving back to Sligo and spreading outward into the infinity of the Atlantic. I was alone in one of the most awe-inspiring places I had ever beheld.

Halfway down a nearby slope some thoughtful locals in 1943 stitched twenty-foot alignments of whitewashed stones into a meadow in a pattern that spelled TIR EIRE. "This is Ireland," it translates from Gaelic. The message was meant to be read by American B-17 pilots heading toward the Allies' airbase in Belfast. The marquee drolly suggested that the white-painted stones' purpose was to proclaim, "We are neutral Ireland, so don't bomb us!"

Finding those runes took some doing since the meadow's grass had clotted over all but a few stones. But I cleared quite a few until the message sang bold in my own mind.

TIR EIRE!

This is Ireland!

TEELIN'S PUB IS CALLED *Cúl a Dúin*, which is Irish for "the back of the fort," and the name rings apt, for the area is an outpost where the native language stubbornly hangs on, at least among certain stalwarts. Even in English, the way people talk evokes a much earlier time, for the Donegal accent is perhaps the most distinctive in Ireland—folksy and twanging of mountains, while hinting of not-so-distant Scotland. Within it echoes the meters of Ulster Gaelic, which is quite different from the Irish idioms of the southerly provinces of Munster, Leinster, and Connaught.

The pub's owner Seamus Healy came to my outside table. "A fine evening now," he started, and the chat flowed, reminding me of Donegal's natural ease and warmth. The bay lapped behind us; Slieve League hulked to the fore, where the last rays of sunlight were making a fist of illumination upon its barren two thousand-foot peak.

A long procession of teenagers paraded up the quiet road before us. It was striking how wholesome they all looked, some even carrying each other piggyback. "They're here for the summer Irish college. They come from all over the country to study the language with local native speakers for three weeks at a time," Seamus explained.

So, up here a thread of continuity still reigned.

Inside the pub later, the conversation grew animated. My first encounter was with a kind of ancient mariner, Standish O'Grady, with a floppy sailor's hat crowning florid cheeks, brooding dark eyes, and a foot-long beard. He lived in Glencolmcille, nearly ten miles further on.

"So why are you drinking here and not there?" I innocently asked.

Matter-of-fact Standish said that he had been barred from most pubs in his village, due to questionable verdicts about his behavior. "But two of them aren't any good anyway," he shrugged.

"Are you from there originally?" I asked, since his accent said otherwise.

"No, Dublin. I came out for a weekend twenty-seven years ago and never left. I was on the fishing boats for a long time, but no more."

"Why?"

Standish O'Grady, named after a celebrated nineteenth-century novelist, worked through half his pint before deigning to answer. "I'll give you three reasons: One, because I got tired of being pulled off the rocks; Two, because I got tired of watching good people drown; and Three, because I got rescued so many times I couldn't take it anymore. That's why I stopped and that's enough questions."

Chastised, I turned to another older fellow I'd seen taking photographs on the cliffs, called Seanie. A few minutes later—conversation being as easy in Donegal as anywhere on earth—I was jawing with somebody else named Paddy Byrne. The latter wore a silver earring and was strong-looking, bow-legged and stocky, and wielded anecdotes by the brace. "That fellow you were talking to, Seanie," he began, "is kind of a local legend."

"What do you mean?"

Paddy jolted his head back and laughed. "Why he's the man who discovered the turbot!"

"I don't get it?" I remonstrated. "A fish?"

My new acquaintance leaned closer. "Aye, neither did any of us at that time. He was out fishing for crayfish as we all did years back, when suddenly he pulls in a rake of weird-looking fish. He doesn't know what they are, but keeps them anyway and heads back to the pier. He unloads a few wee boxes and everybody is standing around looking at them and scratching their heads. 'What are them things, Seanie?' somebody asked.

'Fuck if I know!' said Seanie. 'But I can tell you one thing—there's money in them!' You see, Seanie doesn't have a clue as to what gruesome flat feckers he's just caught. But fair play to him, he brings them to Killybegs and finds out that the English buyers are just dying for turbot. Jeez, within a week we all started fishing for turbot. Seanie's turbot saved our skins."

I laughed heartily and asked, "Are you still fishing yourself?"

Paddy voice raised. "For God's sakes, no! Nobody is. You can't buy an EU quota around here now. Aye, back in the seventies, you went down to Teelin pier, and there used to be thirty to forty half-deckers tied five-abreast in the morning. Now there's not a one. Not one proper fishing boat left! Nobody has any quotas here. This village was nothing but fishing once, and now a whole way of life is finished. You came in this pub on a Friday and every table would be thick with the boys in their slickers, counting out their take for the week. The place would smell of fish. Do you smell any fish now?"

"Well, I had a tuna fish sandwich a while back."

Paddy Bryne slapped a hand on my shoulder. "You're all right. I've got a tour boat and that's about the only boat you'll find at the pier these days, other than those that come up the coast, and some of them would be running drugs now. Why don't you come out tomorrow for a look around?"

This night's entertainment would not stop. In fact, someone to my left was talking in Irish to a friend. I had not witnessed this simple phenomenon in years—a couple of fellows speaking in the tongue of my ancestors. So I butted in.

"This is my language," said Pat Gillespie, "Irish is what we speak in my house."

"Do many around here?"

"Not as before," responded Pat, who said he was sixty-one, but had a playful ease about him. "When I was a wee lad you'd see nothing but donkey carts on the road, and you were proud if you had one, because no one I knew had a motor car. Back then, it was as if the outside world didn't exist. The idea of going to Killybegs, not ten miles away, would have been huge. We'd get there and they'd look at us, with our rough dress and bare feet and talking Gaelic, as if we came from another world."

Pat revealed that he was considered something of a *seanchaí,* or "a person who talks from time"—in other words, a man carrying on an ancient Irish tradition of at once imaginative and yet formal story telling. The seanchaí was a person who preserved legends, spun tales, descried law, and defined the very drift of reality, so I nodded in respect.

"But don't mind that at all," said Pat. "I have a cousin who is much better at it than me—he's four times national champion story teller of Ireland. You've got to meet him and, if you'd like, I will see to it tomorrow."

Well, you still could not beat this Donegal, I thought as I walked out the door into the clear and starry night.

Chapter 18

In the morning, salmon kept leaping in the harbor outside my bed
and breakfast, sudden silver pirouettes that flashed toward the sun.
At the pier, I found my friend of the night before, Paddy Bryne,
organizing some French and Norwegian tourists and sputtering up
the engines of his boat, the *Nuala Star*. "Climb on board!" he called.

The boat rocked as we headed out into the vast Donegal bay. At
the top of one cliff stood an ancient stone chapel, and above the next
reigned a cylindrical stone watchtower, which had been built by
the British two hundred years ago to keep an eye out for Napoleon
Bonaparte's marauding fleets. Rough walls ranged the fields.

Stone, stone, cold, old, and dead stone—Donegal's signature seemed
to be written in stone. At the base of every cliff hulked stones the
size of cars and even bungalows. The Irish people, I thought, come
from stone. This is who we are. A people of stone houses, farm walls
of stone, crosses of stone, tombs of stone. The beauty of the country
is all about stone.

Paddy stilled the *Nuala Star*'s throttle. "See that cliff?" he said
to his rain-slickered throng, gesturing to a sheer rock face at least
six hundred feet high. "There's barely a sheep that can handle that
slope. But such was the poverty here that the women of Teelin used
to scramble down the gap beside it whenever there was a shipwreck

on that beach below. They would risk their lives to retrieve a few timbers or a mere sack of a coal."

Beyond Slieve League, we approached a wave-blasted island where a few peasants would have once subsisted in freezing hovels. Now it was uninhabited. Far across the heaving sea lay America with all its heartbreaks of departure from these shores. And hidden beneath the waters off the coast of Ireland lay other capsules of time—the wreckage of the Spanish Armada, of German U-Boats prowling during World War II, and skeletons of the recent fishing brethren of Standish O'Grady who foundered in the Atlantic's violent whims.

Paddy Byrne said we could go no further, for the sky had gone black. The boat bucked as a torrent fell. I went into the wheelhouse, and we talked some more.

"Ah, Standish O'Grady is considered, I am afraid, a bit of a *pishogue*, which is an omen of bad luck," said Paddy. "When you have three or four boats go down and you swim away from them like some seal but the others don't, well there comes a time when nobody wants you on board. But that's the life we all lived and there are many around here who are crying for it yet. The people of Donegal are people of the sea."

GLENCOLMCILLE (PRONOUNCED "GLEN COLUMN KILL") was my next stop—a village a few miles beyond Teelin where an early Christian visionary named Saint Columba founded a monastic settlement in the sixth century because his wanderings told him that this spot had a strange holiness. The place has attracted countless seekers ever since who have felt the same thing.

As I drove toward it under a lashing rain, sheep smeared with their owners' signature branding colors—blood red, chartreuse, and bile green—munched idly beside highland bogs.

The rain softened and upland lakes emerged like mirages. Stacks of hand-cut turf gleamed black beside the road as it plummeted into a valley fronting an enormous strand. At the floor of this glen, there again lay the story of stone. For Glencolmcille is littered with Celtic crosses, thousand-year-old chapels now crumbling into ruins, portal tombs, dolmens, old crumbling cottages.

Droves of tourists meandered about the main street. They looked like they shared some kind of outback dress code—sandals with woolly socks, nylon pants, heavy sweaters, and knit caps tucked tight over stringy lengths of rain-sodden hair. But they parted obligingly, docile as sheep. At the end of the next lane, an old man was scything hay into glowing ricks, a nearly vanished practice elsewhere in Ireland. The thatched bungalow around the bend sported greying lobster traps and a pyramid of freshly-cut turf on the side field, along with a donkey grazing beside a rusting, miniature tractor that must have been seventy years old.

Further on sat a summer school devoted to the preservation of ancient Irish folkways—*Oideas Gael* was the brainchild and passion of a local priest. Walking up to it, I heard the blood-pumping sound of a dozen bodhrans, or hand-held skin drums, being whacked by people of all ages coming from the nearest room. From the next a chorus of tin whistles sputtered and trilled, further on, another collective were belting out ancient ballads more or less on key.

This, I had heard, was one of the most famed repositories of the old ways left in Ireland, situated in one of the most hallowed destinations in the land. So who were these impassioned seekers, I wondered, knowing almost zero Irish people wear Aran Island sweaters, which are usually made in Malaysia and which were ubiquitous here.

A young woman at the reception desk explained, "People come from all over the world to us."

"Are any of them actually Irish?"

"Well, a few," she paused and averted her eyes. "But mostly they are Americans. We also get some Germans and Dutch and English though. And a few Irish people visit if the weather is fine."

I drove on. Now the light was splashing copper to gold across the crests of fold after fold of distant hills, the effect almost otherworldly. Finally, a perilous V-cut led down into the bustling town of Ardara, where I sauntered into a pub called Nancy's Bar. In 1985, Jamie and I once stopped in here for a pint and left six hours later, so exhilarating was the company we found. Back then, Nancy's was a Dickensian warren with an antique little bar in the front and a higgledy-piggledy half-dozen other tiny rooms elbowing this way and that. We found stools, fell into the flood of conversation, and then the fiddles, bohrans, and flutes came out, followed by baskets of free sandwiches. The owner's real name was Margaret McHugh, and she was a born story-teller with a black dog named Guinness. Sadly, I now discovered that Margaret had recently died.

However, a dish of peppery smoked mackerel, buttery new potatoes and a zesty fresh salad lifted the spirits, as did the still charming ambience of the place. With a wee song in the heart, I strolled after lunch to the adjoining shop, Eddie Doherty's, which like several in Ardara, specializes in hand-woven Donegal tweeds. In fact, the back room featured a table loom the size of a four-poster bed with rolls of brilliantly colored woollen thread stacked upon benches and surrounded by boxes of spindles, shuttles, and cones. The loom's vertical warp threads were stretched taut from the overhead frame to the maze-like "reed" at waist level, where hundreds of lateral weft wires waited for the shuttles and the pedals and treadles to get busy with the next garment. Eddie Doherty, a balding man with azure eyes, came by to say hello. "That's a beautiful machine," I remarked.

"Well, it's been good to me for forty years," said he.

"How fast does it work?" I asked, touching at a lovely scarf in progress.

"A good weaver could maybe produce thirty yards of fabric a day, maybe thirty-two, others less."

Thirty yards a day? The BBC had just profiled a Chinese town called Datang, not much bigger than Ardara, which mass produces *20 billion* socks a year.

At least something in this world was still done with care, I thought, looking around at the stacks of wool on Doherty's shelves. They glowed with a subtle palette from olive to earthy brown, charcoal to gorse yellow and sky blue. I asked Eddie how he chose his particular hues.

"Back a couple of generations, weavers would gather their dyes from what they saw around them—red, say, from the fuchsia; or maybe orange from lichen, a quiet kind of orange; and green from moss. That's what gives Donegal tweed its distinctive look—the nature that's in it. We still like to stay close to the colors we live with here."

The shop, saturated with the earthy, dank sheep scent of lanolin, boasted an enticing array of sweaters, shawls, scarves, and caps. But I was tempted by the multi-hued jackets and waistcoats. A young clerk emerged, freckled and auburn. She had turned on some *femme*-lite version of rap which incongruously made her break into a little step dance. But the girl's eye proved to be superb, and I was seduced. What was on offer here was as pure a product of Ireland as one could find—the wool from the sheep of surrounding mountains, the colors filtered out of local visions, the artistry of the weaving taking place in this very room. I departed Eddie Doherty's dressed in an ochre waistcoat pearled with berry hues and topped by a flaxen jacket—and feeling like a million bucks.

On Adara's high street, my mobile phone suddenly buzzed. "Is this David?" a woman asked, her voice high, quick, and tremulous.

"Yes, that's right."

"Well, I am Jane, the witch John told you about, and he said you wanted to come by."

What to say to the first witch who has ever rung you? May I have three wishes please? Or what's cooking—newts, toads, or adders? No, I just limply responded, "Oh, yes! He spoke of you highly."

"That's very, very doubtful," Jane cackled, sounding genuinely half-mad. "But I understand you want to see me? Does tomorrow night work?"

IT WAS BACK TO TEELIN, back up a steep slope in search of the champion seanchaí Eugene Curran's cottage under the lee of Slieve League. The rain wielded an absurd biblical violence now.

Eugene, a tall man in his mid sixties, hurriedly bid me into his front sitting room. Pine-panelled and nondescript, it offered no comforting fire or slate floor nor any other discernable nod to Ireland's romantic past. A long sofa stretched before the window, and the easy chair beside it looked like the master viewing point for his wide-screen TV.

Regrettably, the conversation began with Eugene describing the strict protocols of the current government-run national story-telling competitions, which are conducted in modern hotel conference rooms.

"The competition is very, very keen. You have to perform for a minimum of fifteen minutes," said Eugene, rifling through various details. Then, like a fiddler tuning his bow, he offered a narrative salted with the doings of mythological heroes, such as Fin McCool and Cúchulainn, and the rest. I liked all of those guys. But still, I was a bit adrift.

Suddenly, a chorus of hoarse adolescent voices erupted behind an adjoining wall, followed by an explosion of thudding rap music. "What the heck is that?" I asked.

Only then did I notice delicate crescent laugh lines furrowing out at either end of Eugene's lips. "Well, we do rooms for the students who come here for the summer courses in the Irish language. There are twelve boys staying with us now, and the Lord above knows what they are up to."

The ice broken at last, he told me of his own childhood. "I was born in this house and this very room we are sitting in is two hundred years old. Look at the front wall there, it's nearly three feet thick," Eugene said proudly.

Soon, he was talking back through the ages. "There were myself and my siblings raised here, but there were eleven children here in my father's generation. In the one before that, there were nine; and the one before that there were eleven again—nine brothers and two sisters—going back to 1821."

Although a thousand people lived in Teelin during the Famine—four times more than now—the community managed all right, Eugene said, due to plentiful fish and a versatile husbandry made possible by a benevolent local landlord. The Congested District Board, an oddly named British attempt to solve "the Irish problem," later funded the construction of a small fleet of successful Teelin fishing boats. These, being black-hulled, were called "Zulus." Eugene told of how three hundred people were once employed in the pursuit of fishing, from the catching to the drying, storing and shipping. "When all of that was gone, the younger generation moved off to the cities and to the ends of the earth," he sighed.

Eugene grew more impassioned as he spoke of the struggle to preserve the native tongue, at first blaming the British for its demise. "There was a time when any school kids who spoke Irish would have a wooden board tied around their neck, and for every word of Irish they spoke a notch was put in that board. At the end of the day the notches were counted up and that child was caned accordingly." Although Irish speaking has withered inexorably—despite its teaching being an intensive part of the national school curriculum—Eugene insisted that his mother tongue will somehow prevail. "The Irish language has survived centuries of British imperialism and all manner of modern threats and yet it is still alive. If it were only taught properly, it could come back stronger yet one day."

Nonetheless, he described how even in a refuge like Teelin, the language has suffered a pitiless attrition. "In my young days, in all this area around here Irish was the everyday language. People went to school without knowing the English language at all. But the threats were everywhere. Going into even the next village of Carrick, they spoke English in the shops. English was like a fancy language, and people talking Irish were looked down upon as being poor, and they got embarrassed. Then families came in who didn't know the language or a local married someone from the outside and people began to feel ashamed to speak Irish in front of them. Now, less than ten percent of people would be speaking Irish every day, although most in Teelin would know it."

I asked how he became a seanchaí.

Eugene took a deep breath. "My mother was a storyteller, my father was a storyteller, and we also had a tailor's house and a shoemaker's house and a forge where the blacksmith worked. In those houses people would sit and talk and there would always be travelers stopping by off the road. You'd hear lots of stories being told in those places when I was a boy."

He brought out a pot of tea.

"Storytelling was considered a special gift. Maybe once a week people would gather together to tell stories. There would be fiddlers and accordion players, singers and poets, and they would all get together on what was called a 'big night.' A house in the neighborhood would be cleared out, and there would be a night's dancing with breaks for story telling or singing. There was no television, and there were only battery radios since there was still no electricity and they were very expensive. During the 1950s, you would pay twenty punts for a radio, which would equal four weeks wages for a working man. Even if you had one, you would ration its use to save the battery. So we entertained ourselves."

Eugene revealed that he had won a prize for telling the best stories among Teelin's children in 1952, when he was eight years old, which encouraged him to keep at it. But the coming of television killed off all desire for home-spun entertainment. Then came the cars and the distant jobs, and the final goodbye to sitting around fires to trade stories in the night.

Had Eugene ever held forth with his tales in Teelin's pub, Cúl a Dúin, I asked.

His answer was depressing. "There would be no one interested in Irish story telling in pubs anymore, like it would be too old-fashioned. The younger generation, they're not interested. It's sad to say, but our culture is dying. I could end up as one of the last of the old story tellers."

As it happens a poet named Art Mac Cumhaigh (c. 1738-73) had said much the same long ago:

> Tà mo chroí-se réabthla 'na mhille céad cuid,
>   Agus balsum fein nach bhfóireann mo phian,
> Nuaira chlumin an Ghalig uilig da tréghbeáil,
>   Agus caismirt Bhéarla í mbleol gach aoin . . .

> My heart is a hundred thousand bits, all burst and broken.
>   And there's no balm that will give me relief,
> When I hear the Irish language everywhere forsaken
>   And a tra la of English in everybody's mouth . . .

Chapter 19

The witch's cottage at the edge of the Poisoned Glen was off any map I knew. On the way north, torrents of rain obliterated all vision of the ocean and the mountains and nearly of the road itself. Directional signs occasionally appeared in the murk, but they were written in Gaelic.

At the end of a mist-shrouded lake under the lee of Mount Errigal, the tallest peak in Donegal, I was supposed to venture through a settlement called Dunlewey until coming upon an old roofless church that had been long-ago gutted by fire. "Just turn down the dirt lane until you see an enormous bank of rhododendrons. I live behind those," Jane Crane explained on the phone. "By the way, I hope you will do me the honor of staying in my guest house."

Somehow, I found my way and parked in the midst of a waiting grove. On one side rose a ramshackle, wood-lathed octagonal greenhouse, while opposite stood a stone hut with its roof a bright red fishing boat hull, flipped upside down. Donkeys brayed from behind a copse, hens clucked, and from a bed of ferns various elf sculptures were giving me the stink eye. By now the rain had softened, allowing the murmur of rushing water to whisper from a source unseen. Ahead lay a gravel walkway toward a vaulted passageway that had been hewn into a mossy high wall.

Suddenly, a large woman with a spectacular frazzle of ginger hair appeared at its opening. Around her flapped a billowing and vaguely medieval green linen dress and cape. She waved and called in a high voice, "Is that David?"

We exchanged greetings.

Jane led me past her guest cottage with an old-fashioned Dutch door. Then it was over a bridge above a brook. Here one confronted a Hansel and Gretel vision of a two-story stone cottage, with a turret rising over the far end and flowers spilling out of various window boxes. A conservatory jutted out from the dwelling's midst, and she opened its screen door.

"Meet Moisteen," said Jane as an old black dog padded across the airy, plant-filled room. "That's Irish for rascal." We sat down at a red-clothed table, and she pushed forward a bowl of blonde nuts. "I hope you like pistachios. These are from Iran, the best pistachios in the world."

The witch wore a hexagram ring and a green amulet on a golden chain around her neck. "I see that you are looking at my trinkets," she chuckled.

"Well, it's hard not to."

"I like to think they convey certain powers," Jane whispered portentously, then cast me a mischievous look. "Would you like to fly?"

At the sight of my obvious confusion—I mean, what had I gotten into?—she burst out laughing. "I gather you haven't met too many witches before."

"You're the first," I admitted.

"Well, don't worry. I'm just a white witch, and I won't cast any spells, or aspersions either—ha, ha! Perhaps you'd like something to drink?" Without waiting for an answer, Jane disappeared to retrieve a bottle of red wine and an ashtray big enough to service a coven. "Your cousin is a wonderful man," she resumed while filling the glasses. "How is John keeping?"

As the talk sped forward the only external sound was of the little freshet that coursed over the sluice of time-smoothed bedrock just outside the door. "There is such a sense of flow here," I commented idly.

"It's funny that you chose that word," said Jane, lighting a cigarette. "Seamus Heaney wrote a poem about this very spot, and it is called 'Sruth,' which is Irish for 'flow.' It's an ode to a friend who died who used to wash in this stream as a girl and fill herself with its spirit."

Inhaling deeply, Jane continued, "The moment I saw this place I knew it had spiritual power—magic, if you like. Strange things do sometimes happen here. Have you ever seen a badger? No? Well, most people haven't, and many claim there are none anywhere near them, which is what a lot say about fairies nowadays. But just because you don't see something doesn't mean it's not there. You just wait, and you will see badgers a plenty outside my door, because they are drawn to me."

We traded our stories, and the odd connections we shared. Jane was in Iran one moment, Malaysia, Cambodia, Hawaii, England, and back in Ireland the next. Before I knew it, this witch, who had a jolly and barely-lined face for a woman of sixty-eight, was making me laugh. She waxed quite theatrical, modulating her voice from a drawing-room English accent to conspiratorial or aghast intonations as her anecdotes demanded.

But the light began to fade, and Jane abruptly shifted moods—as witches might. Without warning, she struck a match to a two-foot-high candle, then put a finger to her lips. "My friend Johan who is a South African heart surgeon is coming by shortly, and preparations are required. You also see that the candle has been lit and that is very important," she said, eyeing me sternly. "The rule of this house is that when the candle is burning everything that is said before it must never leave this room. Will you honor this?"

I nodded yes. What else was I going to do, since I was her guest?

"Some very bad things might come to you if you do not," Jane warned with a look that was half-inscrutable and perhaps also half-facetious. "Tomorrow we can talk about anything you wish 'on the record,' as they say, but I need you to swear that you will repeat nothing you hear while the candle is burning."

"Cross my heart," I said.

My prior journalistic experience offered no guidance on how to handle privileged conversation with mildly threatening Donegal witches. For that matter, I was warming to Jane. Fortunately, just as her stories grew most tempting to repeat, my dilemma was stopped by recalling the tricks of the eighteenth-century novelist Laurence Sterne. The Irish-born author of one of the funniest novels ever written, *The Life and Opinions of Tristram Shandy, Gentleman* (1759), often handled matters indelicate by writing like this:

. . . .

. . . .

. . . .

. . . .

Something of note occurred outside the communication exclusion zone, however. As dusk fell, one, two, and ultimately six furtive badgers materialized from their subterranean "setts" to feed on slices of bread Jane had scattered. Fat and furry with elongated black-and-white striped snouts, the young resembled opossums, while the adults were nearly the size of bear cubs. I wondered how creatures so large and distinctive could altogether evade human sight. Like fairies indeed, they capered about the shadows, then vanished.

Jane's back hallway held some arresting pictures. One showed her as a curly-haired little girl training adoring eyes at her dashing, mustachioed father in his R.A.F. officer suit. In another photograph, she appeared at some gala celebration as a glamorous young woman in a clingy dress, batting eyelashes at Henry Kissinger, former American Secretary of State and a Machiavellian arch-wizard if there ever was one. Jane resembled the glamorous actress Faye Dunaway then. But here was another of her years later with a star-emblazoned scarf drawn around her head and looking outlandish atop a donkey cart. So who was this woman? What was the peculiar animus of her life? And what made her go so weirdly Irish in the end? Finding an answer to such questions had become one of my own passions, because the country is a magnet for thousands of questers from afar like myself.

We said goodnight, and I felt my way through a pitch-black grotto to the stone guesthouse, wherein no light switch would oblige my fingers. The passageway to the bedroom was dangerously low and I banged my head hard enough to see stars. All I could hear as I reeled was the babble of the brook, and all I could see were visions of badgers. I was at once nowhere and everywhere, spinning half-dazed through a secret Irish reality.

THE NEXT MORNING, I EMERGED LIKE A BADGER blinking to life. Jane appeared at the door of the conservatory, exclaiming that she had had a vision—of food. She bid me to fetch bacon-stuffed breakfast rolls from the local convenience store, saying, "Get us a couple of those and we can talk with no candle burning."

The depot was identical to countless others in modern lands— soulless and antiseptic. But at least I could finally see from its parking lot the full, ethereal expanse of the lake and the 2,500-foot heft of Mount Errigal, its quartzite peak shimmering silver in the morning light. Back at the cottage, we munched and sipped coffee as Jane began to tell her story:

Born in Northern Ireland, she had been educated in private schools in England. Her father was not only an officer in the Royal Air Force, but had won a coveted MBE (Member of the British Empire) by the end of World War II. Working for various British newspapers, Jane discovered a passion for adventure writ large and began to travel to exotic destinations like the jungles of Cambodia and the British protectorate of Malaya, then still struggling with a communist insurgency. There, some SAS commandos agreed to give her parachute training, and her story of feminist derring-do captured headlines back in the U.K. In time, she fell in love with a high-bred Iranian and settled in Tehran, where she gave birth to a daughter and began doing "public relations work" for Henry Kissinger's friend, the Shah. After the Islamic uprising, the family retired to a sizeable house in Cornwall in England, where they took in paying guests. Eventually, her marriage foundered and she ended up, for some reason, in Hawaii. "Was all this clear?"

"No," I said.

By-the-bye, Jane discovered some telepathic-like gift. "I have had some strange things happen along the way. I just know things about people. It just happens, and it feels like people are projecting things. I sometimes think I am God's litmus paper," she said, lighting another cigarette.

She moved to London, where a friend made her a present of a crystal ball, which his mother had bought off a gypsy fortune-teller in the Balkans decades earlier. Jane took one look and predicted a certain life-transforming event for her friend, which basically came true.

Half in sport, she began practicing professional crystal-ball-gazing under the campy guise of "Madame Shimigrodska." Before long, she purchased her cottage in Church Hill, the house my cousin had nearly bought from her. There she told fortunes. "It snowballed and got ridiculous. I had mini-buses coming to the house, people banging on the door day and night," Jane recalled.

"I went to pubs as well," she continued, "and would work in the back rooms. I had to make a rule that people couldn't come to me more frequently than every three months, because some would be there every week otherwise. They wouldn't lift a knife or fork unless I said to. All kinds of people came to see me, women wanting babies, people who were ill and didn't know where to turn, and some very famous. Please swear that you will not mention the people I've spoken about."

"Scout's honor."

Theatrical Jane abruptly closed her eyes and began murmuring. "Oh God, there was always this strange music that would come to me, and I would hear voices. It went sort of . . . diddly-eye, diddly-dee." Now, she broke into such scoffing laughter that it was hard to know when she was being straight.

In any case, she became known as a person who revered Donegal's ancient lore as well as its people. But also she became obsessed with fairies, even leaving food out at night at their ancient gathering circles.

"So why did you leave Church Hill?" I asked.

She did not bat an eye. "Well, the fairies told me, 'You must go over to Mount Errigal. You must find an old derelict house and you must find a round tower there.' They said, 'That place has to be protected—it's a portal. Something bad might happen there, and you have to stop it.' So I began to search."

I guffawed. "Do you truly believe in fairies?"

"I believe in the spirit world and fairies are a part of that—they are an expression of other life forms. Think of mushrooms, which are another life form. You know Hare Krishna's are not allowed to eat them. A mushroom isn't a vegetable. They grow better where there have been stallions or rams around, and fairies are associated with mushrooms, aren't they? I think it is quite possible that the 'little people' were a genetic experiment."

Jane pressed on. "If you believe that a mule resulted from a donkey and a horse, then it only takes a little stretch of the imagination to believe that wherever there is the smell of mushrooms, there may be fairies. I know that there are little people because I have seen them. They look like this . . ." Here, she pointed to a cluster of miniature gnome statuary in red caps, sticking their weird eyeballs out from behind various nearby plants. "I made those and used to sell them."

Hmmh, I said.

"No, there is a very serious thing here. Where do the fairies come from? They are another species, the little people. They used to be around a lot more, and every old person in Ireland used to have a story about fairy places. I've seen cruel things happen to people who tampered with fairy circles. There was a family that had terrible bad luck after the father bulldozed a stone circle on the mountain. Two years ago one of the aunts came looking for me. Poor people, they had to nearly carry me to the field because I had hurt my back. I put the family out of the field, and I went staggering around it. I could feel that the little ones wanted the circle back.

"It was the eve of May—the *Beltaine* feast," she said of the point in the ancient Celtic calendar that heralds the coming lushness and joy of summer. But it was also a time of great superstition, and one was that livestock could disappear on the feast's eve due to messing about by upset fairies, called in Donegal the *Slua si*. At Beltaine, heedless mortals could even be dragged away forever to fairy forts or "raths," and letting a redheaded woman into one's house could nearly bring it down. So Jane, with her wild ginger hair, knew that she would be seen as having formidable powers this night, especially after having just supervised the righting of this particular circle's fallen stones, which even the most skeptical Irish rarely tamper with to this day.

"The circle was ready," she half whispered now, "and we had the conch shell to blow and the bohrans to beat. It was getting dark on the hillside. The houses had their electric lights blazing, whereas in the old days it would have been people lighting bonfires on the hills. But we made our own bonfire by the circle, and I thought this is what somebody was doing there five thousand years ago. I just could feel it." The celebration was exalted, Jane said, and the neighboring family returned to health, and new babies were born to them in the sweetness of time.

Nonsense, you might say, but until not that long ago, most everyone in rural Ireland believed in fairies just as Jane Crane said. Witness the verses of the Donegal poet William Allingham (1824–89):

Up the airy mountain,
    Down the rushy glen,
We daren't go a-hunting,
    For fear of little men;
Wee folk, good folk,
    Trooping all together;
Green jacket, red cap,
    And white owl's feather.

They stole little Bridget
    For seven years long;
When she came back again
    Her friends were all gone.
They took her lightly back,
    Between the night and the morrow;
They thought she was fast asleep,
    But she was dead with sorrow.
They have kept her ever since
    Deep within the lakes . . .

Jane sipped on her coffee and continued: "I thought I was going to be the den mother for all the misplaced fairies here in the Poisoned Glen. I thought the fairies were being put out of their fairy places by all the new plastic and cement bungalows arising in the fields, that they were going to come back here and live in the tower I would build, and I would look after them. But it didn't happen. The tower is empty."

So even in this fugitive corner of Donegal, cold modernity came crashing in again. But something marvellous did transpire after she moved into her cottage—the property's ancient title included ninety more acres than she at first anticipated, bestowing annual payments to leave her domain undisturbed as a nature preserve. Nonetheless, she fell afoul of local officials who sought to gouge out a quarry on her land, which pursuit Jane resisted vehemently. "They said I was a 'fucking blow-in.' I said, 'Fine, if your machines start eating away at that mountain, I will go up upon my land and do a hunger strike,' which is a very emotive thing in Ireland. 'Donegal County Council will have success where Weight Watchers failed.' Anyway, they backed off."

Savouring these stories, I walked through her grove toward the lake. A hard wind was whipping white caps across Loch Dunlewey and the scene felt cold and lonely, but cleansing. On the far bank stood a turreted maroon castle called Dunlewey House that belonged to none other than the Guinness clan and was much visited from England by J.P. Donleavy's former wife. Suddenly, my journey seemed to be wreathed by circles.

THE DAY SOFTENED. Jane, arranging her hair into girlish pigtails and donning a flowered dress, suggested a driving tour of the hinterlands.

The first stop was a highland lake shimmering in a vast, uninhabited vale. "This," Jane said, "was once the domain of notorious tricksters called 'the Slashers,' who killed young girls there at *Lughnasa*, the August harvest festival when people would gather fruit and flowers in the mountains and hold crossroad dances."

To the west rose another quartz-flecked mountain, its peak wreathed in filmy white clouds, and its base mirrored by a second long, tree-lined lake called Altan. "The mountain's called Aghla More," Jane explained, "and there's a plateau halfway up where all you have to do is knead the grass with your fingers and crystals and gemstones will arise."

Our progress was soon slowed by a horse-drawn carriage bearing a bride in a white wedding dress and her handsome groom. This was at the edge of the tiny settlement of Church Hill, where I had stayed in 1974. "Hello!" we called and waved.

On then to the little valley which held Jane's favorite fairy circle. We turned past some horrendously garish new houses, twisted up an ancient boreen, then parked. From the adjoining field there immediately emerged a curious hayseed of a fellow who Jane had phoned beforehand—Charlie. He had a thin moustache and grey eyes that looked lost in reverie.

"It is lovely to see you again, Janey," Charlie exclaimed.

Trudge, trudge, we three clambered through the high grass to a fifty-foot circle of knee-high stones, surrounded by an electrified wire.

"You know," Charlie exclaimed, "a cow calved here one time. Granny's mother who was from up above was telling me that."

"The house with the green roof?" asked Jane.

"No, with the grey roof," answered Charlie. "But they kept a cow here. They had fires here, and the mother locked up the place because of the cow being in calf. The next morning the mother came down to find the new calf, and there was a wee string tied to its tail. And Granny was telling me, because she knew there were fairies there then, that the fairies tied the string. Oh, they tied the string!"

"There's nothing bad happening here now?" interrupted Jane.

"Oh God no," said Charlie.

"They just wanted their place back," Jane said of the fairies.

"We were getting it a bit rough here for a while, aye," sighed Charlie, who then pointed to a higher meadow. "Wait, 'til I tell you, Jane. There is a building site up there with a big house in the works. There came a brand new digger, do you see? And I was looking for a wee bit of digging done myself, so I stopped down and the digger man said to me, 'Is it safe to be digging over here with the fairies about this hill?'"

Charlie shifted his feet. "I looked around at what he was destroying, and I said, 'Well, I wouldn't be digging here anyway myself.' I said, 'You topple a fairy tree and your digger might seize up permanently.' And you know what, Janey? The man went ahead, and didn't his digger just seize up, when it was only but a new digger, like. The poor man was terrorized.'"

"Ha ha!" laughed Jane, as if proving a point to me—a point perhaps about the ill tidings that befall a culture too eager to obliterate its past.

I dropped the witch off at her cottage and continued on to the coast.

THE SUMMER EVENING HAD A GOLDEN TINGE as I came upon a beach at the edge of a glittering bay. Climbing over the dunes, I was alone. Just a mile or two out to sea lay a scattering of small islands with names like Inishfree, Inishshinny, Inishmeane, and Inishsirrer, Gabla and Uaigh, each likely a story unto itself. Most would have once held their own people spinning their own tales: The scene ached with both sadness and beauty.

At the nearby village of Bunbeg, a few people in the shops were speaking to each other in Irish, and before a pub, a crowd of young men tossed half-embarrassed bits of it into their English. Fishermen were unloading their catch from small trawlers at the nearby secluded harbor, while boys in wetsuits burst their heads above the surface like frisky seals.

By the time I returned to the cottage, Jane was already enjoying a glass of wine with tonight's dinner guest Anna McClafferty, an attractive middle-aged lady whose right eye seemed strangely inert. She soon revealed a brutal fact: her young brother had impaled that one with a toy gun's projectile during a childhood game of Cowboys and Indians. "I was just learning my first words of English in school when it happened," she said. An agonizing operation in London, followed by months in hospital, saved but a glint of vision in that eye.

Marrying and raising five children, Anna somehow found time to study and work her way into a full-time career as a teacher of Irish language and literature. Then she began tackling Irish-to-English translating. Now she was regularly doing that in Strasbourg for the

European Union, a needlessly expensive pursuit to some.

"Have you ever tasted *poitín*?" Jane asked after dinner, referring to the Irish home-brewed firewater that can make the mind see marvels, perhaps even badgers turning into fairies. The name, pronounced "paw-cheen," means "little pot." Jane produced her own version, flavored with elderberry, and it packed a wallop.

"How did the Poisoned Glen gets its name?" I asked.

Anna told of an ancient king called "Balor of the Evil Eye" who belonged to a race of piratical giants—the Fomorians—who lived on Tory Island off the coast. He kept a beautiful daughter confined in a crystal tower to protect her from hordes of suitors. But a chieftain named Famola broke in and dragged the lass to the Poisoned Glen. Then Balor gave chase, and Famola had to kill him by hurling a giant stone into his face. "A river of blood gushed out of Balor's evil eye and poisoned the entire valley, where to this day much of the water remains unfit to drink," Anna said.

What with the refilled glasses, the native Irish speaker grew expansive. "Even the name of the settlement here, Dunlewey, is part of the story, too. Dunlewey actually refers to Lugh, who was the Celtic god of light, and who was the son of Evil Balor's daughter, the one who got dragged off to the Poisoned Glen. Balor despised Lugh and tried to kill him at birth. So another legend has it that there was a smithy here who made a fearsome weapon called *An Gagh Salash*, 'the lance of light.' Lugh purchased it and waited for Balor, the embodiment of the dark times past, to come around. Then he drove the lance of light into Balor's evil eye, which spat its poison. Afterwards he built a fort here and that is why this place is called Dunlewey—the fort of light."

Though confusing, the ancient stories related to the very place we sat—and almost every nook in Ireland has its own myths, though thousands are forgotten. As time passed, we all listened to the flow of water outside the door, the one pure stream in the Poisoned Glen.

The next morning Jane brought out a book of poetry. Then she turned to a Yeats's verse called "Stolen Child," and beckoned me to read it out loud.

> Where dips the rocky highland
> Of Sleuth Wood in the Lake,
> There lies a leafy island
> Where flapping herons wake
> The drowsy water rats:
> There we've hid our fairy vats
> Full of berries
> And of reddest stolen cherries.
>
> *Come away, oh human child!*
> *To the waters and the wild*
> *With a fairy hand in hand*
> *For the world's more full of weeping than you*
> *can understand.*
>
> Where the wave of moonlight glosses
> The dim grey sands with light,
> Far off by furthest Rosses
> We foot it all the night,
> Weaving olden dances,
> Mingling hands and mingling glances
> Till the moon has taken flight . . .
>
> *Come away, oh human child!*
> *To the waters and the wild . . .*

Parting with Jane was sad, for I felt I had met a sensitive soul, and a person who was that rare thing, a truly original human being. To me, it seemed that her real calling was not witchcraft but to celebrate the spirit of Donegal.

Chapter 20

Alas, the journey home abruptly coursed downhill, toppling out of reverie and into the small lowland town of Letterkenny, close to the border with County Derry in Northern Ireland. The place is ringed with new housing developments and the high-tech assembly plants of multinational corporations. You have your BMW dealer, Yin Yang Chinese restaurant, and Jehovah's Witnesses temple, along with assorted nightclubs, fast-food joints and bars, one of which had just featured a brutal drink-and-drug-fueled killing. For the modern traveller, Letterkenny has some special sport, though. Just drive on for a wee bit, and your mobile phone will ring with receipt of a text message from Outer Space saying, "Welcome to Northern Ireland." Reverse a hundred yards, and it will ring again, saying, "Welcome to the Republic of Ireland." In short, the border towns of this divided land come with twists. This became apparent as I paused before a roundabout, where an automobile whooshed up to within a foot of mine's tail, its exhaust pipes thundering at Mad Max decibels. The car was a gleaming white Honda and low-slung, its driver maybe eighteen—a classic "boy racer" as they are called.

Boy racers are young males who retool old cars into statements of aggression that are meant to petrify the timid and lure the like-minded into late-night duels—sometimes to inadvertent death—on back roads. A "For Sale" sign on a side window, with a mobile phone number for response, represents a coded-message of "Let's get it on!" Though the phenomenon exists across Ireland, Donegal, inexplicably, is the capital of Boy Racing. The result: the highest per-capita rate of vehicular mortality in the land.

The one thing the testosterone-crazed Boy Racer cannot tolerate is a safe driver in his path. Faced with my careful roundabout behavior, this one frantically pounded his horn as if it were a joystick in a computer war game—a remarkable act in itself since people rarely honked their horns in rural Ireland until the coming of the Celtic Tiger, when car ownership tripled and stampedes flooded once empty roads. Irritated, I noted that his registration number was *93DL5160*, signifying that the Donegal-licensed car was first sold in 1993.

At the next roundabout, an even more aggressive Boy Racer materialized, the engine of his still glossier and lower-riding white Honda Civic (again) revving at a level that made my tendons tremble, while rap music thumped savagely from its external amplifiers. As *92DL2410* whipped past, perhaps a dozen blue lights flashed in stroboscopic sequence on the car's rear end, as if to let the world know this was a night club on wheels.

At a blind bend, a certain *87DL5301* blew by in another white blur—the Boy Racers' hot rods are nearly always the same color, the white of a V-2 rocket. Where was I? In the South Bronx or L.A.'s gang-banging Watts? No, this too was Donegal.

I flipped on the radio a minute later and came upon someone crooning a sentimental old anthem as if reality was well and truly scrambled:

> This is my homeland,
> The place where I was born.
> No matter where I go,
> It's in my soul.
> We'll kneel and pray there,

> For those who have gone.
> My Donegal!

"Those who have gone" proved to be an apt phrase, for that week would see one boy racer killed on this very road and a pedestrian maimed by another gone out of control.

Heading south, I considered the tackiest tourist expedition of them all—looking up one's Irish roots. I can't possibly—no, never in a million years, I kept telling myself while entering County Monaghan. But I did, blaming my impulse upon an American relative who had already tracked down the ancestral holding and forwarded directions after his visit. If I was going to get to the bottom of the increasingly unhinged nature of Irish life and restore my sense of meaning about the place, I just had to do this.

Within a hinterland of tranquil lakes and rolling mound-like hills or *drumlins*, I came to a village called Shantanagh (pronounced "SHAN-ta-nah"), near which a farm belonging to one Sean Monaghan was meant to lie. The town was a mere crossroads, with a dilapidated former granary, a few nondescript houses, and no shops nor church nor pub. How'd that Donegal song go?

> This is my homeland . . .
> No matter where I go,
> It's in my soul.

I didn't quite feel the County Monaghan equivalent right now. But into the back country I turned, passing a pretty Church of Ireland chapel and graveyard surrounded by ancient yews.

A steep, manure-clotted driveway rose between muddy pastures. At the crest lay a two-story, white-washed farmhouse, bordered by an old stone barn presently hosting what sounded like a feather-flying chicken brawl. Another shed sat further back, silent. A not unusual disarray informed the farm's yard—a rusting tractor here, a portable cement mixer there, water troughs, herbicide barrels, and last year's fertilizer bags, all looking like they had blown out of a storm and randomly settled upon roosts from which they might never budge for the next hundred years.

No one seemed to be around, so I walked about, thinking. In their boyhoods of long ago, would my ancestors have once worked and played on every foot of ground I traversed? Would they have clawed potatoes from the soil here or whittled a stick while sitting on this wall there, before fleeing for a better life in America, knowing they would never see their parents or this very farm again? Whether my spirit was soothed to be standing on this very soil or not, I felt at once peaceful and curious.

A car abruptly rumbled into the yard, and out of it climbed a slender red-haired woman, followed by three daughters, small to tall. At first, they each cast apprehensive eyes my way.

"I am sorry to intrude, but I think we're related," I started, hurriedly mentioning the previous visit of my California cousin, while explaining that I, too, hailed from the U.S. but now lived in Cork. "I tried to call first, but the number I have didn't work."

The mother Sandra swiftly relaxed. "You're very welcome, I remember Michael well." She wore a slouchy blue cap and looked to be in her forties. Sandra introduced her daughters: brown-haired Kate, seventeen; Sara, taller, though a year younger; and Emily, a freckly ginger sprite of four. They shifted nervously on their feet, shy but curious, as if two sides of the universe—those who had left Ireland and those who had stayed—had just realigned.

The talk started self-consciously. "It's Sean you would want to talk with, but he is after shifting the cows. He should be along soon," said Sandra, originally from County Meath and holding traces of that county's closer-to-Dublin accent.

Her husband soon appeared, and I eyed him as if expecting to find some kind of mirror image of myself. But stout and round-faced, Sean Monaghan bore little resemblance to me or any relative I knew. Yet his greeting was warm. "Why, of course you would want to look us up. Will you come in for a cup of tea?"

The rear door opened to a kitchen with various toys and belongings scattered about. "Sorry about the mess, we just got back from a weekend at the Galway Races," Sandra apologized.

In Ireland in 2008, that event was considered to be nearly a national political convention, a cabal. For here the bigwigs of the ruling "Soldiers of Destiny" party, the Fianna Fail, hosted an enormous marquee laden with food and drink for its patron property developers, many of whom flew in on their private "blades."

"Did you win?" I asked Sandra.

"We did okay, actually," Sean answered for her poker-faced. In this betting-obsessed nation, doing "okay" at the races means that one has done well indeed. But the subject is always handled furtively.

As Sean's wife fired up the kettle, the daughters assumed a ring of inspection about the table. Where to start, when fishing for instant intimacy? I began by speaking of the accomplishments of the "Monagans"—the "h" having been inexplicably dropped by my side long ago—after my great-great grandfather Walter Monaghan followed his brother to America in 1846. There followed backbreaking work in Massachusetts woollen mills and the hardscrabble farming. My great-grandfather became a "master caster," or a kind of alchemist at mixing alloys in a Waterbury, Connecticut brass mill; somehow he'd put my grandfather through the Yale School of Law at a time when very few of Irish descent set foot there. All of this I breezed through, worrying that any prolonged talk about the classic American success story might seem dismissive of this family branch.

My apparently long-lost cousin Sean just amicably exclaimed, "It's amazing that you are now back with us in Ireland."

He buttered a scone. "The idea that your great-great grandfather was born in 1822 fits the history we've heard because it's said that there were sixteen children born in this house around that time, and we know some went off to America. There were only four rooms here then, and this kitchen is one of them. The sitting room beside us and two bedrooms above would date back to that time. The front half we added on some years back."

It was impossible to picture so many children crammed into such a space. "How could a family of that size have managed back then?" I asked.

"That's the thing," said Sean. "They scarcely could have. The farm was quite big for its time, all right—nearly twenty acres. But there is no way it could feed a family that size, not when the English made sure that livestock were always priced beyond the natives' means. That's why most of the young had to leave."

Sean spoke in the sonorous rhythms of County Monaghan, the intonations still resonant with the twang of Northern Ireland, the border to County Armagh being very close. "Your great-great-grandfather would have had no chance to inherit the farm, because no one but the first sons ever did. My own father Pat was the eldest of his lot, so that's why it came to him and next to me. He was born here in 1912 and lived to be eighty-seven."

Sean rummaged about for a photograph of his late father, decked out in a suit and tie and hoisting a glass of whiskey before a Christmas tree.

For a long time, Sean worked the farm with his brother Edward, who died fairly young. Together, they expanded the holding until it could support eighty cows and compete on modern terms. "In this business, you have to keep moving ahead because otherwise you're lost," he said. "So I just built a new barn."

I wanted to see it, to get a feel for the land, and Sean was glad to oblige. Donning Wellington boots, we began a walk into his present— and my past. The evening was moody, the sun nudging nonchalant shafts of light through a mixed-up sky. He gestured toward the next ridge. "You see that field just across the way? There's a mound of stones at the top, and it's said those are the remains of a cottage our family lived in long ago."

My personal Loughcrew, I thought.

Sean said he had two married sisters who had moved a bit away and another who owned a pub a few miles to the west—his only siblings.

We came to his tin-topped, cement-floored new barn. It was as utilitarian as they all are nowadays, but up-to-date-looking. So I complimented Sean for his work.

"It does the job," he nodded modestly, then beckoned me to the back of his land, to where his fields slipped toward a pair of diminutive lakes with more low hills brooding from the back side. Sean pointed toward one of these. "Can you make out the white cottage behind the trees?"

I nodded.

"An old fellow named Jim Monaghan lives there and some say he's our relative, too. Jim Monaghan farmed a long while with his brother Joe—there was just the two of them up there—but then Joe died. So now he's alone. But he's a Church of Ireland man and keeps to himself."

"You mean his line took the soup?" I asked in surprise, using the Irish saying for the attrition of some native Catholics to the Protestant side: the English induced them to do so by offering converts access to soup kitchens, formal schooling, and various other elemental rights.

"We don't know for sure. But he's very sharp and maybe you should look him up."

I FOUND MY WAY TO SEAN'S SISTER'S PUB at Ballytrain Cross— McConnell's. Below lay another small lake—there are eighty thousand lakes in Ireland, and a disproportionate number in Monaghan. Staring into its silvery surface, it occurred to me that this hidden patch of County Monaghan was as unspoiled as the deepest nooks of Donegal.

Children spilled out of the back of a pub and began shouting after a runaway ball. Were these more relatives? I went inside and met the owner, my cousin Mary (Monaghan) McConnell. A waif-like woman, she soon had her youngest girl by her side.

The neighboring lakes, Mary Monaghan said, were joined by a stream called the Owenagh or "River of Owen." My son's namesake Owen Monaghan could have been named after it, but then again this whole part of the county was known in ancient times as *Eoghanach*, or the "Land of Owen."

The next morning I went looking for my other lost cousin, the one whose branch apparently "took the soup." I became hopelessly lost within unmarked back lanes until a tractor driver waved me toward a small break in a distant hedgerow. "He's up at the end of that lane—aye, a good ways up!" he shouted.

That path proved to be blocked by a green metal gate and this was an odd gate indeed, strung with rotting boards scrawled with painted warnings. The first said, "Private—Gate always locked." But this couldn't be true, since the waist-high, rust-weakened gate could barely stand upright and was held together with tape and twine. "No more vehicles up the lane—the Gardai," read the other scribbled placard.

But this did not exactly say "Keep Out," did it? Furthermore, any garda crafting such a bizarrely-scrawled admonition would have had to be some kind of fantastical being as found in Flann O'Brien's surreal novel *The Third Policeman,* wherein the Gardai absorbed so many molecules from their bicycle seats that they became half-bicycles themselves. Reasoning thus and so, I straddled the precarious barrier and began trudging up a long lane which was bordered by thick hedges and topped by a lulling canopy of overhanging branches. It gently lifted into a heather-scented silence, with big fields left and right now only holding a few horses. A sharp bend, and the lane twisted through high pastures—this was a substantial holding.

At last, I could see the homestead, an enclave of white-washed

stone outbuildings encircling the central cottage and all of this
sheltered by a ring of trees. The place was immaculately maintained
and impossibly bucolic. The walls of three surrounding stone barns
gleamed as if they had been white-washed the last month; the case-
ments of their haylofts and stable doors were chocolate brown. The
long, one-story farmhouse itself was nestled into a green slope, with
miniscule windows squinting out at whimsical random heights. From
a chimney wafted curls of bluish turf smoke, casting a sweet, earthy
aroma over the scene—a time capsule, said I to myself, and a tidy
Protestant-seeming one at that.

The main entranceway was around the back, and its outer door
was left open wide, just as one would have found in the rural Ireland
I'd known in the 1970s. In the vestibule, three walking sticks rested
in a wicker basket and through the window above them I could
see a stone hearth licking with flames. I rapped on the inner door,
imagining a quick invitation into this dusky world wherein I would
hear captivating stories, more circles within circles perhaps.

Then appeared the old farmer Jim Monaghan—*my cousin*. What
a beauty he was! Spry and obviously keenly alert; his determined
features showed no trace of sagging; his tousled, sandy hair revealed
scant touches of grey. Outfitted in a green cardigan over a plaid shirt,
this was an old fella who looked after himself.

I said, "I was with Sean Monaghan across the way last night, and he
believes we may be relatives." Then I uttered my own name slowly—as
if to say, *just the same as yours.*

The old man scowled back. "Sean Monaghan sent you?" he finally
asked, fixing me with steely eyes.

"Well, yes, he suggested I might come by to say hello."

Jim Monaghan straightened, "You know, I don't want to be rude
now, but he steered you wrong."

"I don't understand."

Old Jim came right out with it. "Aye, I've got to tell you something now. We don't socialize with them Monaghans over there. We don't talk, we're not friends, and we're no relations at all. We're not from the same tribe."

"Not from the same tribe?" I rejoined.

"Aye, we come from different tribes," Jim repeated and his meaning thudded home. My distant cousin was referring to the age-old religious enmity in the borderlands that had been stoked time and again by the murderous feuding in the North. In County Monaghan thirty percent of the population remained Protestant and a few evidently still entertained a deep hostility to the Catholic majority, considerable numbers of whom had abetted or joined the IRA in times not long past. I was one foot into the ugliness of the North.

A pause—and then he finally offered a note of courtesy. "Did ye walk up?"

"Yes. Your signs down below said no vehicles should enter."

"That's right, aye, because I had trouble with that lane way, the gypsies coming and everything and their type will stay in a place for a long time and make the devil of a mess when they are not robbing you blind."

We looked each other over slowly, Jim and I. Suddenly, he began to resemble my grandfather, a whiskey-drinking and potatoes-for-breakfast terror of Connecticut law courts. And it occurred to me, too, that the act of chasing ancestors comes with no assurance that you will find kind ones. "So I saw that sign and thought I should walk," I said.

Cousin Jim did not yield. "Sean Monaghan and them has nothing to do with us, nothing to do with us at all."

I gave up, realizing this old goat had pegged me as a Papist myself and would be offering no cup of tea. Wanting to depart on a grace note, I offered, "Well, you have a lovely place, and you keep it very well. Are you still farming?"

Jim Monaghan managed a half-smile. "No. How would you be

farming and me eighty-seven years of age?"

"You don't look it."

"If I live to December I'll be eighty-eight," he said, repeating wistfully. "If I live until December . . ."

"Did you farm until recently?" I asked.

"Oh, aye. I farmed until recently and then a nephew of mine has the land now. He leases so much every year, that's the way it works. When you get to be my age, you don't want cattle."

How did he manage his seemingly complete isolation from the modern world, what with the nearest shop at least three miles over the hills? "Do you drive a car?"

The farmer nearly spat his harrumph. "I never drove a car in my life. There wasn't a car about the place ever." Jim hitched his hands to his sides. "I do it all on the bicycle. Yes, the bicycle. I was in with a doctor about something long years ago. He came in, and him smoking a pipe, he just stood up to me and he looked at me and said, 'You were on the bicycle?' I said, 'Yes.' He said, 'Take the advice of me now. As long as you can stay on her, stay on her.' So I do."

With that I put out my hand to Jim's.

A LITTLE FURTHER WEST IN COUNTY MONAGHAN, a curious-sounding literary and musical event was about to unfold on the grounds of a great country estate called Hilton Park. Some of the most famous names in Irish literature were supposed to appear at the Flat Lake Festival, along with an unusual collection of musicians.

Purchasing a day ticket, I parked near the estate's entrance in a village called Scotshouse, where the locals stood and gawped at the afternoon's improbable bustle of activity. A man climbed out of a silver Jaguar and ambled forward, waving a hand towards his vintage car. He had a mane of dark hair, a greying goatee, and bushy eyebrows that wagged as he grinned like the actor Gene Wilder in some of his madder guises. His name was Ambrose.

"Denise has already left so I am your valet today. Climb in and I will chauffeur," this eccentric said, opening a door to the Jaguar's plush interior. Three middle-aged women were similarly bid on board. "No hurry, ladies," said Ambrose. "I've never been in a hurry in my life, so why should I start now?"

Ahead, a disoriented-looking fellow was frantically pushing buttons and adjusting the aerial on an unresponsive walkie-talkie, which he finally shouted into as if the thing were a tin can on a string.

"What's that about?" I asked.

"He's traffic control!" cackled Ambrose, adding, "Don't mind me now, I was up until the wee hours and am still half pissed."

As we passed through the imposing gates to Hilton Park, an antique vermillion school bus approached, its driver as mangy as an Alabama redneck. On its hood white letters painted with a whimsical hand said *Denise*, while its sides were splashed with musical notes and the words *California Dreaming*.

The driveway passed through a grove of towering conifers, the ivy on their trunks strangely luminous despite the dullness of a wet afternoon. For the next half mile, the lane then hugged broad pastures dotted with hundreds of sheep. Finally, the demesne ascended to a plateau where the festival was spread out across vast lawns. In the foreground rose a red and white circus-sized tent. To its side were parked a couple of hundred cars, vans, and caravans, with most bordered by little sleeping tents. Streams of people wandered here and there, shoulders hunched against the rain.

Dominating the scene was the Georgian "big house" of Hilton Park itself, perhaps a hundred-and-fifty feet long and three stories tall, with dozens of pediment-crowned windows and a giant Italianate portico in the middle held up by six Corinthian columns and topped by an elaborate balustrade. Everything seemed delightfully off-kilter, with a bagpiper wailing under a giant oak at the end of the drive. A little sign beside him said *Flower Patch*. It referred not to actual blossoming things but a sea of seed packets festooned into the soil with tiny sticks.

"Enjoy the madness," chuckled Ambrose as we climbed out.

On the far side of the house lay an ornamental garden laid out with artful symmetry. Its maze of low hedges was inhabited by playful sculptures, the oddest one comprised of twin columns of iron scrap, topped off by long rusted armatures with buckets at their ends. They nearly touched in some kind of toast to the exquisitely landscaped and pastoral view of the lake beyond.

Nearby booths were selling all manner of food, with one featuring a giant pig roasting over a sputtering bonfire. I went for a sausage on so-called "artisan bread." Just then, a man asked, "Where'd you get that?" This was the poet Paul Muldoon, winner of the Pulitzer Prize, an Irish-born professor at Princeton and poetry editor of *The New Yorker.* In another minute the Nobel Laureate Seamus Heaney showed up to greet Muldoon. When their conversation paused, I turned to the former and said, "I believe we have a witch in common, one I just visited in Donegal."

"Oh you mean Jane?" Heaney chuckled, not missing a beat.

I followed the poets to a lofty, corrugated-aluminium construction, which a sign called The Butty Barn. Within it a hundred or so people sat on hay bales arranged before an empty stage. A battered former ice cream truck in the Good Humor style lurked in a far corner, with Butty Radio painted on its side. Behind its glass service window sat Patrick McCabe, author of the brilliantly twisted novel of anguished and abused Irish youth in the 1950s, *The Butcher Boy.* Originally from just down the road, he had brought the Flat Lake Festival into being with his friend Kevin Allen, a Welsh film-maker who had married into the eighth generation of the Madden family, which lot had owned Hilton Park since 1734.

At the moment McCabe was broadcasting a hilarious ad-lib monologue from his ice cream truck by way of introducing Paul Muldoon to the stage. Once on high, Muldoon recited a virtuosic poem called "The Old Country" which merrily assassinates about every nostalgic Irish cliché in the book:

> Every malt was a single malt.
> Every pillar was a pillar of salt.
> Every point was a point of no return.
>
> Every cow had subsided in its subsidy.
> Biddy winked at Paddy and Paddy winked at Biddy.
> Every track was an inside track . . .
>
> from the days when every list was a laundry list
> in that old country where, we reminisced,
> every town was a tidy town.

The swelling crowd applauded ecstatically. For here was a mustering of an endangered species in many lands, but not quite in Ireland—the tribe who still cared passionately about language.

Outside, the rain had gone even colder and more virulent. It was enough to drive a man into the drinks tent.

"Ah sure, it's a bit soggy, but what of it?" said a fellow beside me.

In such an Irish venue it is impossible to be alone—or to whine, since the country remains ever stoical about its weather. A friendly character invited me to sit down. "You look like a wet poodle," enjoined this impish fellow sporting an outer rain jacket over an inner rain jacket and, within these, an outer sweater over an inner sweater over an outer shirt over an undershirt— fully prepared, he was, to take on the latest offerings of one of the most miserable summers in Irish history. "I'm Charlie and this is my new friend Claudette Colbert," said he.

"It's Geraldine, actually," laughed the woman at his side.

On the tent's stage, a lass began doing ethereal things with an electronic harp, to which no one paid the least attention.

Introductions were exchanged, and Charles Langan said, "Mainly, I live in Roscommon with my chickens, but I'm multi-cultural actually. When they make too much noise I leave the country."

"To where?"

"Depends on the harvest —if the grapes are doing well I could be in Portugal in August, then maybe France or Italy or Austria next. I follow the vintages.

"I smuggle, therefore I am—a sommelier with a white van. I can collect two thousand bottles at a time, bring them back and sell them at half-price and still make a killing. Look, why don't you try a glass of what I call 'Holy Wine?'"

He filled a cup and handed it to me. "See, most people don't know that there is some good wine, and cheap, to be found around the shrine at Lourdes. So I was making a stop to fill up the van last summer on a right scorcher of a day, when what do you know, but the engine overheats."

"And you prayed for a miracle?"

"Exactly! And that's what I got, because I saw a holy well just up the road and I filled the radiator with fresh water from that. Jesus, Mary, and all the saints, didn't it do the job! The front of the van began to glow, and it ran better than it ever had before. When I came to customs at the Channel they waved me ahead to the front of the queue like magic."

So went the man's rollicking stories. Needing a break, I wandered across the field to the Big Top, for some reason named "The Post-Lounge Tent of Sentimentalism." Inside, several hundred people were listening to a forum on the coarseness of Irish building through the boom years.

"Now we are faced with four motorways traversing County Meath alone," said Frank McDonald, the environment editor of the *Irish Times*. "The Bungalow Bliss, which we used to complain of in the past gave way to Mansion Mania. What we witnessed of course was an unparalleled Squander Mania, during which we realized the value of nothing . . ." Thus the indictment went from a possibly-stacked panel of experts.

Suddenly, a phalanx of sixty aging men in black climbed on stage. Then Patrick McCabe's "Butty Radio" reassuringly crackled its elucidation. "Appearing now is the Neath Male Choir, one of the finest choirs in singing-crazed Wales."

Their music was indeed beautiful, as the three-score men raised the roof with soaring renditions of the Welsh classic "Laudamus," the Negro spiritual "Little Innocent Lamb," and the inspiring hymn, "Every Morning Sings in Every Life." Little did anyone suspect, but the latter was a set-up for the "Pat the Baker" advertising jingle used by a major Irish bread maker of that name, which was sponsoring the choir's trip:

> Who wakes up the morning,
> For a fresher kind of day?
> Who tells the sun to rise.
> Now Pat is on his way . . .

Afterwards, Seamus Heaney offered his gilded exaltations to a rapt audience. Then a blues band came on, followed by a fellow performing Lou Reed's "Take a Walk on the Wild Side." Eventually, the crowd gathered beside a bonfire by the lake to sing and strum guitars with some strange locals on kazoos. With less than military planning, I had to sleep in the car.

The next morning broke shockingly bright, and I embarked on a stroll through Hilton Park's grounds. A jolly fellow in a loud pin-striped suit and sporting a comical bowler hat soon appeared. This was the novelist Patrick McCabe, the co-inventor of this fantasy world, and I said to him, "The last festival I was at was Woodstock, and this one is better."

"Or muddier," he responded with a chuckle.

Once again, yet another face of Ireland—inspirational despite all odds and changes—had been revealed, grinning in the dawning sun.

Chapter 21

One morning at that summer's end, Jamie and I stood beside Cork's River Lee watching our son Owen climb into his sleek scull and make ready his oars. The time for competitive rowing had returned, a passionate pursuit on almost every major Irish river and bay and especially in the country's southwest.

"Good luck!" we called as Owen slipped out into the broad stretch of river below the city center and beside Cork's hurling stadium, *Párc Uí Chaomin*. With young teenage pals bobbing right and left in preparation for the start of a race, he looked back only furtively. Rapidly gaining upper body strength and inner determination, our fourteen-year-old did not wish to reveal softness for dear Mom and Dad now.

"You're off!" a steward hollered over a bull horn and a half dozen young rowers pulled back on their oars.

"Go Owen, go!" I shouted for a moment, but cheering became pointless as he surged beyond hearing and even gained the lead. When managed with a perfect blend of rhythm and strength, sculls are among the most lyrical of boats, sliding forward in great whooshes following every stroke. But sculling is a delicate art, since these fickle craft can lose headway or even topple with the smallest loss of concentration. Getting it just right is an impressive feat at any age.

Alas, Owen faltered at the halfway point and ultimately slipped back into the pack. Still, we felt proud and when no one was looking, Jamie hugged him and said, "You did great!"

"That's not true," he scowled. "I should have been first."

Unfortunately, his passion for rowing presented one problem: The River Lee is not the Blackwater. Suggestions that Owen might switch to a club in the town of Fermoy, eight miles from Ballyduff, were rejected outright. Then he would become caught up in another week on the Lee—training two evenings and every Saturday and Sunday morning. Coaxing him to our supposed family getaway became a challenge.

This day our route to Ballyduff required a stop at the boys' school of Midleton College a half hour east of Cork City, which had just opened its doors for a new year. The first rugby match of the season was about to begin, and watching Harris and friends do their warm-up exercises on the pitch, I was struck by how they had all grown into strapping young men.

As the game's mayhem ensued it became apparent that the other side had a hulking size advantage. Several Midleton boys limped off with various wounds and Harris, a second stringer, was thrown into the breach. WHACK! Here a shout: "You feckin' shite!" Then another: "Cut 'em lads!" THWAP! And there was our seventeen-year-old son lying flat on the ground with cleat marks imprinted on a bleeding thigh. A little bandaging and up you go. BAM! That was his head.

"How are you feeling?" Jamie asked afterwards since he looked slightly dazed. "Just a couple of nicks, but I'll be fine," Harris exhaled.

Laura by now was back in Dublin, gearing up for a second go at the gruelling German exam that she had failed at the first pass. The pressure was intense because the wrong score in a single freshman course at Trinity College can consign you to repeating every single subject for the entire next year.

"Are you doing okay, Laura?" I asked on the mobile phone as the rest of us finally headed over the back hills toward Ballyduff.

"Grand. *Mein Deutsch ist ganz gut.*"

Well, I had my doubts.

Arriving at the cottage felt like reclaiming lost territory, since for weeks now it had been rented to a procession of strangers from foreign lands. But the Blackwater dazzled as ever, and our gardens teemed with produce now. That night we feasted upon steaks from the butcher in Lismore, along with freshly harvested potatoes, tomatoes, and carrots.

We made a campfire by the river, and as dusk fell a turquoise kingfisher rifled past. Owen lifted a flaming marshmallow on a stick and laughed so hard at the disgusting mess, he seemed utterly content. Harris looked lost in dream.

THE NEXT WEEKEND I EMBARKED ON A NEW PILGRIMAGE, this being to visit a priest in Belfast. Father Peter Burns had recently delivered a stirring eulogy at the funeral of a mutual friend in Cork, and in a conversation afterwards invited me to stay at the Clonard Monastery, where he was rector. The prospect was intriguing, for the place lay at the epicentre of the Troubles—the euphemism for the three decades of carnage that left over three thousand dead, and countless more physically and emotionally scarred. When all hope seemed lost, Clonard had secretly nurtured the very beginnings of the progression towards peace in Northern Ireland and helped keep the process alive in the face of repeated relapses into enmity and despair. A kind of triumph ultimately did result, for in 2007 the warring parties' political representatives had joined together in a democratically elected, power-sharing government that would have been unthinkable only a decade before. Belfast's mood, so long festering, had reportedly grown buoyant, and I felt I had much to learn.

Belfast's George Best Airport is named after a soccer legend who drank himself to death. Landing there, I hired a morose taxi driver with a head that resembled a projectile. His eyes were nearly expressionless, his pate shaved to the last follicle, and his vocabulary almost non-existent. The new Belfast? Bullet Head didn't give off that vibe. In fact, this guy seemed to have all the fright-night trappings of a paramilitary killer—cheap leather jacket, bulging neck, forehead scar, and grim lips—except it was apparent that he would never have had the brains for that demanding job, nor for many others. Although Clonard Monastery's steeples dominate West Belfast, and its legacy is written into the city's soul, good old Bullet didn't have a clue as to its location. In fact, he got lost in the warrens off the notorious Falls Road, a snafu that could have got himself eliminated some years before. "Are youse a priest?" he asked as we finally dribbled to a stop before Clonard.

I'd left behind the Ireland I knew, that was for sure. The surrounding area was grim and depressing, its terraces crammed with low-slung brick houses with shades drawn and no sign of life on their stoops. At first glance the monastery itself left me flat, for Clonard's church cannot be confused with Notre Dame, St. Peter's or St. Paul's. No, what I saw was a blocky hundred-year-old neo-Gothic brick cathedral surrounded by a grey asphalt parking lot. Though a massive and ornate roseate glass window brightened the facade, the meagre spires on either side stirred no sense of transcendence.

At the cathedral's rear, a stone bell tower poked a bit higher into the sky, and an austere, L-shaped three-story brick residence hall ran to the right. I knew this church's construction in 1909 was funded by the generosity of poor linen workers and shipyard laborers for whom every shilling came hard. But still Clonard seemed so plain from the outside that I wondered how the Redemptorist brethren of the Congregation of the Most Holy Redeemer found inspiration within. Arriving well ahead of my appointment, I left my bags at the reception desk in order to reconnoiter the neighborhood.

It quickly became apparent that the neater and newer houses nearby were that way only because their previous incarnations had been burned down or blown up. Every fifth or sixth had a plaque at its front mourning the martyrdom of some "Volunteer," a sobriquet for recruits to the guerrilla Irish Republican Army, which waged its rebellion against enduring British rule and local Protestant domination in brutal ways—including assassination, kneecapping, kidnapping, extortion, and robbery.

I came to a side street called Dunlewey—a bitterly ironic reference to the Donegal god of light since it was once a passageway into hell. In August 1975 an IRA hit squad, led by a former seminarian in Wales, bombed a crowded bar in the nearby archly Protestant Shankill Road, then machine-gunned those trying to escape. Five died. Paramilitaries from the "loyalist" side, so named for their steadfast fidelity to the Queen, returned the sentiment on Dunlewey Street two days later with a car bomb that blew apart tenements and a nursing home. A Protestant ambulance driver made three heroic trips to rush the injured Catholics to hospital; on the last one the IRA shot him dead.

Around the corner on the Falls Road rose the famous murals of Bobby Sands and nine other IRA men who starved themselves to death in the notorious H-Block of the Maze prison in 1981. Across the way waited the bowery so-called Garden of Remembrance with its plaques commemorating the violent deaths of dozens more "D-Company Volunteers." A decade on from the vaunted cease fire of 1996, the exaltation of violence remained so vivid that it was enough to crush the heart.

The new Belfast? The police cars on the otherwise bleak Falls Road were certainly outfitted in blithe colors—a checkerboard of robin's egg blue against squares of yellow—in an attempt to make one forget the armoured vehicles that formerly patrolled the ever-flaming West Belfast with machine gunners' fingers twitching. Alas, the cops' barracks still wore yesterday's fashions: Forty-foot-high chain-link fences to thwart the further tossing of Molotov cocktails, with an observation and shooting tower rising higher still.

Central Belfast proved to be another story. The refurbished Europa Hotel, bombed *thirty-three* times between 1972 and 1992, gleamed beside the also-bombed but recently renovated, lovely old Grand Opera House. The only devastation to be found in the vicinity came from jackhammers and wrecking balls rebuilding great swaths of the city. A giant, permanent Ferris wheel, called the "Big Wheel," whirled beside the stately Edwardian city hall, clearly intended to serve as a statement of transcendent urban renewal. Scores of people strolled the adjoining park, serenaded by various buskers. Around another corner rose the massive new Victoria Shopping Centre with a spectacular vaulted glass dome forming an instant landmark. Thanks to hundreds of millions of pounds of new investment, downtown Belfast, the fastest growing city in the United Kingdom, sported a jaunty air—at least physically.

But the underlying mood seemed alien and maybe still restive. People on the thoroughfares kept their voices hushed and faces subtly averted, showing little of the boisterousness of the ebullient South. As if still fearing the slightest confrontation with authority, they obediently waited for traffic lights to turn before crossing the street, almost never indulging in the anarchic jaywalking seen in Cork. Also missing were the bizarre displays of double-parking, forbidden bus-lane parking, and facing-the-wrong way-parking that persist below the border—the helter skelter song of Irish life. On corners, many hulking figures sported the menacing shaved-head look. Thank goodness, garish SUVs and German roadsters were scarcely to be seen, but the tone still felt sullen, perhaps owing to the centuries-old implanting of the region with dour Scots, as well as the lingering vigilance of a populace only recently freed from tribal mayhem.

Yet uplift reigned here and there. On a quiet, sun-filled square a pony-tailed classical guitarist stood playing an elegiac piece I could not make out. "That was very beautiful—who wrote it?" I asked when the musician paused.

"Well, thank you very much, because I did," he smiled, and we got to talking.

I asked how long he had been in Belfast.

Rory, as he was called, responded, "I was born close to here, but split for London in the early 1970s when things became unbearable. But I came back around fifteen years ago and have stayed on ever since."

So here I stood, intrigued by another layer of Ireland's endless intricacies. "Have the changes been as great as they say?" I asked.

"Basically, yes. I mean on the streets right around here every other building was bombed to bits at one time or another, and the violence was so thick no one in their right mind would ever stay in town after dark. But now there's music around every night, and in most places, the vibe is completely changed. In the dodgy ones—well, you just don't go there."

I walked down a pleasant tree-lined street to a pub called John Hewitt's where the lunch-time crowd inside looked bohemian and interesting. But what most caught my attention over coffee was a painting on the wall depicting two men eyeballing each other across a chessboard. Working a black pawn was the salt-and-pepper-bearded Gerry Adams, former commander of the Belfast IRA and head of the arch-nationalist Sinn Féin political party ("nationalist" meaning advocates of a re-united all-Irish nation). Scowling over a rival castle was Ian Paisley, the white-haired, rectangular-faced demagogue of a Presbyterian minister long at the helm of the Democratic Unionist Party (the "union" signifying eternal ties to mother England). These two formerly bitter enemies had just agreed to work together as joint leaders of Northern Ireland. *Pigs Can Fly!* sang a neighboring framed mock newspaper headline.

My walk back to the Falls Road revealed further sights strange and sometimes zany—signatures of an intact older Irish culture that the flashier Republic was busily eradicating. Here was a bakery boasting long shelves of proper soda bread, disappearing from many shelves in the South. The next shop specialized in Mass cards and mourning statuary with ready-made inscriptions, such as a cherub outfitted with this expression of grief: "To the loving memory of a wonderful boy, from dearest Mum." They seemed prepared for early death in the North.

"Kean's Fancy Goods, Toiletries, Lamps, Rugs" was bordered by "Brian Paul Hair Design—Offering Pensionaire's Rates, Chin Wax and Eyebrow Tinting." Better still was a fast-food joint trading under the name of "Ruby Emerald Pizza." *Ruby Emerald Pizza?* Understand that and you have solved the riddle of Ireland.

A few minutes later I met Peter Burns at Clonard's reception desk. His eyes were penetrating yet warm, and his lips had a bemused twist. "You are just in time for our dinner, which we take in the middle of the day," Father Burns said. "It won't be fancy, but it should be filling."

Tall and thin, he was wearing a slate grey cardigan over a white shirt, black trousers, and sandals over grey socks, an outfit that basically cried *priest*. So did the timbre of his voice—sonorous, measured, and quiet—as we walked down the high-ceilinged, statuary-filled corridor of the monks' residence hall.

He nudged open the door to the monastery's dining room, and the airy, long chamber was so still it felt like a chapel unto itself. As we sat down at a table, an elderly woman delivered a pot of tea. Filling my cup, Father Burns spoke of Michael Bradley, our mutual Cork friend who had recently died. "Michael was so full of joy it was extraordinary," the priest sighed. "I miss him deeply."

"I still remember your eulogy clearly," I said. "You built up the idea that he lived life as if it was a feast of gladness to be shared."

"That's my reading of the New Testament, anyway. Some levels of the church hijacked the message into being a call for constant penance and gloom, but I believe that obscures the call to joy and celebration that is repeated so many times in Christ's teachings. The faith should be positive."

The other Redemptorist monks, all clad in civilian clothes, filed in and gathered at a far table to leave us to our privacy. The youngest of the ten or so was perhaps in his late fifties, and a few were ancient.

"How many priests are here now?" I asked, sampling the simple but hearty celery soup that the rector served from a communal food trolley.

"You see, we're itinerants because that's the way we're ordained— to be missionaries to those forgotten by others. Almost every Redemptorist spends years abroad in places like the Philippines, Brazil, or India. When those who are away come back there will be sixteen of us in Clonard again," Father Burns said, filling my plate with steaming chicken with gravy and dumplings, surrounded by drumlins of carrots and boiled potatoes. "There used to be fifty of us here, but times have changed."

As we supped, the rector spoke about his year studying depth psychology at the renowned Menninger Clinic in Topeka, Kansas, and of his affection for America's vitality and especially its jazz music. "But there is an underlying soullessness to your country that I could not countenance," he added sternly.

When the meal was done, we climbed three flights of stairs to enjoy a panoramic view of Belfast, with green hills to the south, the city center to the east, and to the north the beginnings of the bay, beside which all manner of ships, including *The Titanic,* had once been constructed in an industry now vanished.

Below us was a thirty-foot-high, mile-long concrete wall with barbed wire at its top that slashed between otherwise nearly identical terraces of squat cement and brick houses.

"What's this?" I asked, jarred.

Father Burns explained, "It's the dividing line, the so-called Peace Wall and has been here for the last thirty years. The other side is the Shankill Road district or what is called 'loyalist' or 'unionist' territory.

Everyone on this side is at least nominally Catholic—although I have my doubts sometimes. They certainly can all be described as being 'republican' in wanting to re-unite the North with the Republic of Ireland."

Some graffiti scrawled on the nearest flank of the Peace Wall read, "We'll never be second class citizens to you scummy bastards."

"It feels like Beirut," I said.

"I'm afraid so. The wall was built after loyalist mobs came over in 1969 and burnt down every house in front of us on what is called Bombay Street. The monastery itself was under attack and would likely have been burnt if it were not for local men who stood guard. This whole area went up in flames. We had to take the people in and house them for weeks afterwards because they had nowhere else to go."

Father Burns pointed to a portrait of a handsome young priest on the wall behind us. "That was Father Michael Morgan. He was looking out this same window where we're standing in 1920 when British snipers shot him dead. You see the Troubles here go far back." He was of course referring to the 1919–1921 War of Independence that ended with the partitioning of Ireland.

"It is hard to describe the intensity of the hatred that arose here again in the 1970s," continued Father Burns. "Okay, it is gradually breaking down, but there is a very, very major divide between the two districts, and you are looking right into the heart of darkness now."

We descended to a ground-floor reception room for a more formal discussion, a room that I would learn had served as the incubatory for the secret negotiations leading to the gradual triumph of peace in the North. Before getting into all that, I was curious to learn more about my host and asked why he became a priest.

Father Burns, now sixty-four, described a religious retreat he visited as a high school student. He became riveted when an aged Redemptorist father, crippled with arthritis, struggled out of his wheelchair to talk about a higher path. "I thought there was something gripping in this man's speech that had to do with the call to service, to give one's life to the service of people. This priest was in a wheelchair, but he was a charismatic man, a very powerful preacher, and I remember sitting listening to him, thinking I would give anything, and I would go through whatever I had to go through in order to one day be up there doing what he was doing."

Originally from a remote district in Donegal, the Burns family had moved to north Belfast when Peter was ten. The staunch Catholic father brought his sons to a weekly confraternity of male parishioners at Clonard (by the 1960s drawing in nearly ten thousand men and their sons, but now numbering only a few hundred) that managed to captivate his offspring. Now the rector, or second-in-command of the 150-strong Redemptorist order in Ireland, he spoke passionately of his early days at Clonard.

"I first came here from 1972 to 1978, which was really when the Troubles were at their height. It was a very, very difficult and dangerous place to live then. There were soldiers on the streets and explosions going off around us day after day—it was a war zone. I remember preaching in the church here in 1974, when I was thirty, right after the IRA had set off a bomb in a downtown restaurant, killing and mutilating all kinds of people. I spoke out against this passionately, and some people began walking out—which was a sign really that you were preaching the gospel."

"Mind you," the priest continued, "I would have great sympathy for the nationalist cause. A lot of us spent a lot of time in Long Kesh prison ministering to the internees who were often beside themselves with despair. But Clonard has always been respected as a center of welcome and outreach for all, and we were trying to connect with Protestant communities through the thick of it."

Where was the key, I wondered, asking, "Was the very experience of religious faith different in the North?"

"At least in rural areas I think Catholicism runs significantly deeper than in the Republic of Ireland, because the Catholic identity remains very deep and very strong up here. There are historical and cultural and social and economic reasons for this, of course. But I think it all comes down to this: I don't know of any faith tradition that has really flourished or survived in the midst of material affluence. Wealth kills religion. And I think that twenty-first century Ireland is an eloquent testimony to that. The faith has declined and gone down the tubes with such rapidity that it is just mind-boggling."

He fired off another small salvo. "It's like what I saw while studying in Kansas when I preached in a middle-class parish with lots of money. The image that I had was of shooting arrows into marshmallows. You couldn't begin to penetrate because they really couldn't hear the hard edge of the gospel, the real gospel which calls for self-denial and for mortification and pursuing the simplicity and frugality of life, the gospel that speaks so powerfully about the danger of riches and material wealth and the need to constantly search for humility and innocence. But that's happening here, too. The fact is that this is an Ireland which is supposed to be a place where Catholicism lies in the warp and woof of the people—and now it is nothing of the kind."

"But wasn't the ugliness here tied up in the name of religion?" I demanded.

"'The name of religion' is the right choice of words. Just saying you're Catholic doesn't make one so. The IRA went against so many of our teachings you could not count them. Nonetheless, room must be left for people to be changed and renewed, and there is hope around now."

Father Burns had another appointment ahead but offered meaningfully, "I have arranged for you to meet Father Gerry Reynolds this evening and I think you will find him fascinating. Gerry was involved in the struggle toward peace for years and may have much to say."

AFTER WE PARTED, I STROLLED THE MONASTERY'S GARDENS and then entered the church, whose interior proved to be lavishly decorated and quite beautiful. Before a high altar, a collection of elderly people sat praying—perhaps for the memory of loved ones killed during the Troubles.

In the quiet of the monastery's library, I settled into an intriguing history of Clonard. The Redemptorist order, it turned out, had been founded in Naples in 1732 by a minor nobleman named Alphonsus Ligouri. Traveling on the Amalfi coast, Ligouri met a mystical nun called Maria Celeste Crostarosa who told him that he must found a new religious order to attend to the spiritual needs of the most abandoned of souls, and that this need had been communicated to her by a vision from the Virgin Mary. Ligouri obliged and his order, steeped in the writings of Spanish mystics, flourished. In time his followers would fan across Europe and eventually to the sprawling Catholic ghetto of the Falls Road where poverty ran endemic among peasants pouring in from the countryside. It did not take long for the young monastery to galvanize the community, attracting thousands to its masses, novenas, retreats, pilgrimages, and social confraternities and solidarities.

The upsurge of the Troubles in 1969 stoked a contagion of violence across Northern Ireland that soon engulfed Clonard. On the night of August 15th a loyalist mob surged out from the Shankill, beat Catholics outside its doors, and tossed firebombs in all directions. The monks set to furiously tolling their tower's bell in a cry for help. An anonymous chronicler from the Clonard brethren recorded those dreadful events in this fashion:

> The houses on Kashmir Road and on the other side of
> Bombay St. were blazing. One assistant fireman got a bullet
> in the side, was given first-aid in the [monastery] parlour,
> anointed and rushed to hospital. There was smoke coming
> from St. Gall's school, no one could go over to help to put it
> out because there were bullets coming from three directions

protecting the people throwing petrol bombs. There was also a sniper in the trees.

The British army arrived the next year and for a time seized control of Clonard's bell tower—against impassioned protest—as an observation and sniping post. When fifteen-hundred young men, almost all Catholic, were interned without charge in 1971 on suspicion of being potential enemies of the state, the violence grew even worse. With its priests rushing forth into the daily conflagration to anoint the dying and console the grieving, the monastery's stature grew in contradictory ways—as a bedrock of the community to Catholics, a den of "Papist" subversion to the Protestants, and an enclave of deep suspicion to the British army. In those ugly times, the omnipresent paratroopers took to frisking parishioners on their way to Mass and searching the monastery without warning for hidden weapons.

The truth is that the "Paras" eventually discovered hundreds of rounds of ammunition in Clonard's garden shed in December 1972, and over the next twenty years a cache of dynamite beneath a manhole cover, a bomb in a flower bed, and a mass of bomb-making fertilizer beneath Clonard's social hall. The monks of course had nothing to do with any of this.

Walking a few blocks to the busy Springfield Road, I found a bright enough looking pub called The Fort. Once the door closed behind me, the place showed a different guise—chilling and suspicious.

A heavy-set, gloomy fellow eyed me up and down and then demanded to know where I was from. After hearing the basic story, he offered another challenge.

"Then what brings you to the Falls?"

"I'm just trying to understand things," I said.

"Yeah, yeah, me, too. But tell me, do ye have any religion at all?"

Instantly, I knew what he really meant: was I a Catholic?

"Well, I am staying at the Clonard Monastery."

My answer produced an instant double take. "Clonard? That place

performs miracles." Then he told me about his own year of imprison-
ment in the 1970s and more or less the grim story of his life.

Another fellow with a prodigious facial scar and IRA tattoos on
his thick forearms leaned forward to avow his own admiration for
Clonard. After a while I confided that I wanted to get a taste of the
Shankill as well and asked how far away it was.

"Not far enough—maybe three minutes walk," said your man
after taking a long draught from his pint. "It's the getting back that is
the problem. You go into one of their pubs, and your next stop will
be a hospital."

The evening light was strangely serene as I walked through a
prison-like gate in the Peace Wall (one of thirty seven in Northern
Ireland) to the Shankill. On the next corner stood a welcoming
committee of bristle-haired and sweatshirt-hooded teenage toughs
standing close to a graffiti that said "KAT"—short for "Kill All
Taigs," the last word an aspersion against Roman Catholics. Around
the corner there are other scrawls saying "ATAT," for "All Taigs Are
Targets"; and "KAN," for "Kill All Huns," a local slang for Protestants.
On this corner the political dialogue was summarized by a Union
Jack fluttering over a fresh-looking mural that proclaimed:

Ulster Will Always
Remain British
Never Surrender

Later, Father Gerry Reynolds received me in Clonard's social room.

Everything here was maroon. The carpet was maroon, the sofas
were maroon, and the curtains were also decked out in this color that
priests for some reason love. In contrast, Father Reynolds sported a
furze of white beard and moustache and thinning white hair on his
head, along with the traditional black and white garb of his calling.
But what struck me most was the glow in his eyes, the gentle songlike
humility to his voice, and the quiet, indefinable radiance about him.

"A pleasure," he said, extending his hand. "You've travelled, far and

I have had a full day myself. I was wondering if you will join me in a drop of whiskey?"

"I'd love one," I said readily.

"I don't indulge that often," Father Reynolds remarked as he set down our glasses. "But you see, a celebration is in order both in honor of your visit and because this is the fifty-sixth anniversary of the day I was ordained."

Of all the excuses I had heard to take a drink, this was a first. And although I had by now been a bartender in a cathedral, sipped poitín with a witch, and smoked hand-rolled cigarettes with New Agers on the Hill of Tara, never had I drunk whiskey with a holy man in a monastery, much less one located at what was once the epicentre of endless, soul-wrenching carnage. So I hoped for fresh revelations as Father Reynolds, a touch frail but keenly alert at seventy-three, began speaking.

Left fatherless at six, he explained that he grew up on a small farm in Limerick, then focused in upon his vocation as a teenager. "I had no overnight illumination, but I had two uncles who were priests, so the idea of a vocation was welcome in my family. The notion wasn't at all radical or countercultural in Ireland back then, the way it is now. But the truth is that years had to pass after my ordination before I began to understand the true nature of priesthood."

"What do you mean?" I asked.

Father Reynolds began describing seekers who eventually transformed his life, particularly a nineteenth-century French nobleman named Charles de Foucauld. A rank hedonist as a youth, he joined the French Foreign Legion in the late 1870s to straighten himself out. In between campaigns across North Africa and the Middle East, Foucauld developed a passionate interest in the lives of both Jesus Christ and Muhammad and the teachings of various Christian mystics. Then he retired to a life of contemplation at the edge of the Sahara desert, living in a mud hut among nomadic Tuareg herdsmen and camel drivers. There, he developed a network of solitary monks devoted to prayer and impassioned efforts to stop the killing between rival tribes and at the hands of his colonialist fellow French. Although Foucauld was himself shot dead in the Algerian uprising of 1916, his mission was revived by a Frenchman of the next generation named René Voillaume.

"René Voillaume," Father Reynolds explained, "founded a hermetic order called the Little Brothers of Jesus that has quietly been working ever since to bring peace to tormented spots like Belfast. A beautiful nun from the French Basque country named Jeanne Mathilde introduced me to this tradition, and it has had the most profound impact on my life." We finished our drink and agreed to talk more the next day.

Back in my room, the stillness of the monastery felt puzzling, considering that it was located between the pincers of two ghettoes steeped in mutual hatred. As I turned off the light, it struck me that my long journey within my adopted country was being rewarded with more inspiration than I had a right to expect. It was a moment of grace.

In the morning I took another walk along the Falls Road. This time I saw things I had not fully appreciated the day before. As a young employee of Ruby Emerald Pizza opened its doors for a new day, I saw hope. The skinny teenager, no older than my son Harris, was washing the shop's outside windows without a worry about any trouble that might erupt behind his back, whether from drive-by shootings or the harassment of passing soldiers, either one of which used to be a constant threat. Up and down the street people were waiting for buses, pushing prams, or fetching newspapers with a nonchalance that would have been unthinkable but a decade earlier. This was no small miracle.

I joined Father Reynolds in the monastery's reception room, hoping to unlock a deeper thread. A question had arisen when reading about all his ecumenical work on the forbidden side of the Peace Wall, and I went for it: "You could have gotten yourself killed when you began attending to people in the Shankill or travelling around with Protestant clergy. So why would you take such risks?"

Gerry Reynolds hesitated as if parsing memories. "Well, first of all, my predecessor Alec Reid had been making a lot more dramatic and influential gestures than I had for years, so I was a minor player, really. But to me another aspect always had to with the search from within. A turning point in my life certainly occurred when Jeanne Mathilde introduced me to the teachings of Foucauld, who said a true priest should become a universal brother, a brother to all. She also spoke of the power that comes with forming a small confraternity of priests or nuns that is devoted to putting adoration at the center of their lives, and she put me in touch with Foucauld's disciple René Voillaume.

"One of his ideas is that every day should begin with prolonged prayer—an hour of prayer all alone. A powerful idea, certainly. But I tried and tried and finally told him that I found this very difficult. 'Why couldn't I do a few minutes here and there and make up the hour throughout the course of the day?' I asked him.

"He said, 'No, it's necessary to go beyond—*de pas le zon d'ennui.*' Or in another words beyond the 'zone of boredom.' You may desire to pray passionately but find that ten minutes into your morning prayer that you will be thinking of ten things you need to do, but you cannot stop then. No, you must go on because you are offering your own tribute of time to God and for this experience to be full you need to stay with it because there is a sacrificial element at the very heart of prayer. You must get to the state where you can say, 'Right here am I, Lord. I am yours, use me, shape me, guide me,' as in the language of the psalms."

The priest's eyes fixed on some point in the garden outside as he next began murmuring fragments from the impassioned poem "Batter My Heart" by John Donne.

Batter my heart, three-person'd God, for you
As yet but knock, breathe, shine, and seek to mend
That I may rise and stand, o'er throw me, and bend
Your force to break, blow, burn and make me new.

. . .

Divorce me, untie or break that knot again,
Take me to you, imprison me, for I,
Except you 'enthral me, never shall be free.

Father Reynolds described how this process of meditative prayer led him to his initial overtures toward the Protestant churches and people of the Shankill, shortly after being transferred to the monastery in 1983. But his first walks to the other side of the Peace Wall were fearful, and he began to doubt his own moral strength. Finally an episode occurred that changed everything.

"The IRA had shot a part-time British soldier on the Shankill in 1986, and I was very, very upset because this could potentially throttle the small efforts I was making to link up with the clergy on the other side in order to find a way through the darkness. I knew this was a test but I didn't know what to do. But a Methodist minister named Sam Birch suggested I go with him to the house of the man's grieving parents. This was not very far, but in another sense it was very, very far. There was a whole crowd of young men standing around the door and they pulled back and tightened up with menace at the sight of my vestments. But the father of the man who was killed stepped out and asked me to come into the kitchen and meet his wife. Her name was Peggy, and she was beside herself in grief, but she walked in and threw her arms around me and said, 'I am so glad you came.'"

Gerry Reynolds lowered his head and his voice quieted to a whisper as he continued. "I had brought over with me a little carving of the face of Jesus that a priest friend from our fraternity had brought back from Chile. A peasant in his parish had given it to him and asked that he pass it on to someone in troubled Belfast, but he just couldn't do it himself because he had become afflicted with a brain tumor."

Reynolds, who would later battle cancer himself, reached into a pocket for his gift. "I still remember Peggy holding the little carving, and the way she touched it, and her tears falling down. I offered a little prayer, saying 'I hope this can help you see the face of God.' Her eyes then took on the face of God for me, and I will never forget her grief and her tears as she looked down at this little carving of the face of Jesus."

The father of the murdered soldier then produced a painting of the Last Supper that another son, a Protestant paramilitary himself, had recently completed from within his prison cell. "He let me take it back to Clonard," Gerry Reynolds recalled, "where I left it on the front of the altar for weeks. That was the beginning, Sam Birch and I going to that family as Catholic and Protestant clergymen together. It led to many further joint visits afterwards to other bereaved homes, some on the Shankill, some on the Falls, for some years to come. That was the beginning of the bridge building, very much so."

"The political front wasn't really part of it, then?" I surmised.

"No, my interest came from the word of God which I am trying to live, as well as from my sense of the church as the sacrament and the soul of the relationship of people with God and one another. I remember being on a kind of retreat in a place in Galway we call the Mount of Nazareth and finding a text from Isaiah that really spoke to me about the whole situation here. It communicated that the way forward is really the way of God, that tapping the love that God has placed within human beings is the way to transform human life. Obviously, there needs to be transformation of political structures and all that. But these things flow from that deep source, and that's where I come in, by speaking to that and trying to give people encouragement and inspiration to help them to a better sense of where they should go next."

In fact, a more overtly political avenue toward peace had already been launched by that other seeker from within Clonard, Father

Alec Reid. He was the first to draw bitter political and then para-military rivals together to join in exploratory meetings. A man of great perseverance, he worked out the first talking points of potential compromise and launched any number of entreaties to the powers that be in London and Dublin, hammering out a path forward.

But Gerry Reynolds's passion was fostering the spirit of reconcili-ation. When convening meetings between enemies who could barely look at each other, he frequently began by reciting this psalm as he now did word-for-word for me:

> I will hear what the Lord God has to say, a voice that speaks
> of peace, peace for his people and his friends and those who
> turn to Him in their hearts. His help is near for those who
> fear Him and His glory will dwell in our land. Mercy and
> faithfulness have met justice and peace has been embraced.
> Faithfulness has sprung from the earth and justice looks down
> from heaven. The Lord will make us prosper and our land will
> yield its fruit, justice shall march before Him and peace shall
> follow in His steps.

The triumph of peace in Northern Ireland was agonizingly slow, but its roots lay in this unassuming urban monastery, along with fellow Protestant churches. Later, I gazed at the perpetually spinning Ferris wheel in the heart of downtown Belfast, that symbol of hope in a city torn asunder, and knew that I had found its true engine—the bravery and devotion of those with faith in their fellow man, and perhaps God. It felt as if my own sense of Irish identity was coming around again itself. But now I wanted to go still deeper into the North.

Chapter 22

Are you cooking dinner for us or what?" barked Liam, the former IRA volunteer who had invited me to spend the night in his rural hideaway.

Even though he had claimed to be a gourmet chef, I wasn't surprised, for this particular gourmand had no food in his house and a shoebox of a kitchen with no frying pan and a total of one pot and two plates. He did possess a rather powerful cork-screw, and the frequency of its use was beginning to worry me, owing to his violent mood swings.

We had just been sitting outside eyeing one of the most extraordinary sights I had ever seen in Ireland—Scotland. Up here in a coastal village in north Antrim, that mirage of hazy mountains across the Celtic Sea had kept flickering on and off throughout the golden afternoon. I had always thought of Scotland as a far-off land, but now it loomed close enough to almost touch one moment, then vanished the next, as if it wasn't there at all.

"I don't think anyone can understand Ireland until you see this," I had said to Liam as we had lifted a fresh glass of wine to the slowly setting sun. "I mean you could sail across in an afternoon. No wonder all those Scots came here."

"Well, I don't like those bastards, and I'm getting fucking cold," he said, turning his back on the incandescent sea as if the idea of anyone arriving from over yonder polluted the entire ocean. "Let's go in and start a fire."

That job took some doing since Liam had resumed his penchant for inexplicably trembling. He got a flame going fast enough but then began dropping lumps of coal all over his rug. Ignoring them, he plunked his wiry frame upon the living room's single chair, while directing me to the battered sofa. "Three for a tenner, you can't beat it," Liam exclaimed about the blessed trinity of bottles on our side. Then he refilled our glasses so hurriedly that wine splashed onto his table and onto one of his stacks of poetry.

"Not a bother," Liam laughed, grinning sheepishly as he rubbed a sleeve over the mess. As it happened, a book had first united us. Traveling light—which is to say with only a toothbrush in my pocket after leaving my suitcase at the monastery—I had hopped on a bus for the Glens of Antrim, a series of nine lush vales that accordion out of a stark hinterland to a spectacular rocky coast.

"What's the best village to visit in the Glens?" I'd asked a fellow with a long pony tail, the only other passenger.

"Carnlough."

"Why do you say that?"

"Because that's where I was born."

So advised, I disembarked beside a pretty harbor, admired the Zen-strokes of Scotland across the sea, and followed a walkway back into the glen for the simple reason that it was there. An ideal choice, for this former one-track rail line to a limestone quarry led in a couple of miles to a magical glade ending in a spectacular waterfall. At the base of the torrent lay a deep, adamantine pool in which salmon were surely lurking. The scene was transfixing.

On the way back, I happened upon an old man with two sheep dogs, and we fell into a talk. Once Hugh McBain started, I could barely fall out of it. "I live a mile and a half further up the mountain, way past the waterfall, and right on up," said the geezer, "and though I'm seventy-two I keep three hundred sheep and walk back and forth to the village everyday. You can go straight up, och, and you will be able to see straight across the water to Scotland, and it is something powerful."

"I might like to do that tomorrow," I said.

"Mind you, those Scotch Protestants are a fierce tribe now. They are against our religion, they are against our ways, they are against Ireland, and they are against about everything you could name. They are a negative people."

"*They* are a negative people?" I repeated, my irony unregistered.

"They came over here with only one purpose, and it was to make our lives miserable," said Hugh, who then proceeded to tell me about his father's service to the IRA in 1920 and the rest of twentieth-century history. Sheep bleated, birds criss-crossed the gentle blue sky, and it was hard to square the serenity of this green hollow, with the sun-tossed waves doing jigs on the ocean below, with the man's rant.

But at least he was entertaining. Perhaps it was the purl of the stream beside me, but I had a skip in my step as I descended to a row of cottages on the outskirts of Carnlough. Wouldn't you know it, but a pub called The Waterfall sat at the end of the lane, awash in light. Chiaroscuro was added by an identically butter-yellow house across the road whose rounded corners were splashing mellow photons this way and that.

The moment I stepped into The Waterfall, the pub shot to the Top Ten list of all those that I had seen in Ireland. It was shadowy and still, and you had to duck for fear of hitting the ceiling rafters, plus the floorboards were so old they creaked to the step. The huddle of men at the bar spoke in hushed tones, as if in tune with the ancient artifacts gathering dust in every corner; a grandfather clock ticked, and a peat fire fluttered. Sipping at a perfectly poured pint, I sidled into the conversation, then described my meeting up in the hills.

"Oh Hugh, don't mind him, he's so much money, counting it gets him half twisted," chuckled the nearest patron.

"But he's just a shepherd, right?"

"A shepherd, me arse. That man is worth at least three million sterling."

Laughing, I turned toward the casement windows which were playing prism with summer's end. Sitting before them was a man leafing through *The Collected Poetry of Patrick Kavanagh*—the former IRA recruit I was destined to befriend, Liam. My first impression was that he resembled a barn owl, thanks to his salt-and-pepper hair; deep, dark elliptical eyes; and gaunt, almost concave face.

"It's rare to see someone reading poetry in a bar," I intruded jovially as I headed past to have a cigarette outside.

"But that's the only writing that matters," he said, and then wandered out to join me. With the strike of a match, he asked, "Where are you from?"

"I live in Cork now, but am from the States originally. How about yourself?" I asked as Liam exhaled.

"The Falls Road," he said, his eyes burrowing into mine.

"I was just staying there in the monastery," I mentioned with feigned nonchalance, knowing the comment would be a depth charge.

Liam snapped to attention. "You mean Clonard?"

Nod.

"And did you meet Gerry Reynolds?"

"At length."

"Well, that man is a saint, and he saved my life," declared Liam so abruptly that I began blurting out questions in return. His responses were shatteringly honest and arresting.

"I was in trouble a while back, all right, and under a death threat from a splinter group of the IRA. No one on the Falls would talk to me because of a hard fellow claimed I was after his lass. I knew I was about to be killed and went to Gerry Reynolds because my friends said, 'He's the only man who can save you now.' I never met anyone like him, anyone who listened so deeply. Well, he listened to me even though I was a wreck, and he cared, he fucking cared. Then he made his phone calls or whatever he does and got it sorted. He said it was in the name of Jesus. The spirit of that man is incredible—he's a fucking saint, that's what he is."

"I think I saw the same thing," I murmured, feeling privileged to be brought into a stranger's anguished confidence.

"I'll tell you what—he held me together when I was about to go over the edge. He made me rethink my entire life when I was about to lose it all."

Over a pint inside, we talked literature for a while and traded some laughs. Then, to keep things easy-going, I told Liam how much I admired this pub, little suspecting his next revelation.

"It's a great place, but it's changed a bit, too. The previous owner was a gas man if ever you saw one, and he kept the place beautifully. He would be telling jokes all the day and walking about with a pet monkey on his shoulder that he kept just for laughs. But then one night he walked up to the waterfall and hung himself from a tree. A few years later, his son did the same thing somewhere else. The mother finally sold it, but she's still alive."

"Christ, it seems like there's a lot of hidden darkness up here," I muttered.

"You got that right," said Liam as he began to reveal the story of his own life. A decade younger than me, he looked a decade older, which is what growing up in troubled Belfast once did to many the young male—obliterate twenty years of the spirit, if not entire lives.

"Okay, I was in the IRA for a long time—I was a *soldier*, a loyal soldier. Almost everybody my age from the Falls did the same, because we were at war and felt we were defending our families. But I tried to turn my back on those assholes a long time ago. The problem is that they will never let you go. So I came up here to get away."

I told Liam of the many emotions I had felt back on the Falls Road, the fascination and the horror, and even strange surges of sympathy.

"But you can't possibly imagine what it was like, the sense of threat that followed you like a fucking shadow every single day of your life. The loyalists used to snatch people off the streets downtown with their fake taxi cabs and bring them back into one of their little dens to well and truly find out whether they might be Catholic."

"How could they tell?" I asked, ordering a round.

"They'd demand that you spell the words 'Hail Mary.' Everybody from the Falls would pronounce the first letter as 'haitch' and with that one slip they would be at you with their clubs at your knees. Fucking unbelievable, no? Then there were the cops who were supposed to protect us. Oh, they were vigilant all right. They knew my father had been in the IRA long ago, so they would break into our house without warning and tear the place apart in front of us six kids. They would rip up the floorboards in their search for weapons, and even if they didn't find anything they would pull down their pants and shit into the gaps in the floor, just to make a little statement, like. That was their version of peace-keeping."

I told Liam that I had been mystified by the tattoos of a Belfast man I had asked for directions the day before. "There were three black dots on the back of his hand and a little triangle above them."

"Oh that sign, with the wee triangle!" Liam laughed. "That's a Protestant paramilitary tattoo that means 'Fuck all Taigs.' You say the wrong thing to that one, and he'd be after fucking you over big time."

I half closed my eyes in consternation. "His head was so thick it looked like it came out of a foundry."

"Ah you're a good man," Liam grinned as he threw out a hand, "and you will stay in my house tonight. It's nonsense to pay for a hotel, especially when I've just well and truly cleaned up for my son who's visiting from Belfast tomorrow. What do you like to eat?"

"Filet mignon," I said.

"What a coincidence!" he laughed, "I've got loads of it."

I took the dare but insisted upon buying some groceries. Now, after a long trek by the sea and up a lonely hill, I was dumping sausages and eggs into the former IRA man and gourmet chef's single pot. Liam had just keyed up a *Dubliners* CD to that aching ballad Luke Kelly once sang: "A Song for Ireland."

> Dreaming in the night,
> I saw a land where no one had to fight.
> Waking in your dawn,
> I saw you crying in the morning light.
> Sleeping where the falcons fly,
> They twist and turn in your air-blue sky.

"Do you have any butter Liam?" I called out, and my host appeared at the little kitchen's door with his eyes tearing.

"There's a wee stick in there somewhere," he said, then turned away to crank up the volume.

> Living on your western shore,
> Saw summer sunsets, I asked for more.
> I stood by your Atlantic sea,
> And I sang a song for Ireland.

Somehow, I managed to deliver something edible. Then I innocently inquired, "What part of the Falls are you from anyway?"

"Just off the Springfield Road."

"Really? I stopped in the Fort Bar there the other night."

"Yeah? Well, it used to be called Maguire's and McGuigan's before that. That place saw some nasty times because there used to be a British army barracks across the road."

"Oh?"

"Yeah, I was once sitting there on a Saturday afternoon as nice as this and enjoying a piss up with a couple of my mates. They said, 'Hang on and we'll be back in a bit.' I said, 'Fine,' and off they went. Sure, I heard a boom after that but we didn't think much of that in

Belfast then because it happened all the time. So I had another pint. But then the phone rang, and it was Danny on the line."

Liam was now chucking the bits of coal he had spilled back into the fireplace where they belonged. "So Danny said, 'Liam, I need some clean clothes and can you help me because mine are all covered with blood, and I am in a desperate state and cannot go back to my digs now because they might be waiting for me.' I said, 'No problem, but what's the trouble?' He said, 'Well, me and Finbarr went across to the lane by the barracks, and Finnbarr was after tossing over a coffee jar bomb when it exploded in his hands. He went to pieces, fucking bits and shreds, man, and now he is dead.'"

Liam's eyes had gone bulging and I had no idea what to say or do next. It almost felt like the man was trying to confess to me, and so the next question sailed forth. "Did you ever kill anybody yourself?"

He put a hand to one cheek, and it went black with soot. "I couldn't quite bring myself to ever shoot a British soldier, because they looked just as young and confused as I was myself and most of them just wanted to get the hell out of the North as fast as they could. But I didn't like those fucking peelers, not at all," Liam said, using the Northern slang for invariably Protestant policemen. He had a hard, almost terrifying squint on now. "What those people did to our lives they deserved whatever they got. Okay, I helped kill one of them, and I would do it again, but I didn't do much otherwise."

Although stunned, I pressed on. "I have to ask why you are telling me all this. Weren't you guys sworn to secrecy?"

Liam didn't retreat. "I was a good soldier right, and I did my job for thirteen years, thirteen fucking years of my youth I gave those bastards. But it's all over now, and I don't give a fuck anymore about what they might do to me, and I will say what I fucking want—do you hear me? If I met Gerry Adams tonight I'd shoot him without a second thought, that ego-maniac prick bastard. He and the rest of his lot sold out what so many fought and died for. We gave them everything, and they sold us out, and the Republic of Ireland doesn't give a shite about us either. We've just been left alone with these Protestant savages."

I felt for this man, but his rage was gathering such force that I wanted to get away. What if he turned on me next? What if he decided I had learned too much? I edged to the door and casually announced, "Look, I need to take a walk."

A full moon had risen to paint a luminous sheen across the ocean and the headland to the south. Trudging back into the village I passed a graveyard and lonely cottages that on this night felt like they might harbor ghosts. Eventually a sprawling Malibu-styled flat-topped house emerged at the crest of a small rise. Spot lights illuminated its sloping rose garden whose shrubs had been manicured so as to spell out this message: "Love Is The Answer."

How strange could Northern Ireland get?

Two minutes later I got my answer. Back in the Waterfall Bar, I chanced to meet the author of that bizarre statement of horticultural hope: a nattily dressed and obviously gay interior designer splitting his time between Carnlough when not doing up palatial hotels in booming Dubai, where the Irish were then investing like mad. "That's an incredible thing to come across in the night," I told him, "especially after what I have seen in the last few days."

"Look, things in the North are improving all the time," enjoined the amiable fellow, sipping at a glass of whiskey. "It was so much worse before, that what looks rough to you is a world better now. Anyway the Glens never had all that much trouble. Just give the place a few years, and it will be sorted."

Back in the cottage, Liam was passed out on the sofa so I slipped into the bed he had made up for his son due tomorrow. And *mirabile dictu*, Liam was a new man, cheerful and engaging, when we returned to the village for coffee the next morning. Then we visited a family in a bright new house above the sea with children happily playing on the lawn—other escapees from Belfast as it turned out. They had a drawing of a rural church on one wall that looked strangely familiar.

"What's this?" I asked.

"Oh, that's where we got married in Donegal," said the mother. "It was in a wee place you probably never heard of called Dunlewey."

"After the god of light," I murmured. "I was just there."

Circle unto circle, again.

We all sat outside, and the loveliness of the day made for easy conversation. A pint followed. When the time came to leave, Liam and I exchanged a warm handshake. He had moved me enough that I wondered what I would have been like if I had grown up upon his street, and what dark deeds my own hands could have wrought.

Over the next few days, I toured some more of Northern Ireland. The Giant's Causeway, an hour north of Carnlough, was as spectacular as guidebooks claim, with its baffling fifty-million-year-old basalt columns descending into the sea, but far too tourist-infested. The nearby village of Bushmills, home borough of spade-faced Ian Paisley, the Protestant Darth Vader, was bedecked with so many Union Jacks, banners of the aged bonny Queen, and for some reason, placards with the face of Johnny Cash, that I couldn't leave it fast enough.

Back in Belfast, I fell in with a jovial bunch gathered around tables outside an ancient pub called Kelly's Cellars, and they were a cosmopolitan and welcoming mix. A city planner named Mark Hammil spoke of exciting urban renewal projects he was involved with, and an Indonesian described some head-scrambling work he was doing for Apple computers. As the sun lowered, sea gulls swarmed overhead, and I remarked that I had never seen so many in any city ever.

That night I was drawn to take one last look at the city's lower depths, to try to take the full measure of Belfast as it was now, and as it had been, without the guide book glossing-over. One stop was an IRA-frequented bar called McGuinness's that had been the scene of a savage murder just two years earlier, which fifty-six patrons had witnessed only to undergo collective amnesia when the police arrived. I met a double-talking one of those accomplices to savagery who reserved his outrage for the five sisters of the thirty-three-year-old victim, Robert McCartney, who had travelled to New York and the steps of the U.S. capital in Washington, D.C., to denounce the still festering violence of the IRA and the other side. My host hated them with a passion.

I next entered a most boisterous bar on the Falls Road, The Celtic. The crowd was in a fever due to the drum banging and wicked fiddling of a band stomping the stage to the refrain of, "Fuck the UDF!" They were referring to the Ulster Defense Force, a cluster of Protestant paramilitaries headquartered half a mile away.

"Now *everyone*!" cried the leader. "Fuck the UDF!"

"FUCK THE UDF!" at least three hundred people screamed, and it got worse.

This place has barely healed one bit, I thought.

Thank goodness, I met Father Gerry Reynolds again the next day, and he extended a handshake of hope. "Sure there is plenty of darkness left," he said, "but I have loads of faith in the future here. Give us a few years, and we'll get there."

Chapter 23

Oh, country of bouncy castles and misted mountains, zany Joyce effigies and peace walls slicing through seething rancour. I thought I was beginning to know Ireland intimately as I headed back to Cork. Arriving, I felt renewed. Down on the River Lee, gulls darted above the *Asgard II*, the brig on which our son had joyously sailed around Northern Europe. (Alas, a year hence it would sink off the coast of France like an effigy to Ireland's mounting troubles; but at least no hands were lost). No, on this day the vessel and the Ireland I carried in my head still glowed with promise.

Then the phone rang, the daughter calling. "I'll be at Kent Station in thirty minutes. Can you collect me?"

My pulse quickened as I approached the dreary train platform, for there was a bad omen in her tone: Laura had refused to say a thing about the results of her gruelling repeat examinations at Trinity college in Dublin. The doors split open and throngs spilled out. Where was my daughter? Scores of people shuffled past before I finally caught sight of her struggling forth with a heavy suitcase.

How lovely Laura looked at nineteen, with her long, luxurious red hair and fair, freckled cheeks, her blue eyes reaching out to mine—the face of Ireland was hers. Praying that she was saving her good news until we met, I stepped forward to hug her.

"Hi Dad," was all she offered, as she turned away, lowering her gaze.

"How'd it go?" I implored.

"Well I even passed the Statistics this time."

"Congratulations."

Now Laura paused. "At least that makes four out of five."

"The German?"

"I failed by three points," she said in a voice that was barely audible.

I could feel her spirit sinking and reached for reassurance. "That's next to nothing. We'll find a way around it. There's got to be a way."

"I don't think so, I really don't think so," Laura grimaced. "They're so nasty, they're unbelievable. Eighteen out of the twenty-five of us failed. It's like they wanted us to fail."

I put her bag in the car, and we drove off. "Okay, so where does that leave us? Do you have to repeat the first-year German?"

"No, that's not it. Didn't you listen? I'm supposed to repeat the *entire first year.*"

I nudged the car up the hill, turned the corner. A pebble-dashed wall was stained with fresh graffiti. Instead of "Kill all Taigs," it said "Hire new Cork prison chef!"

"That's brutal, Laura," I murmured, shifting numbly.

"It's nasty, and I am not going to do it, I'm not going back," she responded with a finality that was frightening.

"But you must. This is about the rest of your life."

"You can't make me, and I'm not going to do it."

In America, our daughter's problem would be but a hiccup in a student's progress. You badger the professors, the deans, and all the way through to the university president, if need be, until you get "yes" for an answer and work out some accommodation, perhaps entailing a make-up course. But in America, parents pay up to fifty thousand dollars per year of college and wield personal clout. Not in Ireland, where the tuition was almost free and the system is stone rigid. You make the grade or risk being cast out into the cold.

I rang Jamie, and she rushed home from work. At least Laura let her mother offer a warm embrace. "Look," Jamie said, "We'll fix this."

"It doesn't matter, it's done," Laura shook her head. "I've talked to some friends, and we're going to save some money and go to Australia for a while. That's all I want to do now. I'll go back to college next year, but not Trinity, never."

"Oh my God," groaned my wife as Laura fled to her room. Her shadow followed her out the door, the shadow of her vanishing youth. What had our great experiment abroad wreaked?

More guilt, and more struggle. We tried, frantically, to fix the situation but nothing worked. "Look, this sounds like a cull to me," said a Cork professor I knew. "This is very unusual. But don't let her shag off on some La-La Land journey, because they never come back."

Alas, Laura, stubborn Laura, would not be dissuaded from her Australian dream—which is in fact a classic escape dream for thousands of Irish young people. So with bitter irony our daughter had in fact gone so native that she was vowing to leave Ireland to follow fancy to the other side of the earth.

Despondent, Jamie and I headed out to Ballyduff that weekend with our dog Rudy—the teenage boys once again having other parent-abandonment plans. Continuity was what we craved. Instead, we made another crushing discovery: the hound was two-timing us.

Oh, we should have seen the warning signs, which had been apparent for weeks. Once at the cottage Rudy would bolt off toward the trail by the river, vanishing for hours. Then things grew more suspicious, with his disappearances lasting until dark, ending with a skulking return to his dogbed. He stopped eating and began whimpering to be let out every morning at precisely seven a.m., his internal alarm clock precise.

The next morning I drove to the village shop. Mysteriously, a half dozen For-Sale signs in Ballyduff had disappeared all at once, while scores of flower pots had materialized from the bridge to the top of the T-junction, and a baffling number of houses seemed to be simultaneously getting fresh paint—that's the way reality can spin on its head in Ireland, still. Buying a newspaper, I asked a droll local what was happening. "Yerrah, they're all after the national Pride of Place award, and the judges are about to come by for an inspection," he scowled. "So it wouldn't look too good if the whole village was on the block."

Chuckling, I headed back to our cottage. The leaves glowed in their autumn hues, birds were in serenade mode when my eye caught the riddle-some Rudy trotting beside the road, tongue flopping as if he had just breakfasted upon a confit of rabbit. Worse, he was on a leash being gripped by my next-door neighbor, a retired Englishman whose doings were normally hidden behind a substantial hedge. So there it was—*in flagrante*. I felt jilted.

Delivering coffee to Jamie, I huffed, "Things are going to hell in a hand basket. You won't believe this. I just caught Rudy walking on a leash with another man."

"So he *has* been stepping out on us. With whom?"

"Noel, from behind the hedge."

The wife, who often laughingly told our human offspring that Rudy was her favorite child, shot out of bed and feigned the reaction of a woman scorned. "The next-door neighbor? I should have seen it!"

The situation was soon resolved, yet its merry insouciance did seem to hold some small omens in itself. You head off for an adventure abroad and even your dog won't stay on the leash.

No one knew that Christmas 2007 would be the last chapter in the great Irish fairy tale. No matter if the overheated construction industry had gone quiet as homes stopped selling, and the Irish stock market, long viewed as the one of best plays in the world, was in free fall. It was just an inevitable correction, the banks' forecasters insisted; a respectable growth rate was predicted for 2008, or at worst a "soft landing."

So off to Boston and New York again went the wives of plumbers and farmers, the daughters of builders and bankers, spending the equivalent of nearly five billion dollars on bargain presents. It was buy, buy, buy abroad once again as the sidewalk Santas' bells rang outside Macy's and the snow fell. "Ah sure, the government's crooked anyway!" was the refrain in the here-come-the-gals drinks lounges of JFK, where price tags were ripped off that might alert sleepy customs inspectors at Dublin and Shannon airports back home as to duties to be paid.

In January, the first alarm sounded with the revelation that a Dublin solicitor named Michael Lynn had flown the coop after single-handedly borrowing eighty million euros to finance his property scheming. Many erstwhile kingpins of the Irish boom would repeat this latter-day Flight of the Earls, with Interpol on their heels. It turned out that the first absconder, Michael Lynn, had leveraged some purchases by refinancing the same properties with two and three identical lines of credit at a time. Then he'd gone on a property-buying spree around Ireland, Spain, China, Dubai, and Eastern Europe, wherever his fancies carried him. Lynn, it suddenly became clear, was the avatar of the Celtic Tiger's greedy rot. Eventually, unpaid creditors raised the alarm. When the authorities came knocking on the door of his lavish South Dublin residence, nobody was home and nothing was left in it, except twenty cases of French wine and a Hoover. The Gardai did discover that the fellow had made an advance purchase of two hundred and fifty thousand euros worth of time-sharing on an executive jet service.

Interpol sightings of this wild goose began filing in from Budapest and Lisbon, Barbados and New York, but nobody could extradite him back to Dublin, due to legal arcanery. Eventually, Lynn gave a phone interview from Point Unknown to the London *Daily Mail*, in which he called himself "a product of the system."

> It was the way things were in Ireland. . . . The banks were . . .
> very excited . . . by the amount of money that could be made
> and we were all—including myself—following the trend. I was
> the Celtic Cub out of control in hindsight. And I was greedy
> and over ambitious. . . . We were all part of a mythical illusion.

A mythical illusion. Is this what Jamie and I had led our children into? Is this all modern Ireland was? Across the pond, the giant American investment bank Bear Stearns foundered, and the shock waves reverberated across our adopted country. On St. Patrick's Day 2008, as things would have it, the pot of gold at the end of Paddy's field began to vaporize: Anglo Irish Bank, first-stop for speculators and one of the largest banks in Ireland, lost a whopping fifteen percent of its value in the time it takes to run a parade. That collapse was labeled "The St. Patrick's Day Massacre."

Three months later, the Minister for Finance acknowledged that growth in the property sector, the tax-incentive-fed backbone of the economy for nearly a decade, had come to a "shuddering halt." By then, the collective value of Irish banking, long fingered as a sure play, plummeted. By Christmas 2008, Irish bank shares were trading for handfuls of pennies. The house of cards was collapsing.

But give this to the Gaels: When trouble hits they revel in it as if misery is their birthright. So by the spring of 2008 every next fellow in the pub was proclaiming, "Yerrah, I could see it all coming long ago."

Right.

Further revelations emerged about the prime minister Bertie Ahern's suspect relationships with his property developer friends, and he ultimately resigned in disgrace. His successor Brian Cowen's first highly symbolic act was to close down the lavish party tent at the Galway Races where his ruling party traditionally feted its property developer friends. A giant sucking sound issued from the Bouncy Castle culture.

At least there was some good news in Ballyduff. Never too distracted by the giddy consumerism of the boom, the community took cheer from indeed winning the national village Pride of Place award.

Meanwhile, our cottage held its peace, and as spring came it was time to turn the soil. The cheating dog Rudy had vanished per usual, and Laura had indeed gone off to Australia. The boys were at school, Jamie at work. But I had the river beside me, the swans and terns winging past, and at my feet a pile of rotting seaweed gathered from the nearby coast. I set to pitch-forking it into an asparagus patch in the making, in the old Irish way of sweetening the earth. Ancient Kerry men and Aran Islanders used layers of this nutrient to bring fertility to miserable, sandy soil, and that was good enough for me.

Suddenly, the mighty splash of a spring salmon turned my head. It felt like a call. So I donned hip waders, I readied a split cane rod and tied on an exotically colored fly. Then I stood in the surging currents of the Blackwater, casting and casting for a new breath of life. At last, there was a take and my reel screeched as a fish who had traversed thousands of miles to come back to this island—this place beside the ancient Blackwater—grabbed my fly and ran, veering and leaping twice, three times, like some wild figment of the imagination. Then heart-sickeningly, he broke free, this shape-shifter like myself.

THAT FRIDAY JAMIE ARRIVED FROM CORK not only with the boys but five female friends in a convoy. Steaks were flopped on the grill, the wine was unleashed, and didn't the gals all talk for Ireland as we gathered around the picnic table on that gentlest of April evenings.

"Did you ever see anything more beautiful than this!" exclaimed Miriam, a black-haired lasher.

Sinead, a delightful, improvisational young thing, started telling stories about her youth in her hilariously-pronounced "Waatefiyord" as if she were inventing a surreal world with every recollection that darted into her train of thought.

And here was Jamie following with gloriously campy renditions of Joni Mitchell songs, singing as if, for this moment, she didn't have a care in the world.

"You're the cut off her head, dolly bird!" clapped rambunctious Sinead.

Before I knew it, there were owls hooting from the trees, ladies hooting from the kitchen, and a campfire glowing by the river. The economy might be crashing, but the country's spirit surely wasn't—not tonight, not yet. There were no people more exuberant or resilient than the Irish, no people anywhere with whom Jamie and I felt so at home, I kept telling myself.

A week later, another vision emerged from the edge of our garden: a white-bearded man with a floppy hat, hip waders and khaki gear, who was snapping pictures of our house. I walked out halloing, "How are you doing there?"

"I was just having a look about, and I hope you don't mind. I am Hans Christian Andersen," the man said. Not, obviously, the fellow one-hundred-and-thirty-years dead who wrote all those fables, but the other Hans Christian Andersen who used to own this place.

"I have heard about you! They say you took all the salmon from the river!" I exclaimed.

He quickly accepted my offer of tea. As the pot steeped in the kitchen, I showed him the changes the previous Scottish owners had wrought. Hans Christian Andersen looked so pleased, I asked why he left.

"You know, we never wanted to," he sighed as we sat down in the dining room with it windows eyeing the river. "But then the grand-children came along and that changed everything. My wife wanted to be close to them, so we moved again to Sweden, just across the bridge from Copenhagen."

"Has it gone well?"

"Yes, very well."

We chatted on. He said he had barely caught a salmon right off our banks—they moved too fast there, and he fished other beats, and this gave me relief since I had struggled to capture their magic myself. The subject turned to the sweeping changes that had come over Ireland, and at first Hans Christian only offered cautious observations. "It upsets me to see some good things disappearing, certain things particularly. I am thinking of right here in Ballyduff with Maura Lindsey's pub, and my God, Pad Flynn's hardware shop gone. These things make me sad. But it was beautiful to live here, yes, the every day for seven years."

I looked this curious visitor in the eye, and said, "Maybe that's the best thing about this place, the way it holds you in the present."

Hans Christian nodded. "That is so. But there has been too much change too fast around the country. It sometimes felt like it was deliberately losing its soul."

He fingered some fresh tobacco into his pipe. "But it is still like nowhere else. You see, when I come back, I do not return for just a few days, no. I like to get the feel of it all again, the whole island," he said, spreading out his hands. "And this time I have been driving around the island for weeks, staying in the mountains, by the coast and in Sligo and Wicklow and lots of places maybe not so many people go to. I love how much things still change in such short distances, the accents, the outlook, the things they do. Everything is just different all the time, and you can never stop being interested in Ireland. Some say it is a small place, but it will never be that to me. I think it is one of the largest places I have ever seen."

That, I thought, summed it up.

Oddly, Hans Christian Andersen's quiet dignity made me think back upon some of the earlier lunacy I'd seen in the name of Ireland. Just a few years earlier I'd been in Chicago, thousands of miles from simple Ballyduff, just before Patrick's Day.

The waiter serving the hotel breakfast explained to my consternation that the river was about to be "slimed."

"Slimed?"

"They dye the Chicago River green before every Paddy's Day—been doing it for forty years—and it's going to happen in about an hour, just a block away. We take our Irishness very seriously here."

"Really?" I guffawed, thinking of how rather more gravely my own family was confronting that issue.

"See, it's the perfect river for painting green cuz it has locks in it and is the only one in the world that can flow backwards, so that the dye kind of just sits there," the gnomic fellow explained. "And that's why Chicago is the biggest place for celebrating St. Patrick's Day anywhere. We go green, we stay green."

So educated, I had hurried off. Thousands of people were already pushing frantically ahead on the street, Japanese, Chinese, Hispanics, American blacks and whites. All were dressed in green. They wore green jackets, capes and dresses, and were doing jigs and beating bohrans and blowing kazoos. There were black transvestites sporting green eye shadow and green wigs. Many marchers were wearing T-shirts that said, "Kiss Me, I'm Wasted!" Hucksters were selling green floppy hats and green sombreros and green Stetsons.

To me then, looking at the Blackwater River that was not ever green but black as peat, that memory felt like a journey into a separate reality, the indomitable kitsch of make-believe Irishness.

But that Sunday morning, the Chicago River lay just ahead. Up and down its cement banks, there must have been a quarter of a million people gawping into this urban sluiceway.

A flotilla of a half-dozen speedboats roared out from under the nearest bridge, each one's bows emblazoned with green lettering saying "Blarney Island." The boats weaved crazy eights as their crews began dumping buckets of dye right and left. Horns blared, sirens screamed, and bagpipes bleated, and a quarter of a million people set to hollering from the top of their lungs. For lo, the river was *green*!

Green confetti fell from the sky, and there were kayakers in green vests and red wigs paddling around in loony circles in the river that had become an icon of human silliness.

Dumbfounded, I headed off in a taxi for the Irish American Center in some distant suburb of Chicago where the lawns were blanketed in snow that, thank God, was not colored green. The organizers promised that three thousand people would be on hand in this enormous former high school, and that perhaps seven hundred would appear in the auditorium wherein I would soon speak about what Ireland had come to be.

Not quite. Before me lay a sea of empty seats. One row did host old geezers who looked as if they had strolled in for a nap. In the aisles, children played. Whoops of laughter erupted from the bar to the left of the stage—the assembly point for the missing legions. Suffice it to say that hardly anyone cared to know about reality on the other side of the ocean.

The next thing I knew I was in a smoky Italian tavern called Richard's, happily nodding to Frank Sinatra tunes at closing time. The bartender was smiling and, as the day required, I was working at being carefree, too. The problem was that a man was walking around on top of the counter and threatening to knock over my beer. Worse, he happened to be three-feet high and was frocked in—what else—green. He also sported a fake red beard, pointy ears, and a kind of dunce cap, and was now sticking his eejit grin into my face, trying to tell me leprechaun jokes.

"For Christ's sake," I thought. "Is this what Ireland has come to mean to the world—a cartoon dressed in green?"

Recalling all this as I waded into the Blackwater for one more go at the elusive salmon, I felt relieved to be right where I was.

Chapter 24

As 2008 drew to a close, no country in Europe suffered a more meteoric crash than Ireland. Its hyper-inflated property values dropped by between thirty and fifty percent in the next twelve months, a rate of decline steeper than almost any Western economy had experienced since World War II. New housing developments across the land, utterly uninhabited and dubbed "ghost estates," stood forlorn, with their unpaved access roads littered with debris. Glassy office blocks and thrown-together manufacturing plants cried out for tenants. Rows of repossed SUVs brooded on car lots, and you could buy a used Mercedes, those signature chariots of the boom, for a song. So many hotels had been levered into construction that the country had almost twice as many guest rooms as it could fill, and huge numbers of foreign tourists stopped visiting. Banks tottered—even XCES Projects, Tom Harding's nemesis, collapsed.

Like an amateur at a poker game, the country had made the fatal mistake of sinking its aspirations into a single hand—the construction industry. In fact, the latter half of the Irish boom was so tied up in building that an amazing twenty-five percent of the work force became dependent upon it, whether directly or through related services. The gaudy profits and extravagant wages to be reaped from building had become the life blood of the nation—bolstering the trade of restaurateurs and taxi–drivers, sofa sellers and Bouncy Castle vendors, almost every reach of the economy. It was as if a colossal pyramid scheme had just fallen apart.

Frank McDonald of the *Irish Times* put it this way: "What kept the boom going for so long [was] the almost infantile notion that there was only one way the property market could go, and that it was up. . . . The banks kept throwing money at their developer clients even though these men with the Midas touch were leveraged up to their eyeballs."

In roughly a year's time, one hundred and fifty thousand Irish construction workers—about one out of every two—would lose their jobs. A quarter of the country's realtors, forty percent of its architects, and droves of young lawyers followed. Unemployment soared to thirteen percent, draining the once-flush exchequer of billions in lost taxes and added social welfare payments. Once waved in with open arms, the Polish and Estonians, Lithuanians and Slovakians got the message, with thousands quickly heading back home, and another twenty-five thousand registering for the dole. The bitter pill was that Poland, so long destitute, began hosting employment fairs for indigent *Irish* workers. The next generation, my children's, was about to suffer the age-old Irish indignity of having to flee for work abroad, but with few avenues of escape left now. My wife and I worried often.

As government tax receipts dried up, Leinster House began issuing new emergency budgets—one, two, and three in seven months, each based on more dire forecasts and Draconian tax hikes than the one before. People were being told to expect worse ahead, due to fears that the entire economy might be taken over by the International Monetary Fund. In a moment of candor, the nation's finance minister, Brian Lenihan, acknowledged that Ireland was "now at the hangover stage as the party went a little too far."

Who blew the dream? The populace wanted scapegoats and briefly took to street marching. Teachers upset about increased class sizes, the elderly angry at the proposed end to their free medical care, students worried about new tuition fees, taxi-drivers demanding higher fares, and the bloated civil service unions hit with ten percent pay cuts all had their days on the pavement. The letters page of the *Irish Times*, always a national sounding board, erupted with daily outrage, with one Pat Murphy of County Wicklow wielding a particularly poisoned pen:

> Madam . . . Your correspondents are not railing against mediocrity. They are railing against: the mire of floundering leadership; the mire of ignorance; the mire of profligate waste . . . the mire of Government dithering; the mire of cronyism; the mire of cynicism and embitterment; the mire of denial and delusion, of blather . . . ; the mire of pessimism; the mire of hubris; the mire of injustice; the mire of incompetence; the mire of despondency and dejection; the mire of social unrest.
>
> Then there is the inability to make a moral judgement, the alarming and reckless exposure to endless debt, the lack of "regulation," the loss of trust, the fears of the vulnerable, the hopelessness of the unemployed, the lost opportunities.
>
> Some are born mediocre, some achieve mediocrity and for some, at best, mediocrity remains just an aspiration. —Yours, etc.

"Ah, it's so fresh today, and you would never get sick in such weather," said an old lady at the corner shop as I began walking into Cork late one December morning. And she was right, because a heavy coat of frost lingered on the hills, as happened so often lately that the worriers claimed this too was diabolically unnatural, perhaps even divine retribution for Ireland's profligacy.

Turning the corner, I nearly tripped over an unshaven homeless man who was sitting on a stoop with a bottle of hard cider in one hand. The other held the end of a smoke possibly started on someone else's lips. Though his dress was ragged, he was humming contentedly. This was nice to hear, because I had last seen him lying in the road in the black of night. I and several other passers-by had hurried over to roust the man lest he be killed. Getting no response, we worried that he was dying and called emergency services. The ambulance was slow to arrive; worse, the paramedics traded small talk as they took their sweet time readying a stretcher to handle this sad figure. All the while, the driver was grinning at some text message on his mobile phone.

"This is an outrage," I said to a woman nearby.

"It's nasty and feckless, that's what it is!" she seethed. "The essence of everything wrong with the way this country has gone!"

But wait. One of the paramedics leaned over the near-corpse and bellowed. "How are you, Frankie boy? A little too cold for you tonight, is it?"

What the hell? But the man opened his rheumy eyes and nodded.

"Okay, Frankie boy. Hop in now, and you'll be looked after, nice and cosy like."

With that, the homeless fellow clambered into the back of the van with a twinkle in his eyes, as if his ruse had been repeated many times.

This being Ireland, apparent tragedy was laced with comedy. On the other hand, maybe there would soon be a lot more Frankie boys littering the streets, considering the drastic changes afoot. A friary in Dublin had recently opened an old-fashioned soup kitchen and found seven hundred souls taking up spoons and bowls the first day, many looking like ordinary citizens who had just lost their jobs.

In any case, I gave Frankie boy some coins and pressed on. The pawn shop down on McCurtain Street seemed to be doing a brisk trade, and the neighboring porn palace now boasted "360 Videos Inside!"—even in recession there was money to be made. The expensive Turkish Barber across the street looked half empty, which was another good sign, for Ireland had gone manic about self-pampering lately, with every major hotel opening extravagant spas. A number even offered "Detox Weekend" specials, which had to do with immersion in seaweed or mud. But they were all closing down.

Though dotted with shops advertising liquidation sales, Cork's central esplanade of Patrick's Street still had a buzz. There were so many buskers you would think a bus brought them in. A clutch of hairy Italian jazz musicians rooted and tooted "Santa Claus is Coming to Town" before Marks & Spencer, the department store chain whose windows featured mannequins in see-through harem gear. A stout man in a furry cap was keeping warm by banging spoons on his knee before McDonald's, which had just slashed its "euro saver" burger prices to better fit with the beleaguered times.

On the lane ahead, a wandering minstrel produced an eerie, wailing music by bowing a bent carpenter's saw. A stringy Welshman, he showed up in Cork but once a year to play "Silent Night" and "Wish Upon a Falling Star" with such a yearning melancholy that people stopped in their tracks. A lonely man making music with a saw seemed like the right touch for the season.

Outside the central post office, a dwarfish fellow hawking a Cork newspaper called "Echo . . . oh, Evening Echo . . . oh!" over and again.

I turned the corner and found the wispy-haired Brian O'Donnell standing sentry before his pub, The Hi-B, scowling at the world at large.

"A nice day," I offered.

"It's not so nice if you are in my trade. People are forgetting how to drink."

What he said was partly true, for the windows of the bars and restaurants that I had been passing reminded me of those little snow jars that go still once the last flakes settle after the capsule is given a shake. Here were a pair of pubs with only a somber customer or two perched on their stools. It was obvious that this Christmas the citizenry were staying home. I kept scrounging around half-filled warrens, looking for a present or two.

Ah, but seek and ye shall find. The centrepiece of Cork is the English Market, a vast, vaulted, and teeming arcade filled with shouting fishmongers, butchers, and sellers of fresh bread and produce, delectable Irish cheeses and exotic imported olives. The place is a hidden urban nest in which ancient ways flourish. Its culture, characters, and aromas bring one back through time, back to the communal market at the center of the hungering world. The English Market boasts one white-haired vendor so intimate with his fruit and vegetables that he accurately predicts the exact weight of every bunch of produce in a customer's hands before examining his scale. Inside the English Market, the dismembered heads of sharks and ugly monkfish cast ghoulish eyes. There are bleeding red carcasses on tables and bowls of worm-like white pig intestines awaiting transformation into the old Cork specialty of tripe and drisheen, a sweet oleaginous dish dating to impoverished earlier times. Here, the blood and guts of human predation wear no plastic wrappers.

Entering the arcade, I was confronted by rows of slain turkeys and still-feathered geese hanging from vicious hooks. One had had its neck wrung on our behalf, since Jamie, who loved these particular vendors, had ordered a big tom to be hung and dried for our Christmas dinner. I bought a hefty grilled sausage on a roll slathered with sweet chilli sauce, red peppers, and onions—yummy fare. A woman further on was selling steaming hot carrot soup, and why not have that, too?

"I had great success with growing carrots this year, but, with it being so wet, the slugs got almost everything else," I told her.

"Ah, it was a beautiful year for carrots, love, one of the best ever," the cheery old dolly bird said. "But it was the year of the slug, the banker slug."

How much I still loved the bite of Cork wit. A foot forward, a soup slurp, and suddenly I began to make out a crescendo of song reverberating from the second chamber of the English Market straight ahead.

High on a balcony beyond the next archway, there stood two-dozen men, none young, draped in red scarves and belting out Christmas carols. And I knew nearly every singer, so deeply had we fallen into Cork life. Why, there was grizzled Ray Lloyd and my neighbor Pat Lynch making choir boy "O's" with their lips from the back of the rogue's gallery. With the rigor of a drill sergeant, a talented pianist named Anth (for Anthony) Kaly had somehow turned this questionable bunch into a disciplined chorus bent on raising funds for a hospice for the terminally ill.

At the edge of the throng of listeners I noticed more friends. One was Peter Harding cradling his infant granddaughter. Beside him stood his brother Karl, a man of quiet dignity who had recently volunteered to cut a day or two off his work week—as tens of thousands of Irish were being forced to do now—to help his bookstore employers forebear through troubled times.

"How are you boys?" I said.

"Getting by, getting by just grand," said Peter.

I had arranged to meet a musician friend named Ricky Lynch in a nearby pub where he was soon to perform. As always, rabbinical-looking, frowning and bearded, Ricky wore his signature black jacket, trousers, and cowboy boots, crowned by a black hat. A kind of local cult hero, his sixtieth birthday party became a Cork Woodstock with a succession of eighty musicians performing on stage. Now he ordered a brandy and port.

"It's strange out there," I said. "Half quiet, yet there is a good spirit around, too."

"Ah well, that's Cork. The tides are always coming and going here, you know," Ricky sighed. He was a man I listened to closely, since he always spoke from the heart. A skilled artist, he made his living by singing Bob Dylan and Hank Williams numbers—and now his own lyrics—over his fiery guitar with the accompaniment of his two sons in a group called the Lynch Mob.

"But have we reached the ebb?" I asked worriedly.

"Who knows? I'm trying to tell myself there must be good in this.

This whole Celtic Tiger thing was like a hallucination, and change was overdue."

The doors of Canty's began thwacking open as people piled in with their Christmas packages—the town was coming alive at last. Jamie, done with her day's work, appeared holding a holly wreath and wearing a crimson jumper for the season.

"What a day! We had a thousand kids in for the Panto, and what a bunch of screamers!" she said, referring to the riotous, audience-participation-required pantomime production that is a Yuletide theatrical tradition in Ireland and the U.K. The recipe calls for a vaudevillian rendition of a familiar, old-time fairy tale (this year *Sleeping Beauty*), camped up by brawny but rouged cross-dressers in dresses and corsets, barking nonsense lines that school kids shout to correct. Then they give way to children's choruses and ballet dances by troupes of little girls in pink tutus.

"It was huge fun," my wife enthused. "On a day like this I wouldn't live anywhere else."

Whop, went the doors and in spilled more friends. Ricky Lynch climbed onto the stage and tuned his moody guitar. "This is for all of us now. It's a song from Appalachia by Stephen Foster, but it's Irish to the core. 'Hard Times,' it's called." Then he began plaintively:

> Let us pause in life's pleasures and count its many tears,
> While we all sip with the poor.
> There's a song that will linger forever in our ears.
> Oh, hard times, come again no more.
>
> 'Tis the song, the sigh of the weary.
> Hard times, hard times, come again no more.
> Oh hard times, come again no more.

"That was beautiful, Ricky!" Jamie said afterwards. "It went to the essence."

"Well, who do you think I played it for?" he laughed. "I knew it was one of your favorites."

On the way up the hill afterwards, we paused to look back over the city that had been our family's home for almost nine years. That new seventeen-story glass apartment tower, pretentiously named The Elysian, now dominated Cork's once modest skyline like a monument to both enterprise and folly. Its antenna-thin spire had recently begun luridly glowing in a sequence that switched back and forth from crimson to purple and green. "A new kind of living!" cooed its signage, draped with images of imaginary young sophisticates. So far the owners had sold precisely one apartment out of 256.

"'The Idle Tower,' people are calling it now," Jamie whispered.

Alas, the joke was on us—because it was our fate that hung in the country's balance as well. Back in our own house, the boys and Laura, recently back from Australia, were busy trimming our Christmas tree with ornaments that had been given to us by family and friends now scattered far. Those little trifles shone like points of renewal tonight. They also brought nostalgia for all we had left behind.

At Christmas, we went to church nearby and met neighbors and friends, some regulars and others not. Afterwards, Jamie served up a crackling golden turkey, with savoury satellite dishes at its side. As usual, Owen made us all laugh. Peach fuzz blossomed above his lip now, and his voice croaked a bit as he ripped off the wrapping of his heftiest present—a giant jar of Skippy Peanut Butter, which is hard to get abroad. "There is a Santa Claus!" he exclaimed. "Forget the recession!"

And God bless us, every one, I thought.

Chapter 25

Talk about happy, happy talk. At the beginning of 2009, Cork was besieged by howling storms and one ninety-mile-an-hour blow ripped the slates off our roof. Then the muffler fell off the car, the boiler broke, the heat failed, the hot water tank tanked, the dishwasher went kaput; my eyeglasses, bank accounts, and a tooth cracked.

Oh, for the life of street bum Frankie boy!

The news grew so bad you could laugh for crying. As tax revenues dried up, the country's most ambitious schemes for the future shut down one-by-one. Manufacturing plants slammed their doors; urban redevelopment schemes and support for the arts, road works, and soaring bridges all dematerialized. The six public libraries in my ancestral County Monaghan were told they could buy no new books in 2009, *none*. In the more prosperous county of Galway, the book budget was cut by only eighty-five percent. Our local butcher began selling trays of hearts and tongues. Porridge reappeared on breakfast menus.

In February, the police raided Anglo Irish Bank, where a "Golden Circle" of directors had helped themselves to millions of euros in sneaky interest-free "loans" in order to purchase a huge chunk of the bank for their own delectation. Not that this bunch were good at math: They had also extended loans of more than 500 million euro each to fifteen property developers who now had virtually nothing left between them. The day of the bank raid, February 24, 2009, the Irish stock market fell for the eleventh straight session. The *Irish Examiner* reported:

> Dealers said investors at home and abroad were selling Ireland across the board. "We get on our clients in the US and we are trying to sell stocks in Kerry Group or Paddy Power and they are just blanking you," one Dublin based trader said. "They are saying 'Irish? We don't want to know.'" Another trader said: "It's as if the Celtic Tiger never happened."

By the next morning, the entire appreciation of Irish equities over the fourteen years of the boom disappeared into thin air. The sky was falling, and the populace retreated into doom-saying. An international survey suddenly ranked the Irish, crowned the happiest people on earth in 2004, the most pessimistic of all Western nationalities. The country, just yesterday a fabled economic miracle, was now being classified as the worst basket case in Europe after Greece. Even in the small crucible of our cul de sac, people began to look increasingly downcast. Plainly, they were worried about their jobs. Above all, what would become of the children? New college graduates were already queuing at the airport terminals for London and Toronto, Berlin and Melbourne. Was this the future we had bequeathed to ours?

I WENT TO DUBLIN IN SEARCH OF ANSWERS. The first stop was the flashy new headquarters of a company called Treasury Holdings that claimed to control five billion euros of prime real estate from Sligo to St. Petersburg and Shanghai. Upstairs sat the central morgue of the Celtic Tiger, the now-closed private investment offices of Allied Irish Bank. On floor one, all was sun, thanks to the morning light streaming through the glass lobby walls. The outside terrace contained a strange mixture of Irish and Oriental icons. Half-Zen garden, it boasted bamboo nooks and meditative stone arrangements around a reflecting pool. To the right loomed a giant horse's head, a brooding and menacing lead sculpture that evoked half-demonic visions from the ancient Celtic past. At the entrance, a fearsome bronze warrioress with stupendous breasts and rippling thighs stood with a falcon on her shoulder and a spear and severed ram's head in either hand. In the old priest-ridden Ireland, this ode to the wanton Queen Maeve would have been deemed obscene. But Treasury Holdings embraces the spirit of venture capitalism with a vengeance and answers to its own self-selected gods.

On pedestals inside sat the company's true idols—architectural models of colossal projects either in the works or in drawing-board stage. One was of a massive new convention centre in Dublin's formerly derelict docklands. The scheme was both daring and odd—a giant box with a hemispheric glass-enclosed atrium listing into it at a half-cocked angle. It looked as if a drunken building had found a sober one upon which to lean. This miniature tableau was surrounded by a Legoland of office and apartment blocks on the rise.

A Versailles of a new Ritz Carlton hotel in County Wicklow and various projected shopping centres topped other pedestals, each surrounded by miniature cars and tiny smiling people. Who makes all these minute beings that dress up property developers' dreams, I wondered. What would Jonathan Swift, who didn't find all his Lilliputians to be kindly, think of these cheery, miniature fantasy lands?

Real people were scurrying past in various postures of urgency. But my eyes remained fixed on a model of a vast scheme envisioned for fifty acres of prime real estate on the River Thames, perched close to the Houses of Parliament like a statement of ascendant Irish power. Though the land around the former Battersea Power Station is worth a queen's ransom, Treasury Holdings' ambitions were not to flip it but to construct there a new carbon-neutral principality, fed by its own biomass-based generating plant, Tube station, and four billion euros of further investment drawn from around the globe.

Earlier, the group came close to purchasing the Millennium Dome, one of the most iconic structures in modern London, and, around the same time, the former headquarters of the Conservative Party. Old Tories were no doubt cringing at the gall of the new Irish, formerly relegated to mixing cement and hauling rubble for British builders (as they would be again).

A voice sounded behind me. "David?"

It was Richard Barrett, the co-director of Treasury Holdings, a sinewy figure with piercing eyes, who didn't look quite as I had expected. Though a visionary entrepreneur possessing a fortune thought to be worth 200 million euros, his dress was entirely casual. His black-bearded and luxuriously-maned partner, Johnny "The Buccaneer" Ronan, sports killer bespoke suits and a six hundred and forty thousand euro Maybach car (among others) and lives in grand pink-walled digs that Dublin wags call "Saddam's Palace." But Barrett is cut from different cloth.

Barrett wore neither jacket nor tie. An avid swimmer, he exudes supreme fitness for a man of fifty-five—but fitness that runs to gaunt-ness in his cheeks and furrowed brows, fitness that looks a bit driven at first sight. He invited me into a nearby conference room.

In the jittery spring of 2009, I wanted to meet figures who thought large about the economy and was particularly interested in Treasury Holdings' global scope and futuristic undertakings. But repeating all that to Barrett did not seem to get me far; in fact I felt like I was silently being sized up by a man of sharp intelligence but perhaps limited patience. Yet people said Richard Barrett loved language and literature and wrote poetry on the side.

For openers, I asked about Barrett's upbringing beside the River Moy in County Mayo, the most prolific salmon river in Ireland. It seemed to be a theme of so many encounters in my path.

"Our family house was right on the river, and we fished a lot, because my father was a very accomplished angler," Barrett said, brightening as if re-envisioning childhood scenes. "In fact, he was so good that he once caught forty-seven salmon in one day and that stands as the all-time record."

For a moment, Barrett's smile was unrestrained. "It sounds incredible, but it happened. My father taught me a lot. And I caught fifty-six sea trout one time on the Moy myself, which, may I say, is another record."

A numbers man, I thought.

"Do you still keep a house on the Moy?"

"No, we sold it," was all Barrett offered. First trained as a barrister and educated in Ireland's finest schools, he is the originator of more than forty law suits on behalf of Treasury Holdings and has walked away from most leaving rivals counting their fingers, a talent at which the best Irish entrepreneurs excel.

"Where do you live mostly now?"

"In various houses, one in Dublin."

In various houses, one in Dublin.

This Irish tendency to avoid being pinned down and talk straight is well known. But it had now become apparent that a lack of frankness and love of sky castles had much to due with the country's current problems. In any case, I found out that Barrett's residences include ones in London, Ibiza, and a substantial home in Shanghai, where Treasury Holdings retains sixty staff to help with its push to move up from third-in-line to become the largest Western property developer in China. Everyone said that he was fascinated by Chinese culture, and I asked about that.

"Yes," he smiled. "I've grown very interested in the way the Chinese do things because it is so different. Every business deal is based upon establishing personal relationships and rapport. The language itself is coded, and you need to interpret their intent closely, all of which makes things interesting."

"How so?"

"The meaning of what is said can change with the juxtaposition of a few words—the same phrase can mean 'yes' or 'no' depending how it is said. For example, the word for 'crisis' in the written form is two symbols—the first means 'danger,' the second 'opportunity,' and people in this country should think about that now. But when they speak, it is just one phrase full of buried nuances."

Like Irish speaking, I was thinking.

Barrett described his meetings with fantastically wealthy Hong Kong brothers named Hwang who sold the Battersea power station—the largest brick building in the world—and surrounding lands on the Thames to Treasury Holdings for £400 million.

"It was tricky at first," said Barrett. "They wanted to know a lot of things that required personal interaction." The process didn't sound exactly painful, however, as it entailed attending lavish dinners to feel out the verities of Barrett, a connoisseur of fine wine and student of Chinese (who is also fluent in French and Spanish). The eldest of the four Hwang brothers, Victor, boasts one of the greatest wine collections in the world. In one session, he served vintages worth thousands each—including a Chateau Mouton Rothschild (1989). The ten-course, seven-hour banquet was capped off by heirloom 1891 Havana cigars. Clearly, a new kind of Chinese hit it off with a new kind of Irishman, and, two years later, the deal was done.

Once the talk turned to business, Barrett bristled with eagerness and élan. One minute we were in Sweden, where Treasury Holdings was orchestrating a sprawling resort development, and the next outside St. Petersburg where five hundred acres of fallow land was set to be transformed into a Jack Nicklaus-designed golf course with five-star hotel, apartments, and villas.

A more ambitious project is to create a giant wind energy farm in the often gale-tossed Celtic Sea south of Dublin in conjunction with a Norwegian builder of offshore drilling platforms. "Altogether, it will include seven-hundred turbines generating twenty-three-hundred megawatts of power into a submarine electrical grid that may be fed into not only the Irish system, but also the British one. It will be on sand banks seven miles offshore and out of sight from land," Barrett said. "We've actually acquired more than a hundred patents dealing with renewable energy and have assembled a huge team of consultants so that we can make major moves in this area. We're trying to take a very long-term view with our biggest projects now."

The company's most interesting scheme lies in China, where it has bought a desolate Yangtze River island across from Shanghai. When a massive thirteen-kilometre bridge to the mainland is completed, Treasury Holdings intends to build there what Barrett called "the biggest eco city in the world." He continued, "It was certainly the largest real estate purchase in the world and took an incredible amount of work to put together." The idea is that the new metropolis, to be built from the ground up with funds from a consortium of international institutional investors, will generate all its own power from renewable sources and cut carbon emissions to near zero.

Barrett acknowledged that some of Treasury Holdings' heavily leveraged projects at home were in jeopardy, given the Irish economy's dire straits. But this company's salvation, he said, was that it had diversified so widely ahead of the crash. "You just could see that it was impossible for the appreciation levels in Ireland to continue rising. I mean you had dentists becoming property developers, people paying more for land in Dublin than in Paris or London or New York. It was crazy. A sort of national fever broke out, and people got very careless with their money. There are restaurants in Dublin where no dessert cost less than twenty-five euros and nobody thought twice about it. In hindsight, Treasury should have disengaged earlier and even more substantially than we did."

What then was the way forward, I asked, seeing as the company's model could scarcely apply to many other Irish businesses. Barrett grew silent as he reflected. "Well, for now we can redouble our efforts to better serve incoming industry from abroad. But we also need to make better use of our universities and young, educated population to get in on next-stage technology, like nanotechnology and harnessing wave and tidal energy to generate power. Our universities are pushing leading research in that area, but we're nowhere near converting it into reality like the Danes already are doing now."

The clock was ticking, so I asked, "Are you optimistic about Ireland's future?"

"For the short-term, no. For the long-term, yes. There's plenty of opportunity here still," Barrett said, standing up. With that I shook hands with this exemplification of his generation's most grandiose ambitions during the boom, consumed like so many with the idea of lifting a once obscure little country onto the world's stage.

I walked off past blizzards of "For Sale" signs on nearly every street; past posh restaurants that had shut their doors at the Celtic Tiger's swan song; past Leinster House, the seat of government, wherefrom very little was being said for a long while. After a quick lunch, I tried to make contact with another businessman with a singular perspective on all this, a sixty-year-old named Ben Dunne with whom I'd been attempting correspondence. Like some fictional character who had risen too fast and too far, the once fabulously rich Dunne embodied every excess that had come with the boom, then blew up his own life. But he was now surging back into prominence by launching a series of imaginative recession-fighting enterprises—supposedly including cut-rate burial plots in a London sports ground.

No prima donna, Dunne was born into a Cork family whose father started out as a bootblack. But the old man found his way forward and grew to control more than half of all Irish supermarkets-cum-department stores, and the chain bought up a dozen major outlets in the U.K. and Spain. The tough, no-nonsense patriarch saw to it that his children never lost sight of the endemic poverty of an older Ireland and insisted that they taste humility by starting out by stocking shelves.

The boisterous, plain-talking second son, Ben, became the heir apparent. Even as substantial earnings came his way in the late 1970s, Ben Dunne remained a fairly regular guy, devoted to his growing brood. But in 1982 he was kidnapped for a heavy ransom by the IRA, as many magnates were around that time, along with even the famous racehorse Shergar owned by the Aga Khan (which was killed when no money was forthcoming).

Released after a harrowing ordeal, Dunne resumed steering the family empire so successfully that its annual sales reached $1.5 billion. His personal fortune grew, and in time he began to spend it profligately—on a big house beside Dublin's Phoenix Park, lavish foreign holidays, and the white powder that vanishes up nostrils and destroys lives. At the dawning of the Celtic Tiger, Ben Dunne fashioned himself as a man who could make his own rules, glorious and free—the perilous penchant of the new Ireland. Wags called him "the King of the Aisle."

In February 1992, Ben Dunne set off for a golfing holiday to Orlando, Florida, with a coterie of friends and a lot of just-in-case cash, roughly fifty thousand dollars. After settling into a pricey suite in the Hyatt Regency Grand Cypress, he headed out to the links with his pasty-skinned countrymen.

Party time came next, drinks to be clinked through the night. Eventually, he slipped back to his suite for an assignation with one Denise Wojcik, occupation prostitute. Waiting for her was a bottle of Dom Pérignon and the largest sachet of cocaine this working girl had ever seen. "Hello, would you like a drink?" smiled Ben at the door. He brought the bubbly into the enormous bath for a rub-a-dub-dub.

Eventually, Ben Dunne became stoned out of his mind. He imagined that invisible people were closing in, just as real ones had when he was kidnapped. And where was that fat satchel of cash? Ben Dunne flipped his lid and began banging on the hotel room's safe, screeching at the inanimate box he could not open—just the way much of the

Irish populace was doing now. Then he broke furniture. "He was like some crazed King Kong jumping up and down and swinging this chair leg over his head," his consort later recalled. Ben Dunne had become a harbinger of the dark forces gathering within Ireland.

Around sunrise, the King of the Aisle lurched onto his balcony seventeen stories above the hotel's atrium and began to scream incoherently. Shirtless and shoeless, he bayed, "Help me! Help me!" Then he scaled the railing and tottered on the narrow outer ledge as if preparing for a leap into the Beyond, or perhaps to Disney World across the street.

The police coaxed Dunne off his ledge, but then found his drugs and dragged him away, hog-tied, to the clinker. At this point, his obligatory phone call was made not to his lawyer or family, but rather to the crooked godfather of the Celtic Tiger, the just-stepped-down Taoiseach named Charlie Haughey. In any case, the prime minister got on the telephone, and the Irish embassy worked its strings. Dunne was soon jetting home to Dublin, sweating bullets.

"I made a terrible, bloody blunder," he said on the national airwaves. "I was weak and stupid. I have fallen a long way, in front of my wife, in front of my kids, in front of myself." His blunder would become a larger metaphor.

Ben's siblings in Dunnes Stores' management summarily drummed him out of the family business.

Dunne fought back like a man cornered, and the legal imbroglio that followed led to the release of a Pandora's Box of secret files. Some of these revealed the cronyism and greed at the core of the Celtic Tiger. For Dunne, it turned out, had personally given the luxury-loving taioseach Charlie Haughey nearly two million dollars in "contributions" that promptly disappeared into hidden offshore bank accounts. Such unholy alliances in pursuit of political favors, called the "brown envelope culture," shadowed much of the Irish economic miracle.

So there I was trying once again to ring through to a man who might answer some of my adopted country's riddles, including how to jump back into the fray when your dreams have gone bust.

"Oh yes, we've had your letters," his secretary Nancy Delaney said. "I am afraid Mr. Dunne has been very busy but he wants to get back to you soon. Can you hold for a moment?"

Waiting, I thought about her boss's current schemes. They weren't futuristic like Treasury Holdings, but rather in the survival-of-the-fittest street-trader mode. Ben Dunne was now peddling mass-produced sandwiches, half-price fitness club memberships, and cut-rate suits on line, tweaking established interests with a defiant flair. One day he was agitating comfortable London homeowners with his plans to pack dearly beloved cadavers into a neighborhood sporting ground, the roll-out for what might be a chain of supermarket-styled cemeteries. Then he opened an art gallery under his mother's name, slashing the standard forty percent commissions of the trade by half. There was no telling what this shape shifter might do next.

The secretary came back on the line. "I'm afraid Ben is booked all afternoon. Would there be another time that would suit you?"

Not likely, I thought, again detecting that annoying national penchant for avoiding discussing things unpleasant. To Ben Dunne I was perhaps that worst being—a person unknown and un-vetted by friends and thus unpredictable. So why should he tell me a thing? "Say nothing" and "pretend you don't hear the question" was advice I myself had received before numerous challenges. It was the Irish way. The government was doing the same talk avoidance all the time now, had been at it for years—despite the population's rising ire. "Say nothing" and the crisis will go way seemed to be the thinking.

In any case, I made another call that brought me to the other side of the river, my directions leading to a 390-foot spire meant to symbolize Ireland's grandiose new ambitions. Inevitably, witty Dubs liked to disparage it as the "Stiffey by the Liffey." Nearby waited a fellow said to be one of the more brazen but clever entrepreneurs in the land, a businessman named Cathal O'Connell with a chain of hostels he dared to call *Paddy's Palaces*—a name as jarring to most Irish people as the worst racial slurs are to blacks. The so-called "palaces" were the magnets for an outlandish-sounding travel business called *Paddywagon Tours.* But perhaps, I thought, there might be lessons to be learned here as well.

The flagship Paddy's Palace proved to be just a four-story, soot-stained brick former tenement. Deliberately kitsch, it was draped with green and golden banners sporting images of red-bearded leprechauns in stove-top hats, grinning over clay pipes. From there, the backpacker residents board "Paddywagon" coaches for a week-long run to well choreographed stops—Killarney with its lakes and tourist hordes; Blarney Castle with its gab stone; the Cliffs of Moher, and Cathal's own fluorescent green "Randy Leprechaun" pub on the Dingle Peninsula where they drink evil concoctions called "Car Bombs." Young Aussies, Kiwis, and Yanks apparently go for all this, however.

The lobby of Paddy's Palace was festooned with memorabilia from heroic moments in Irish history—images of James Connolly and the other soon-to-be-shot martyrs of the 1916 Easter Rising being marched out of the decimated General Post Office, and figures from the Fighting Irish Brigade in the American Civil War among them.

Cathal O'Connell, who goes by the name "Charlie" for tourists, soon appeared. About forty, with short brown hair, stolid face, and a stocky frame, he looked unremarkable in every respect save one: he was wearing a green T-shirt with yellow letters proclaiming the one desperately clichéd phrase no one in Ireland itself ever, ever utters—*Erin Go Bragh*.

How low could one sink, I wondered. Was Cathal proffering nothing more than a clown image of Ireland such as I encountered in Chicago on St. Patrick's Day?

We sat down before a table full of marketing plans and began to chat. To my relief, the man was nothing but straight talking and probing.

"Okay," Cathal began, "people say I'm playing 'stage Irish' and embarrassing the nation and all that. But they don't know what they are talking about—it's just begrudgery against anything new or different. What we're doing here is in jest, a harmless gimmick. I mean, who's Colonel Sanders atop the KFC shops? And who cares? Anyway, people should be grateful that I'm bringing in thousands of visitors who would never come here otherwise, because they're ignored by the rest of the hotel industry."

"But the leprechauns and all that—isn't it demeaning?" I protested.

Cathal scoffed. "Paddywagon Tours is a great name for a great service for young people without much money. I spent a lot of years servicing the backpacker crowd abroad myself, and it suddenly hit me one day in New Zealand. It was obvious that young backpackers were magnificently looked after everywhere else, except for here—so how do you draw them in? Then I began to think about what Ireland really means anymore to the rest of the world."

I straightened over in my seat. "What's the answer?"

"Well, mainly we're a place that's supposed to make people laugh and that's it. Otherwise Ireland's nothing but a blip on most people's radars. Our customers come to Paddy's Palace because we offer value for money and because all they are looking for is laughter and a good time. They want to see the beauty of Ireland without having to read *Finnegans Wake* first. And they don't care about Joyce either. Most of our crowd don't know a thing about Ireland beforehand and haven't read any Irish literature at all. But so what if their heads are full of clichés? Don't they have a right to come here, too? Anyway, we found a way to draw them in, and they learn a little while they're at it."

I thought: This prospect couldn't be more screamingly different than the visions that drew me to Ireland.

And yet the man's notion of "re-branding" Ireland, as is said in

corporate speak, was being tossed about in 2009 as a potential panacea
to the country's ills. A hot-shot young economist gone TV presenter,
David McWilliams, kept pushing the notion that Ireland needed to
better reach out to the seventy million offspring of the Diaspora and,
toward that end, eventually organized a brain-storming conference of
bigwigs from around the globe of Irish descent. Participants urged all
kinds of pie-in-the-sky ideas for rejuvenating the country's economy,
including a worldwide Irish "recovery bond," an entrepreneurial Irish
institute in Silicon Valley, and the founding of a great Irish university
of the arts. For some reason they did not invite Cathal, who seemed
to me more grounded in the here-and-now than a lot of the others.

I asked to see one of Cathal's buses—his version of the "re-branded
Ireland."

Waiting at the corner, as it happened, was a gleaming green coach
plastered with preposterous leprechauns and yellow lettering on
its side shouting *Paddywagon Tours*. "She's a Mercedes," O'Connell
explained proudly, "and rock solid unless parked in Belfast. We had
a coach happen into a Protestant district there, and it got burnt for
looking too 'Republic of Ireland.' We didn't care, because that gave
us worldwide publicity, and we have twenty-nine others."

We chatted for a while, then abruptly Cathal offered, "Would you
like a lift to the train station in your private Paddy Wagon?"

How ridiculous. But off we went, and I could see various drivers
eyeing the clownish bus and chuckling, as if the country hadn't lost
one ounce of its wit. In fact, another fellow was about to open a
"National Leprechaun Museum" in search of his own pot of gold.

"I can tell you that this business is not only thriving, it's growing
exponentially," Cathal pronounced in his vehement way, shifting
gears, "which of course the back biters also don't like. I suppose we
undercut their market, but the days of Rip-Off Ireland are done. This
country has to get competitive again fast."

It was a mind-jolt, running up the River Liffey's quays in this gaudy vehicle. The new Dublin with its glass towers and bright shops was all around. But I kept detecting whispers of an Ireland old and deep as we progressed, a defining vista of the city I had known as a youth. We passed an ancient pub called The Brazen Head, now become as self-consciously stage-Irish itself as a Paddywagon bus. I had once met a young woman there who had spent her infancy sleeping in a dresser drawer, so destitute were her origins in a family of thirteen children with a father who couldn't hold down a job. When she became a teenager her parents forced her into a nunnery—which she soon fled. The old Ireland was not exactly glory days for the likes of that one.

Across the way was the former Collins Army Barracks, the walls of which I had once scaled in the dead of night to steal a bulging sack of carrots espied in the yard. Pissed to the gills, naturally, and with a Communist party rebel as my accomplice—the year was 1973. My old friend Bun Wilkinson said he needed a lot of those tubers ("as leathery as you can find") to make a decent batch of carrot whiskey. "The carrot will be ambrosia if you find the old ones. It will be enough to kill a hardened sinner."

Now Cathal parked before Heuston Station where impoverished countrymen used to arrive on battered trains from the West seeking any work they could find in the so-called "big smoke." Some were so desperate they wore ropes for belts. No one, but no one, wanted to go back to that time again.

"Tell your friends this is one Paddy Wagon you *can* escape from," Cathal laughed as the door opened.

Whichever way you cut it, this had been a successful day. Ireland, although bowed with duress, was still shape-shifting, bafflingly creative, and resolute against its old stalking horse of adversity, let loose from the barn again.

Chapter 26

With the coming of summer, the national mood grew puzzling. As if by some unspoken cue, people nearly stopped talking about the appalling economic news, which the newspapers were by now rendering with nearly black comic headlines: *Housing Prices in New Collapse! Foreign Travel Down Forty Percent as Tour Operators Close! Ireland's Debt Worst in EU!*

"Flights Over Island Twisting Upside Down, Passengers Falling Out! Radioactive Gaels Gone Mad on Ground," my friend Ray Lloyd said as we looked over one morning newspaper in his mad kitchen. Then he scoffed: "Feck, we've been here before."

Silences seemed to grow longer in the pubs, partly because fewer people came out to talk. When they did, the subjects were usually kept small. It felt as if the collective psyche had retreated into older habits of detachment or perhaps what the romantic poet John Keats described as Negative Capability. "That," he explained, "is when man is capable of being in uncertainties, Mysteries, doubts without any irritable reaching after fact & reason."

Meanwhile, our children remained studies in motion. Laura, the oldest, was working in a restaurant in town and about to head to Canada. Determined Owen kept busy bicycling off to his precious rowing four and five days a week. Harris, having completed his gruelling leaving-examinations from secondary school, did what vast numbers of the young Irish do at that stage—join fourteen friends on a cut-rate flight to Crete where they learned ancient rituals such as competitive shot drinking at the font of Western civilization. By day, his gang swam in the Aegean and then turned to new variations on Gravity Defiance such as bungee jumping from insane heights. Harrowing stuff, but these boys faced an uncertain future—only three of the fourteen had managed to land summer jobs, and all would have to wait for two months before the bizarrely last-minute Irish educational system let them know their examination results and which university course, if any, they qualified for. Their identities had switched, but into what they did not yet know.

An added anxiety was that the government announced that free tuition would soon end. Or might end: this group of politicians, with fingers ever lifted to the winds of change, was not often straight.

Sometimes I wondered where Jamie, our family stalwart, found her reservoirs of verve and daily passion for her work at the Cork Opera House. But then I was wondering about a lot now. A funny thing happens when approaching your twenty-fifth wedding anniversary: The enigma of your life deepens yet again. How did we get so far? How in fact did we get all the way to Ireland? And should we stay?

"Do you ever wish we were back in America these days?" I asked Jamie one night, this being a subject so tender we generally had avoided it of late.

"It still breaks my heart being so far away," she sighed. "Just to think of all the reunions and weddings and funerals we have had to miss. And you know how painful it is for me to be away from Mom."

I nodded, for I still felt a yearning myself that had never gone away.

"But where else would we go? And we're so tied up here. But with everything happening right now, I still just love Cork. And what town in the States would be so much fun?" Jamie asked.

My wife had let her blonde hair grow long and was in high spirits since the annual Midsummer Arts Festival had returned to Cork. There were plays in the park, on stages large and as small as the living rooms of a dilapidated Georgian house; and music on the streets, in a glass-walled *Spiegeltent*, and in a giant marquee by the river. Brazilian samba, avant-garde Catalan dance with an S&M touch, bizarre Irish street theatre, the latest almost-farewell tours of aging 1960s and 70s rock stars like Crosby, Stills, and Nash, and James Taylor—Jamie had seen it all and I'd joined her a couple of times, too.

"Where else would you get that?" she asked after one street performance.

In truth, I felt slightly crestfallen at her enthusiasm, since it meant she was still far from ready to contemplate a full-time move to Ballyduff—that vision of possible permanence I had so coveted, that place that vanquished fretting.

Another evening I joined Jamie for a performance by The Dubliners, the most rousing traditional music band Ireland ever launched. Hard-drinking, bawdy rogues with wild beards and outrageous manes of hair, they became icons of Ireland to hundreds of thousands of fans around the world beginning in the late 1960s. Unfortunately, three of the original five had died. The first was Luke Kelly, a man who sang with such searing, raw power and exultation that he was perhaps the best ballad singer of all time. He collapsed with a brain tumor on the Cork Opera House stage in 1980. Next to depart was the tin whistle player Ciarán Bourke who had collapsed during another performance. Finally, the guitarist Ronnie Drew, whose voice was as rough as a pirate's, succumbed as well.

Tonight's performance was to be a journey through The Dubliners' legendary past, a memorial led by two of its founding members—Barney McKenna and John Sheahan—and the "new" recruits who had generally been around for about thirty years. The evening light was a shimmer when Jamie and I entered the lobby of the Cork Opera House, which was already crammed full of chattering ticket holders.

No question, she looked beautiful in her embroidered black and white dress as she floated about the room, attending to various needs.

"Jamie, how are you dear!" enthused a director of a modern dance troupe, kissing her on both cheeks.

Now she was holding the hand of a swarthy man aptly named Brian Hand, The Dubliners' promoter.

"You've done a brilliant job getting so many people in here," he said. "It's going to be mighty."

I stood in the background, eclipsed.

A moustachioed figure in a jacket and tie approached with his wife at his side. Jamie introduced him as Finbarr, the owner of The Flying Enterprise bar.

They started talking about some joint promotion. Jamie by now had organized more of those than I could keep track of. One day she would be touring the city with a hairy wizard named Gandalf, the next orchestrating photo opportunities with a hundred identical twins or two dozen men with shaved heads—whatever it took to draw attention to some new performance.

"How's everything going, Finbarr?" asked Jamie.

"Grand altogether! We just bought the entire block behind us and have already landed a major tenant and an apartment scheme that is always full."

There was that resilient Irish tone. Recession? What recession? Everything was *grand*. That spirit was sporadic now, but it might be the country's saving grace, I thought, not knowing how much worse things would still get.

Perhaps, I pondered as well, my wife had gone more Irish than I had myself. Our plunge into a new life abroad still held a particular rightness for her.

"*Ladies and gentlemen, please make your way to your seats. The perform-ance is about to commence!*" commanded an intercom voice.

Jamie and I stationed ourselves at the balcony's front row. On the stage appeared five men gone salt-and-pepper to shocking white in the hair department. Two fiddles, two guitars, one banjo. On a chair sat a man of about seventy in a black leather roadster hat, black leather vest, black shirt, black pants, and cowboy boots. This was Barney McKenna, one of the band's founding members, now half-blinded by a stroke.

To his left, a fiddle-wielding John Sheehan, plucked the first notes of a now bouncy, and now meditative reel called "Fermoy Lassies."

Projected on a screen behind them was a black and white photograph from the early 1970s of the original minstrels—*A Time to Remember* the banner said. Their faces were rugged and virile then, their gazes burning with the defiance of youth. And, my, did these boys have hair, especially Luke Kelly—his head and chin were wreathed in an electric frazzle of Age of Aquarius red curls.

The "Fermoy Lassies" took on a prancing gait as the newer members of the band joined in—Sean Cannon on guitar, and a lilting vocalist; Eamon Campbell, a fellow traveller since 1977; Patsy Watchorn a rousing singer newly recruited. The next number was "On Raglan Road," a Dubliners' classic whose aching lyrics come from a Patrick Kavanagh poem:

> On Raglan Road on an autumn day I met her first and knew
> That her dark hair would weave a snare that I might one day rue;
> I saw the danger, yet I walked into the enchanted way,
> And I said, let grief be a fallen leaf at the dawning of the day.

The night grew wings, for these men were singing for Ireland— grand and melodramatic, tender and raucous and gay. A video clip on the screen showed Luke Kelly, from years past, singing in paroxysms of inspiration, his eyes jumping as if his very spirit was leaving him for some other place. This after all was the same land in which ancient poets used to lie all night at the base of waterfalls in search of divination.

John Sheahan offered odes to his departed band mates. "Ah, we were a great group," he said. "But you know, Ciarán Bourke was the only one of us to have any higher education. He did something with the agricultural science before he joined up and dropped out of Trinity. What a great player! But then he took a mighty interest in drink. It was almost scientific the way his interest grew in its various flavors and permutations. I remember one night we were someplace in France and about to have a glass after a session, and he started eyeing the big shelves behind the bar holding lots of different fluids he had never seen before. 'What will you have?' I said. 'I think I'll start with the left-hand side,' he said."

Funny stuff, but Ciarán Bourke more or less drank himself to death.

Ballads rollicking and poignant followed—"The Wild Rover" and "The Rare Ould Times" among them.

Stocky, tuft-bearded Barney McKenna, once one of Dublin's most Rabelaisian spirits, stood up for a solo. A master of malapropisms, he related, "This is a lullaby that my grandmother used to sing to me. Some of you may have heard it, but if you haven't, this will be your first time. It's called 'I Wish I Had Somebody to Love me.'"

And with that, the aging vocalist set to singing with his arms outstretched, as six hundred citizens joined in.

> Meet me tonight in the moonlight,
> Meet me tonight all alone,
> I have a sad story to tell you,
> I'm telling it under the moon . . .
>
> I wish I had the wings of a swallow,
> Fly out over the sea,
> Fly out to the arms of my true love,
> And bring him back safely to me.

Barney McKenna's voice was time-ravaged. One eye sightless and gait awkward, he struggled to reclaim his seat; but his banjo plucking was wizardly, and his lullaby moved every heart.

Luke Kelly's brother Jimmy offered the next song and was followed by an impassioned young balladeer. The old was becoming new again, and there next appeared the son of Ronny Drew, Phelim, a darkly handsome movie actor, singing with a voice that eerily resembled his father's. We will all carry on, was the group's message of the night.

AN ALMOST-FULL MOON DANGLED OVERHEAD as Jamie and I parked outside the Ambassador Hotel, five hundred feet from our house. Its lambent light illuminated a long redbrick building that had once served as a hospice for the British army, including those maimed during the rebellion.

We, the outsiders, had been invited to join what was very much an inner sanctum, because here The Dubliners and assorted musician friends were gathering for an after-hours private party. A small crowd was buzzing in the front lounge, at tables or at the bar, as Jamie and I sidled forward.

The night porter, Martin, looked stupefied by this sudden crush of customers—normally he'd be thinking of laying his head down by now, rather than pulling pints. With worry strings of black hair running over an otherwise bare scalp, he looked to be a certifiable eccentric himself.

Martin turned to Phelim Drew, blurting, "I knew your Da, Ronnie. What a great man he was for the onion sandwiches! Every morning he was here he would call for a black coffee and onion sandwich."

"It was more than an onion sandwich he was after needing," muttered The Dubliners' promoter, Brian Hand. "I remember phone calls from the prisons in Norway, and every other feckin' country they toured, with his little problems."

The Irish will say about anything to be funny, I thought—loving this trait still, for perhaps comedy conquers all.

Jamie and I sat down beside the guitarist Sean Cannon. With penetrating blue eyes and weathered brow, the musician proved to be droll. "I think by this point we have celebrated our past so much this will be the last one of these affairs. It's time to let our old ghosts lie and just carry on making music for whoever will have us."

"And how far would that take you nowadays?" Jamie asked.

"Spain and Austria next, I think. Vienna, after that, then Scandinavia and, I don't know, Mongolia or Vietnam, wherever they'll pay us."

Glasses were clinked, and I spoke of a hidden pub a few hundred feet up the hill where men in their eighties still gathered in a back room on Sunday nights to recite poetry and sing unaccompanied songs one-by-one. The question was whether the demise of the flash new Ireland might somehow revive the older values, the ones of creativity and endurance against all odds.

Sean Cannon responded solicitously, "You should treasure it now that it's gone so rare. But you know, when I was young, everyone used to sing in the pubs and at home, because that was the culture then. Let's pray that maybe we'll see more of that in these times ahead."

The surrounding tables were elbow-full of young musicians who by this hour should have been fearlessly singing themselves. But none was, and a disappointed Jamie had to leave. It was nearly three a.m. Flummoxed, I finally I tapped the arm of George Murphy, the young balladeer who had enthralled the audience earlier. "You are the youngest singer here. Would you give us a tune to get things started?"

With that, the twenty-four-year-old lashed into Johnny Cash's "Folsom Prison Blues." He sang with such transporting power, with his gaze and hands uplifted, it felt as he was calling to the spirit of Luke Kelly, too.

Sean Cannon then uncased his guitar and offered more quietly beautiful songs. One was an exquisite ballad by the Scottish lyricist Phil Colclough named "The Call and the Answer."

> You are the call, I am the answer
> You are the wish and I am the way.
> You are the night and I am the dancer.
> You are the night and I am the day.

For two hours the music erupted without cease, and the scene was as spontaneous and joyful as it ever could be in this country that so often grasps magic out of darkness. A night to remember, it was that, and I felt exhilarated. The problem was that Martin, the night porter, was well past his bed time. Suddenly, just before five a.m., he blurted, "Would ye all be away now!"

Okay, Martin the night porter and the ghost of Luke Kelly and all ye merry Dubliners dead and living still, goodnight, I muttered. Goodnight then to another ode to the wild spark of life itself. I went out the door, not wanting time to stop. Already, night had changed to day; already the sun was burning mist off the River Lee and strewing incandescence upon the distant harbor. The green hills across the valley were aglow, the flowers along my path were on fire. It was all so beautiful I had time to rejoice. Ireland's spark had transformed my family's lives, that spark of inspiration that kept dancing through these uncertain days.

On our lawn there still stood our trampoline, a platform pointing to the skies. I looked at it, contemplating a private bounce, all alone. But all I did was lift an arm in gladness and tiptoed up the stairs to bed, savouring our new world perhaps more clearly than I had done for years. Somehow, I thought, Ireland will prevail again, because it must.

Epilogue

hroughout 2010, the Irish economic crisis grew steadily worse. The government's vow to prop up the sinking banks at all costs proved to be as profligate as the ludicrous property schemes they had financed—an estimated 20 billion in bad debts became 40, then 80 billion euros and more. Meanwhile, empty fertilizer bags whirled through two thousand empty "ghost" housing estates as the developers either went belly-up or fled the country.

Salaries and social welfare were sliced, taxes scheduled to be raised hand-over-fist, stealth fees arriving for the smallest things as the bankrupt Irish government desperately struggled to make ends meet. The word came down that the citizenry would have to cough up an average of 40,000 euros each to fund the bailout—far more than most everyone's grandparents made in a life time—and a penance to hang over every head for years.

In the autumn, the Taoiseach Brian Cowen said everything was stabilizing and there would be no need for foreign help, even as he worked the phone to the impresarios of the IMF and the European Central Bank. They soon arrived in Dublin with plump attaché cases, promising 85 billion euros of murderously leveraged loans to keep the bankrupt country afloat, while dictating what Ireland precisely should and should not do for the next three years.

"Was it for this?" railed an editorial in the *Irish Times*, harkening

back to the Easter Rising of 1916 in which so many martyrs offered their lives for the cause of Irish independence. "Having obtained our political independence from Britain to be the masters of our own affairs, we have now surrendered our sovereignty to the European Commission, the European Central Bank, and the International Monetary Fund. . . . The true ignominy of our current situation is not that our sovereignty has been taken away from us, but that we ourselves have squandered it."

THE WEATHER AT THE END OF 2010 WAS FITTING. A relentless chill fell over Ireland, and the previously rare phenomenon of snow fell time and again. Haunting lines from James Joyce's "The Dead" came back to me: "Snow was general all over Ireland; it was falling on every part of the dark central plain, on the treeless hills... and far westward, falling into the dark mutinous Shannon waves... falling like the descent of their last end, upon all the living and the dead."

Newly unemployed neighbors were walking their dogs through the snow when they should have been at work. I saw many elderly faltering on sheens of dark ice—they whose pensions had recently been slashed by 40 percent or so. The used car lots were choking with row upon row of mementos of the boom, Mercedes Benzes and SUVs that nobody wanted any more, deflated Bouncy Castles each and every one.

Farmers along the Blackwater insisted that even the birds—the swans and the terns and the starlings—had been behaving strangely, coming and going at the wrong times. Much, much worse, thousands of young people with little hope of employment had flown off to London or Sydney or Berlin like lost birds themselves.

Even the pub trade went into freefall, bereft before the falling snow—the menacing and comforting snow. Cowboy movies hit the screen in my Cork local, since nobody wanted to hear the news anymore.

"It's like we've floated back in time and don't even know where we are landing yet," said a friend named Kevin. "But all this travail could be the best thing that ever happened to us, or at least be what we need now. Maybe we will get back to who we were meant to be."

EARLY IN DECEMBER, MY FIRST COUSIN, John Hurst, the seller of rare books in the lovely town of Westport, County Mayo—my parallel dreamer—died. And the journey to his funeral proved to be one both into darkness and into light.

As I headed north beyond Galway, the landscape grew somber, with fog banks slipping off the Connemara hills and blooming gloom over distant lochs. In the middle of nowhere lay more ghost estates.

But on the boggy road, I saw one remarkable sight—a druidic stone circle that had ages of detritus newly cleared from around it, as if to let the old spirits breathe, as if the spirit of my white witch of Donegal, Jane Crane, was at work.

Arriving in Westport, I walked to my cousin's bookshop, where I found his friend Jim Smyth leading John's giant black-on-white English sheepdog, "Rebel"—so named because my southern cousin, was enamored of the glorious lost cause of the Confederacy. Through the Mass-to-be, Rebel was to sit in John's bookshop, with its disembodied knight in armor standing sentry outside.

There are few sights sadder than a dog of such regal stature padding down into the last remnants of his owner's dream. And now where would the dreams fly again? Where do all the dreams go?

My cousin—they say we were look-a-likes—arrived at St. Mary's Church beside the town's tranquil river quays as the darkness was falling, too. This time, so different from our joyous last visits, he was in a box—and one that was due to be set on fire in a crematorium the next day.

It's funny how light people are when lifted into a church by a collective of caring hands, even into a church of no return. So many people were inside, so many pairs of anguished eyes. And then the priest settled in, the reassurance of ritual. And I was thinking, what is Ireland about. What is it really?

After a dirge that would turn any soul, a flute lilted forth, keening and traipsing between more stars than you would find in the west of Ireland on a winter night. Matt Molloy of the celebrated Chieftains band was playing the ancient air "The Parting of the Friends" for his friend, my cousin, John.

I thought again that there was an inimitable and indomitable spirit yet in Ireland. Because it had developed the same day that one of Matt Molloy's prized ancient flutes was about to ascend like my cousin into outer space: The acclaimed flautist had gifted it to an astronaut who wanted to play diddly-eye music somewhere far above the clouds.

We all went to Matt Molloy's hallowed pub after the funeral procession was finished. And there was laughter, and there was song. I finally confessed that I was feeling guilty about enjoying myself so much, at this moment, in this town and among these people who John so much loved.

"Ah, forget that," said a friend of my cousin's named Brendan Hafferty. "On these nights, we don't mourn the death, we celebrate the life."

This night was as true as I ever found in my adopted land.

Tir Eire!

The swans were still white, the river was still black, and the starlings would return.

DECEMBER 30, 2010

Notes

P. 51. This speech by Emily O'Reilly, Ombudsman for Ireland, was excerpted in the *Irish Times*, November 8, 2004 and June 14, 2006.

PP. 43-44. The comments by Seamus O'Donoghue, head of the Irish Vintner's Association, were reported in the *Irish Examiner*, March 3, 2006.

P. 44. Curious events in a Mayo pub were described in the *Irish Times*, October 26, 2005.

PP. 46-47. The entrepreneur Donal Caulfield's comments were reported on in pp. 266-267 of *The Builders,* by Frank McDonald & Kathy Sheridan, Penguin Ireland, 2008.

P. 51. The speech on emigration by Mary McAleese, President of Ireland, to the Irish senate was reported on in the *Irish Times*, February 3, 1995, and revisited September 26, 2009.

P. 75. This description of the Blackwater River valley is drawn from William Thackeray's *The Irish Sketchbook*, London, 1843.
A further reference to the Blackwater's beauty is drawn from *A Hand Book for Travellers in Ireland,* Dublin, 1844.

PP. 119-120. Seamus Heaney expressed his dismay about the desecration of the Hill of Tara in the *Sunday Times* (UK), March 3, 2008.

P. 120. On the same subject, Jonathan Foyle was quoted on the BBC News, March 1, 2008.

PP. 120-121. For the verse "Exiles" see George Russell (1867-1935), *Collected Poems*, London, MacMillan, 1926.

PP. 121-122. W.B. Yeats (1865-1939) poem "The Two Kings" from *Responsibilities and Other Poems*, MacMillan and Company, New York, 1916.

P. 170. Lines from Art Mac Cumhaigh (1738-1773) were brought to author's attention by Paul Muldoon's *To Ireland I*, Oxford University Press, New York, 2001.

P. 179. From "The Fairies" by William Allingham (1824-1889) as drawn from William Allingham, *Poems*, MacMillan and Company Ltd., London, 1912.

PP. 261-263. The story of Ben Dunne's rise and fall and rise again has been told by many parties, including in his own speeches to the people of Ireland. Particular scrutiny was paid to reports closest to the scene regarding the Orlando episode. Among these were in-depth reports from the *Orlando Sentinel* on February 24, 1992, May 20, 1992, and July 12, 1992; plus a comprehensive account from Desmond Murphy in the *Irish Independent* on December 3, 1992; and a later *Irish Times* reprise by Vivion Kilfeather on May 22, 2001. Also see "Dunne and Dusted," Desmond Murphy, *The Independent* (UK), December 13, 1992; "He that Filches from Me My Good Name . . . Makes Me Poor Indeed," Jody Corcoran, *Sunday Independent*, December 24, 2006; "Ben Dunne's Online Shop to Compete with Family," Gavin Daly, *Sunday Business Post*, February 2, 2008; "Show of Horror at Dunne's Graveyard Shift," *Sunday Times* (UK), April 20, 2008; "Ben There, Dunne That: Business Tycoon Dabbles in Art and Death," Maxim Kelly, *Sunday Tribune*, May 24, 2009.

PP. 139 and 263. The Charlie Haughey story has been expanded upon by any number of journalists. Primary sources here were drawn from a many newspapers and books. See in particular a lengthy *Sunday Times* (UK) profile on July 13, 2003, by Christine Toomey entitled: "Charles Haughey: Scapecoat for Scandal? "

PP. 255-258 See "Treasury and Its Holdings," Ted Harding, *Sunday Business Post,* September 10, 2000.

For further information on the property boom and crash, see "The Irish Economy's Rise was Steep, and the Fall was Fast," by Landon Thomas, Jr., *The New York Times*, January 4, 2009. Also, "Fitzpatrick 'Addicted to Money' says Ben Dunne," Ronald Quinlan, *Sunday Independent*, February 8, 2009.

P. 237 The Michael Lynn story is many-layered and continuing. Among many sources for it are reports from the *Sunday Business Post*, October 21, 2007; *Irish Independent*, December 16 & 17, 2007; *Irish Times*, July 6, 2010; and Irish Independent, August 30, 2010.

P. 246. Frank McDonald quoted from *Irish Mail*, October 18, 2007.

P. 247. Pat Murphy letter to *Irish Times*, October 24, 2009.

P. 273. Kavanagh poem quoted by kind permission of Eilean ni Cuillean, executor of the Kavanagh estate.

P. 274. "I Wish I Had Somebody to Love Me," more often called "The Prisoner's Song" was apparently first recorded by Guy Massey in 1924, but earlier variants were recorded by others at least a decade earlier. It was a massive hit in the early years of the last century.

Further Reading

ALLINGHAM, WILLIAM:
   Poems, Macmillam, London, 1893.

CRONIN, ANTHONY:
   No Laughing Matter: The Life and Times of Flann O'Brien, New Island
      Books, Dublin, 2003.
   Dead as Doornails, Lilliput Press, Dublin, 1999.

DONLEAVY, J.P.:
   The History of the Ginger Man, Viking, London, 1994.
   A Singular Country, Ryan Publishing Co. Ltd, Peterborough, U.K., 1989.
   The Destinies of Darcy Dancer, Gentleman, Penguin Books,
      Harmondsworth, Middlesex, England, 1977.
   The Onion Eaters, Eyre & Spottiswoode, London, 1971.
   The Beastly Beatitudes of Bathalzar B, Grove Press, New York, 1968.
   The Ginger Man, Corgi Books, U.K., 1963.

FOSTER, ROY:
   Luck & the Irish: A Brief History of Change 1970–2000, Allen Lane,
      London, 2007.

GRANT, JAMES:
   One Hundred Years with the Clonard Redemptorists, Columbia Press,
      Dublin, 2003.

HEANEY, SEAMUS:
   New and Selected Poems, Faber & Faber, London, 2009.

KAVANAGH, PATRICK:
   Collected Poems, Allen Lane, London, 2004.

KINSELLA, THOMAS, translator:
  The Tain (from the Irish epic Táin Bó Cuailnge), Oxford University Press, 1969.

MAHON, DEREK:
  Collected Poems, Gallery Press, Loughcrew, Co. Meath, Ireland, 2003.

MALONEY, ED:
  A Secret History of the IRA, W.W. Norton, New York, 2003.

MCCABE, PATRICK:
  The Stray Sod Country, Bloombury USA, 2010.
  Breakfast on Pluto, Picador, London 1998.
  The Butcher Boy, Picador, London, 1992.

MCDONALD, FRANK; SHERIDAN, KATHY:
  The Builders, Penguin Ireland, 2008.

MULDOON, PAUL:
  To Ireland, I. Oxford University Press, Oxford, U.K., 2000.
  Horse Latitudes: Poems. Farrar, Straus and Giroux, New York, 2006.

O'BRIEN, FLANN:
  At Swim Two Birds, MacGibbon & Kee, London, 1968.
  The Third Policeman, Plume, New York, 1976.

O'SULLIVAN, MELANIE; MCCARTHY, KEVIN:
  Cappoquin: A Walk Through History, self-published, circa 2000.

POUCHIN MOULD, DAPHNE D.C.:
  Discovering Cork, Brandon Books, Dingle, Kerry, Ireland, 1991.

RUSSELL, GEORGE:
  Collected Poems, MacMillan, London, 1917.

THACKERAY, WILLIAM:
  The Irish Sketchbook, London, 1843.

YEATS, WILLIAM BUTLER:
  The Collected Poems of W.B. Yeats, Macmillan Publishing Co. Inc, New York, 1974.

Acknowledgments

As readers will see, *Ireland Unhinged* is a hybrid, mixing memoir and impressionism; yet it is ultimately a work of serious reportage. However, some names have been changed to protect the privacy of certain individuals where doing so seemed right.

But nothing substantive in this book—other than perhaps the details of a "beard convention" or the look on a president of Ireland's face at a certain time—should be regarded as fiction. *Ireland Unhinged* took shape through painstaking research. Even the comedy is based on fact.

This book could never have come to be without the support of many people to whom I owe lasting gratitude. My greatest thanks are due to my wife Jamie, and our children Laura, Harris, and Owen, for their enduring support. What a Bluebeard's Castle is the writer's life.

I offer heartfelt gratitude to Barnaby Conrad III, my editor to whom this book is rightfully dedicated. Barney is remarkable for his exquisite acumen, tireless diligence, steadfast loyalty, and dedication to every nuance of the word.

My agent Joelle Delbourgo has also been a godsend—an enthusiast of the old school who embraced every challenge, some quite unforeseen. Thanks are due as well to the good people from Council Oak Books, led by Maurice Kanbar, Paulette Millichap, and Sally Dennison. My Irish version editor Brian Langan is a wiz of endless help.

So many people have lent inspiration to this book, it is impossible to name them all. The larger-than-life Bill Griffin, the illustrious Harding brothers, the colorful Ray Lloyd, have been as steadfast as can be. Thank you all, and thank you also Patrick McCabe, Malachy McCourt, Bill Barich, and Ken Starr for your reviews.

I cannot say enough about the welcoming spirit of the people of Ballyduff in west Waterford. They inspire me constantly. But this book came to be through a lot of open doors: from Teelin in rural Donegal; from the likes of J.P. Donleavy; a certain Jane Crane, most loveable witch; and from some remarkable avatars of Ireland's best hopes who made generous time for me in the "big smoke."

I would also like to offer extra thanks to those saintly figures from the Clonard Monastery in Belfast, Peter Burns and Gerry Reynolds. They taught me things.

So many others opened themselves to me. What one loves about Ireland is that it talks as readily as it breathes.

Cork, Ireland, December 2010